Russian Regional Politics under Putin and Medvedev

Many authors have alluded to the unique nature of Russia's dual transition and its difficult task of simultaneously reforming its economy and polity. But there is in fact a third transition still far from completed that is of no less importance, the need to reconfigure central-regional relations and to create a stable and viable form of federalism. There are vast economic, demographic and political variations across the Russian federation. Therefore an understanding of regions, and the causes and consequences of cross-regional diversity, is a vitally important dimension of Russian politics that should not be overlooked. It is only by studying regional level politics that we can gain a full understanding of the complexities of Russia's protracted transition.

This edited volume examines regional politics and centre-regional relations over the period 2000-2010, including the most recent developments which have taken place under the new dual leadership of Medvedev and Putin. All eight chapters have been written by leading experts in the field of Russian politics. In addition to chapters on regional elections, parties, regional governors and local politics, there are three chapters devoted to the important developments which are currently taking place in the Caucasus.

This book was published as a special issue of *Europe-Asia Studies*.

Cameron Ross is a Reader in politics at the University of Dundee, UK. He has taught politics at the University of Cambridge, the College of William and Mary (Virginia, USA) and Oberlin College (Ohio, USA).

Routledge Europe-Asia Studies Series

A series edited by Terry Cox, University of Glasgow

The **Routledge Europe-Asia Studies Series** focuses on the history and current political, social and economic affairs of the countries of the former 'communist bloc' of the Soviet Union, Eastern Europe and Asia. As well as providing contemporary analyses it explores the economic, political and social transformation of these countries and the changing character of their relationships with the rest of Europe and Asia.

Challenging Communism in Eastern Europe
1956 and its Legacy
Edited by Terry Cox

Globalisation, Freedom and the Media after Communism
The Past as Future
Edited by Birgit Beumers, Stephen Hutchings and Natalia Rulyova

Power and Policy in Putin's Russia
Edited by Richard Sakwa

1948 and 1968 – Dramatic Milestones in Czech and Slovak History
Edited by Laura Cashman

Perceptions of the European Union in New Member States
A Comparative Perspective
Edited by Gabriella Ilonszki

Symbolism and Power in Central Asia
Politics of the Spectacular
Edited by Sally N. Cummings

The European Union, Russia and the Shared Neighbourhood
Edited by Jackie Gower and Graham Timmins

Russian Regional Politics under Putin and Medvedev
Edited by Cameron Ross

Russian Regional Politics under Putin and Medvedev

Edited by
Cameron Ross

Routledge
Taylor & Francis Group
LONDON AND NEW YORK

University of Glasgow

First published 2012 by Routledge

2 Park Square, Milton Park, Abingdon, Oxfordshire OX14 4RN
711 Third Avenue, New York, NY 10017

Routledge is an imprint of the Taylor & Francis Group, an informa business

First issued in paperback 2018

This book is a reproduction of *Europe-Asia Studies*, vol. 63, issue 3. The Publisher requests to those authors who may be citing this book to state, also, the bibliographical details of the special issue on which the book was based.

British Library Cataloguing in Publication Data
A catalogue record for this book is available from the British Library

ISBN13: 978-0-415-68890-1 (hbk)
ISBN13: 978-1-138-37723-3 (pbk)

Typeset in Times New Roman
by Taylor & Francis Books

Disclaimer
The publisher would like to make readers aware that the chapters in this book are referred to as articles as they had been in the special issue. The publisher accepts responsibility for any inconsistencies that may have arisen in the course of preparing this volume for print.

Contents

List of Contributors

HELGE BLAKKISRUD is Head of the Department for Russian and Eurasian Studies at the Norwegian Institute of International Affairs, Oslo, and editor of *Nordisk Østforum*, a Nordic journal for East European studies. In 2009–2010 he was a Fulbright Visiting Scholar at ISEEES, UC Berkeley. His research interests include the development of Russian federalism as well as state building and nation building in Russia and Eurasia in general and in *de facto* states in particular. Recent publications include 'History Writing and Nation Building in Post-independence Tajikistan' (with Shanoza Nozimova), *Nationalities Papers*, 2010, and 'From Secessionist Conflict towards Functioning State: Processes of State- and Nation-building in Transnistria' (with Pål Kolstø), *Post Soviet Affairs* (forthcoming). *Address*: Norwegian Institute of International Affairs, PO Box 8159 Dep, NO-0033 Oslo, Norway. Email: *hb@nupi.no*.

VLADIMIR GEL'MAN is a Professor at the Department of Political Science and Sociology, European University at St Petersburg. He was also a visiting professor at Central European University, Budapest, at the University of Texas at Austin, and a research fellow at the University of Essex, Harvard University and the University of Notre Dame. He is author and/or editor of 20 books in Russian and in English, including *Resource Curse and Post-Soviet Eurasia* (Lexington Books, 2010) and *The Politics of Sub-National Authoritarianism in Russia* (Ashgate, 2010). He has also authored or co-authored more than 120 articles published in international scholarly journals as well as numerous edited volumes. *Address*: Department of Political Science and Sociology, European University at St Petersburg, Gagarinskaya 3, 191187, St Petersburg, Russia. Email: *gelman@eu.spb.ru*.

GRIGORII V. GOLOSOV is Professor of Political Science at the Department of Political Sciences and Sociology of the European University at St Petersburg and Project Director at the Center in Support of Democracy and Human Rights *Helix*. He is the author of *Political Parties in the Regions of Russia: Democracy Unclaimed* (Lynne Rienner, 2004) and several other books and he has published extensively on Russian politics, political parties and elections, including articles in *Comparative Political Studies*, *Europe-Asia Studies*, *Government and Opposition*, *International Political Science Review*, *Party Politics*, *Political Studies* and other journals. *Address*: Department of Political Science and Sociology, European University at St Petersburg, Gagarinskaya 3, 191187 Russia. Email: *ggolosov@gmail.com*.

ARKADY LYUBAREV was awarded a PhD in Biology (1993) from the Bach Institute of Biochemistry (Russian Academy of Sciences) and a PhD in Law (2004) from Moscow University of the Humanities. From 1990 to 2001 he was a member of a number of electoral commissions in Russia, including the Moscow City Electoral Commission. He is the author of several books and dozens of articles on elections and electoral law. He has played an active role in formulating electoral legislation at both the federal and local levels, including Moscow City Council. From 2005 to 2008 he was Head of the 'Programme for Monitoring Electoral Campaigns' at the Independent Institute of Elections in Moscow. Since 2008 he has held the post of Senior Expert at the Russian Association of Non-profit Organisations, 'In Defence of Voters' Rights "GOLOS"'. *Address*: Association of Non-profit Organizations 'In Defense of

Voters' Rights "GOLOS"', 8 Pokrovsky boulevard, Building 2a, 109028, Moscow, Russia. Email: *lyubarev@yandex.ru*.

CAMERON ROSS is a Reader in Politics at the University of Dundee. He has taught politics at the University of Cambridge, the College of William and Mary (Virginia, USA) and Oberlin College (Ohio, USA). He has published widely in the field of Russian regional and local politics. His most recent books are: *Local Politics and Democratization in Russia* (Routledge, 2009), *Federalism and Local Politics in Russia*, co-edited volume with Adrian Campbell (Routledge, 2009), and *The Politics of Sub-National Authoritarianism in Russia*, co-edited with Vladimir Gel'man (Ashgate, 2010). *Address*: Politics, School of Humanities, University of Dundee, Dundee DD1 4HN, UK. Email: *c.z.ross@dundee.ac.uk*.

JOHN RUSSELL is Professor of Russian and Security Studies at the University of Bradford. He is the author of *Chechnya—Russia's 'War on Terror'* (Routledge, 2007) and a considerable number of journal articles and book chapters on Russia, Chechnya, the former Soviet Union, terrorism and East–West relations. He has presented papers on these topics at international conferences (ICCEES, ISA, ASN, BASEES, PSA), at leading research institutions (RIIA, IISS, SIPRI, START), and in universities in the UK, Russia, France, Germany, Sweden, Finland and the USA. He addressed NATO's Parliamentary Assembly Political Committee in the Reichstag, Berlin in 2008, and he is currently researching '9/11—ten years after', the 'Eurasian factor' in East–West relations and a monograph on Ramzan Kadyrov. *Address*: Peace Studies, University of Bradford, Bradford, West Yorkshire BD7 1DP, UK. Email: *jrussell@bradford.ac.uk*.

SERGEI RYZHENKOV is an acting associate professor at the Department of History, Political Science and Law of the Russian State University for Humanities, Moscow and editor-in-chief of the website *demagogy.ru*. Formerly he served as a deputy director of the Centre for Modern Politics Studies, Moscow, and was a visiting fellow at the Centre for International Studies, London School of Economics and Political Science. He is editor/co-editor of 16 books and has authored/co-authored more than 100 journal articles and book chapters, published in Russian, English and German. *Address*: kv.42, d.17 korp.2, Sormosvkaya ul., 109444, Moscow, Russia. Email: *r_s@nm.ru*.

RICHARD SAKWA is Professor of Russian and European Politics at the University of Kent and an Associate Fellow of the Russia and Eurasia Programme at the Royal Institute of International Affairs, Chatham House. He has published widely on Soviet, Russian and post-communist affairs. Recent books include: *Postcommunism* (Open University Press, 1999); *Contextualising Secession: Normative Aspects of Secession Struggles* (Oxford University Press, 2003), co-edited with Bruno Coppieters; the edited volume *Chechnya: From Past to Future* (Anthem Press, 2005); *Russian Politics and Society* (Routledge, 4th edition, 2008); and *Putin: Russia's Choice* (Routledge, 2nd edition, 2008). His book on *The Quality of Freedom: Khodorkovsky, Putin and the Yukos Affair* was published by Oxford University Press in 2009, and his study *The Crisis of Russian Democracy: The Dual State, Factionalism, and the Medvedev Succession* came out with Cambridge University Press in 2011. *Address*: Rutherford College, The University, Canterbury, Kent CT2 7NX, UK. Email: *R.Sakwa@kent.ac.uk*.

ROBERT BRUCE WARE is Professor of Philosophy at Southern Illinois University Edwardsville. Since completing his doctorate at Oxford University in 1995, Robert Bruce Ware has conducted field research in the North Caucasus. He is the author of numerous articles on the region, and co-author of *Dagestan: Russian Hegemony and Islamic Resistance in the North Caucasus* (Sharpe, 2010). He is also the author of *Hegel* (Edinburgh University Press, 1999). *Address*: Philosophy Department, Southern Illinois University Edwardsville, Edwardsville, IL 62026-1433, USA. Email: *rware@siue.edu*.

Introduction

CAMERON ROSS

MANY AUTHORS HAVE ALLUDED TO THE UNIQUE nature of Russia's dual transition and its difficult task of simultaneously reforming its economy and polity. But there is in fact a third transition still far from completed that is of no less importance: the need to reconfigure central–regional relations and to create a stable and viable form of federalism. With a population of 142 million citizens, made up of 182 nationalities, and covering an area of 170 million square kilometres, Russia is one of the largest and most ethnically diverse multi-national federations in the world. The 83 federal subjects vary widely in the size of their territories and populations, their socio-economic status, and ethnic makeup.[1] The Russian Federation is also constitutionally asymmetrical. Whilst Article 5.4 of the Constitution declares that all subjects of the federation are equal, in fact the ethnic republics were granted far greater powers than the territorially defined subjects. Socio-economic and constitutional asymmetry in turn generates political asymmetry and variations in the levels of democracy and authoritarianism in regional polities.

An understanding of regional politics, and the causes and consequences of cross-regional diversity is, therefore, a vitally important dimension of Russian politics that should not be overlooked. It is only by studying regional level politics that we can gain a full understanding of the complexities of Russia's transition.

Since the election of Vladimir Putin as president in March 2000, Russia's nascent democracy and federal system has suffered major setbacks. Putin's primary objectives were to create a unified economic, legal and security space in the federation and to tighten the federal government's controls over the regions. But the president's attempts to reign in the power of the regions and to reassert what he called a 'power-vertical' made a mockery of the principles of federalism and democracy. Far from removing the authoritarian features which the new regime inherited from the Yel'tsin era, Putin widened and deepened authoritarianism in the regions. The president's initial reorganisation of the Federation Council, his usurpation of unilateral powers to

[1]The Russian Federation currently comprises 83 federal subjects (originally 89). These are divided into six sub-categories, three of which are based on different levels of ethnic autonomy (republics, autonomous *okruga* and one autonomous *oblast'*) and three purely administrative categories (*krai*, *oblasti* and cities of federal importance). In this volume these entities will be referred to collectively as 'regions'.

dismiss regional assemblies and chief executives and his creation of seven unelected super-governors in the federal districts (now numbering eight) were all major setbacks for Russian federalism and democracy.

In the aftermath of the Beslan hostage crisis of September 2004 Putin was granted powers to appoint the regional governors and this was followed by major new legislation on parties and elections (adopted over the period 2003–2006) which has thwarted the development of democracy at the regional and local levels. Across the federation there are now many different types of authoritarian and semi-authoritarian ('competitive authoritarian', 'electoral authoritarian') regimes, with the greatest levels of authoritarianism to be found largely in the ethnic republics, and particularly those republics which are situated in the Caucasus.

In March 2008 Medvedev was elected president and Putin moved to take over the post of prime minister. In this collection we examine regional politics and centre–regional relations over the period 2000–2010, including the most recent developments under the new dual leadership of Medvedev and Putin. Whilst under Medvedev we have begun to witness the emergence of some small green shoots of liberalism, as the essays in this collection demonstrate, the fundamentals of Putinism remain firmly in place.

In the opening essay on Medvedev's new governors, Helge Blakkisrud discusses the transformation of the gubernatorial corps during Medvedev's first two years in office, 2008–2010. The study focuses on the following key questions: how do Medvedev's appointees differ from the Yel'tsin- and Putin-era governors they have replaced? Does the Kremlin have a preference for a certain type of candidate? Does the change in nomination procedures affect the kind of candidate put forward? And what can the appointments policy tell us about the current direction of centre–periphery relations in Russia?

As Blakkisrud demonstrates, the main trend in regional elite recruitment has been toward greater turnover among the incumbents. Likewise, the previous trend of parachuting in outsiders which was prevalent under Putin has now abated, with the Kremlin increasingly relying on local cadres for gubernatorial posts. Thus, for example, whereas 'Putin reformed the structure but generally refrained from changing the personnel, Medvedev has been systematically replacing the old incumbents'. By the end of May 2010, 41 of the 83 regional heads of executive power had been selected by Medvedev.

The new governors come from diverse professional backgrounds. However, 'one thing many of them have in common is that they have spent part of their careers in private business before turning (or returning) to elected or administrative positions'. A typical 'career trajectory involves holding a position such as mayor of a regional capital or as local head of executive power *en route* from a business position to being appointed governor'. Whilst 'the Kremlin continues to put on a show of regional involvement in the selection process, emphasising party involvement in the nomination procedure and encouraging the practice of "voluntary" resignation of unwanted governors', it is Moscow which clearly has the final word. However, as Blakkisrud concludes, the Kremlin is not able to 'hire and fire governors at will'; it has to find 'candidates who can win the endorsement of the regional elites'.

In his statistical analysis of 66 regional assembly elections conducted over the period 2003–2007, Grigorii Golosov demonstrates that the authoritarian transformation in contemporary Russia was achieved largely because the resources and practices of regional regimes were incorporated into the 'vertical of power'. The formation of the political monopoly was facilitated not only by the strategies of the federal centre that uniformly influenced different regions, but also by region-level factors. Here, the most important role was played by the governors who exercised their powers to prevent intra-elite splits, and to provide support to United Russia (*Edinaya Rossiya*). Whilst, 'it is true that the political monopoly was not feasible without the federal centre's effort, it is also true that this effort probably would have been fruitless without the co-optation of resources and mechanisms of regional authoritarianism'. Golosov's sophisticated statistical analysis demonstrates that 'the ultimate breakdown of Russia's electoral democracy' was a joint operation between the centre and the regions.

In his study, Arkady Lyubarev provides a detailed examination of the Federal Law, 'On the Basic Guarantees of Electoral Rights and the Right of Russian Federation Citizens to Participate in a Referendum'. In particular, the essay examines the impact of this framework law on regional election legislation. This comprehensive study of regional election legislation shows that, even under the highly centralised politics of the 'power vertical' under Putin and Medvedev, there are wide variations in regional electoral laws and norms. Important regional variations are found; for example, in the type of electoral system (a fully PR system or a mixed PR/first past the post majoritarian system), the size of the electoral threshold, the type of party list (open or closed), the method of distributing seats between lists, and the size of electoral deposits. In this study Lyubarev also provides a novel account of ways in which electoral legislation has been adapted and manipulated by regional elites in order to favour the 'party of power', United Russia. This study clearly shows that if we want to gain a full understanding of the electoral process in the Russian Federation it is vital that we include the regional dimension.

Cameron Ross examines the problems of institutionalising and nationalising parties in Russia's regions and he traces the development of the party system from the period of fragmentation and high levels of volatility under Yel'tsin, to the monopolisation of power under Putin and Medvedev. As is demonstrated, Russian parties, with the exception of United Russia, currently suffer from very low levels of 'party nationalisation' and 'institutionalisation'. Moreover, under Putin and Medvedev we have witnessed a massive reduction in the number of parties at the national and regional levels. To a large degree only those parties which are sanctioned by the Kremlin are allowed to register and compete in elections. This has been especially the case since 2005 when the president was granted the power to directly appoint regional governors (subject to the consent of the regional assemblies).

In the absence of strong parties, clientelism, not party politics, dominates regional politics. Competition between regional elites takes place not only between parties but within parties, and the composition of regional legislatures largely reflects the makeup of the respective elites. Whilst United Russia dominates regional assemblies it is far from united and indeed, it would now appear that there may be as many different United Russias as there are regions. Such developments have seriously compromised the ideological foundations and political identity of many of the regional branches of political parties and dealt a serious blow to the consolidation of a nationwide party system in Russia. They have also thwarted Russia's democratic transition.

In their study of local politics Vladimir Gel'man and Sergei Ryzhenkov employ the theoretical literature on 'urban regimes' to throw new light on the development of city politics in Russia. A 'local regime' is defined as 'a complex of political institutions, actors, and the resources and strategies available to them, which determine the conduct of local politics, local policy and local governance'.

As Gel'man and Ryzhenkov demonstrate, the trajectories of local regimes have swung back and forwards like a pendulum. Thus, for example, in the early 1990s

> the collapse of the Soviet Union, the breakdown of communist rule, and the launching of market reforms caused spontaneous decentralisation and democratisation at the local level. These trends occurred against the background of protracted economic transformation, the decline of coercive and distributive capacities of the Russian state and deep conflicts among local economic interest groups.

During this period 'the key actors of local regimes were involved in "the privatization of gains" . . . and "the socialization of losses" . . .'. These local regimes 'emerged in the majority of Russia's cities and regions and demonstrated the predominance of local-based distributional coalitions . . . , which involved major dependent social groups such as pensioners and public sector employees, local businesses closely linked with local authorities . . . , and also criminal "violent entrepreneurs"'.

However, in the 2000s, the dynamics of Russian local regimes qualitatively changed. During this period, according to Gel'man and Ryzhenkov, the institutions and actors of Russia's local regimes, as well as the patterns of local governance underwent radical changes which included:

> the shift from local autonomy to the partial re-establishment of a hierarchical model of regional and urban governance ('power vertical'); the major decay, if not the total elimination of electoral contestation in local as well as in national politics . . .; and the abolition of popular elections of regional governors and, in many cases, of city mayors.

Moreover, as they note,

> the tremendous economic growth in Russia (until the 2008–2009 economic crisis) accompanied by the large-scale recentralisation of governance and the rise of authoritarian tendencies, led to a major shift of Russia's sub-national authoritarianism from decentralised to a centralised party-based model. . . . For local regimes—first and foremost, in Russia's large cities—these changes led to the emergence of elements of regimes of growth and development. They were based upon booming construction, real estate, retail and related sectors of local economies.

Throughout the study the authors stress the centre's use of the 'carrot' as well as the 'stick'. In the 2000s they detail how the centre was able to construct the 'power vertical' using the informal institutionalisation of political rents, the spoils of which were shared between local regimes and the centre.

Richard Sakwa, in the first of three essays devoted to the study of the Caucasus, argues that the recognition of the independence of Abkhaziya and South Ossetiya on 26 August 2008 created a new dynamic in Russia's politics and its role in the broader region. This conflict brought to the fore the role of competing regionalisms. The Caucasus has become the focus of four overlapping zones: the micro-regional, focusing on sub-national politics; the meso-regional, which treats the Caucasus as a single security and political complex; the macro-regional, in which the larger region is involved and in which regional hegemons seek to assert their power; and the mega-regional level, which is the natural sphere of the European Union and the United States. At the macro-regional level Russia and Turkey have emerged as the two main forces, engaged in a growing rivalry with potential outside powers. Within Russia the war in Chechnya is effectively over, but this has brought to the fore the contradictions of the 'Chechenisation' policy, while at the same time raising the salience of the broader regional dimensions of the continuing insurgency in the North Caucasus.

The essay examines the implications of the Russo–Georgian War at all four levels of regionalism, and notes that only when the multi-level political dynamics of the region are recognised and given political valance, can the first steps be taken towards the resolution of the multiple conflicts in the Caucasus. Sakwa concludes by stating that the existence of sub-national struggles can be understood only in the context of meso-regions, and the recognition of competing regionalisms is only the first, but necessary, step to overcome the clash of regionalisms.

In his contribution, Robert Ware considers the extent to which instabilities in the North Caucasus and the evolution of the Russian Federation have shaped each other reciprocally since 1999. Whereas many studies have examined the effects that the Russian Federation has had upon events in this region, there has been much less attention to ways in which the causal relationship has also been reversed.

The study addresses the following key questions:

> Did Chechnya Chechenise Vladimir Putin before Putin Chechenised Chechnya? To what extent was Vladimir Putin's approach to the administration of Russia, and particularly of the North Caucasus, influenced by crises that he faced during his first formative months of power in 1999? Did the Kremlin's Chechenisation programme become a template not only for the stabilisation of Chechnya, but for the long-term administration of its North Caucasian neighbours, and finally for the reconstitution of the Russian Federation? How have instabilities in the North Caucasus been affected by the evolution of Russian federalism, and how have they affected that evolution? ... Has there been a tendency to view the peoples of the North Caucasus in primarily passive roles, receiving policy directives and reacting to changes imposed upon them from Moscow, rather than as reciprocally causing important changes in the Russian Federation itself?

As Ware demonstrates, events in the North Caucasus have had a major impact on national level politics. Thus, for example,

> Putin became Russia's prime minister in August 1999, just one week after Chechnya-based militants invaded Dagestan, and his administrative style was cast in the opening months of the ensuing war. Second, shortly after his presidential inauguration in May 2000, Putin announced the reorganisation of the Russian Federation on the model of Russia's seven military districts. Third, on 13 September 2004—barely one week after the Beslan hostage crisis, and in explicit response to 'terrorist' threats—Putin announced the centralised appointment of Russia's regional governors, and an overhaul of the Russian electoral system that promised additional strength for the party of power. Fourth, in January 2010, President Dmitry Medvedev announced the formation of the North Caucasus Federal District with a focus upon the endemic problems of the region.

Ware also stresses the fact that the recentralisation of powers under Putin and Medvedev, have 'inadvertently contributed to regional problems of corruption, alienation, and extremism. The Russian Federation appears to have fallen into a vicious cycle of horizontal resistance and vertical reaction that places it starkly at cross purposes with itself, a cycle that seems to be as self-perpetuating as it is self-defeating'.

In the final essay, John Russell provides a highly nuanced account of the Kadyrov regime in Chechnya and the relations between the centre and the Republic. In particular, the study examines the advantages and disadvantages to the centre of Kadyrov's idiosyncratic form of authoritarian rule which Russell defines as a type of semi-warlordism. The study also assesses the degree to which Kremlin policy towards Chechnya may become a template for future Kremlin policies in the North Caucasus.

The study addresses four key questions:

> Is Chechnya, as Putin claims, a full-fledged region, or effectively is it already beyond Kremlin control? Is the political situation in Chechnya the result of a unique set of circumstances that cannot be repeated elsewhere in the other North Caucasian republics (which, as will be argued, cannot have a 'Kadyrov' of their own)? Does the longevity of the rule of Kadyrov depend primarily upon the sustainability of his special relationship with Putin personally rather than with whoever is Russian President? And, finally, is Ramzan Kadyrov politically astute enough to continue the delicate balancing act between being the supposed passionate supporter of Russia's territorial integrity and great power ambitions, on the one hand, and the 'energiser' of Chechnya's national and cultural renaissance, on the other?

Russell argues that whilst the Kadyrov regime has brought stability to the Chechen Republic, Kadyrov's authoritarian style of leadership is now acknowledged by Medvedev, to have been 'directly responsible for the growth of Islamic radicalism throughout the rest of the North Caucasus'. Whilst Medvedev 'has made several attempts to limit Kadyrov's power, notably by the appointment of Aleksandr Khloponin as presidential plenipotentiary for the North Caucasus region in January 2010' the 'Russian President has not thus far shown any inclination to unseat Kadyrov'. Any moves to remove Kadyrov from power 'runs the risk of plunging Chechnya back into violent confrontation, thus derailing Chechenisation once more and potentially robbing Putin of his greatest domestic political triumph—the successful ending of the Chechen war'. The citizens of Chechnya, it would appear, will have to endure life under this corrupt and authoritarian leader for some time to come. However, as Russell concludes, there appears to be no plans to use the Chechen experience as a template for policy in the North Caucasus.

The essays in this collection demonstrate that the relationship between the regions and the centre is a two-way flow. Thus, for example, whilst authoritarianism at the national level has bolstered authoritarianism in the regions, it is also the case that the creation of authoritarian regimes in the regions has given succour to the development of authoritarianism at the centre. Moreover, the conclusions of these essays indicate that whilst there have been some positive developments in the direction of liberalism and democracy under the Medvedev presidency, it will be difficult for Russia to extricate itself from this vicious circle in the near future.

University of Dundee

Medvedev's New Governors

HELGE BLAKKISRUD

ON 7 MAY 2008, DMITRII MEDVEDEV WAS SWORN IN as the third President of the Russian Federation. Under his two predecessors, the relationship between Moscow and the regions had undergone cataclysmic changes. Boris Yel'tsin's rule had ushered in a period of unprecedented, albeit unsystematic and *ad hoc*, decentralisation (Teague 1994; Lapidus & Walker 1996). Moreover, although the 1992 Federal Treaty had prevented further fragmentation of the state, it also laid the groundwork for a fundamentally asymmetric federal structure, later further differentiated through the conclusion of bilateral power-sharing treaties between Moscow and selected regions (Solnick 1995, 2000; Kahn 2002). At the regional level, the governors soon emerged as the focal point of political power, and, somewhat reluctantly, Yel'tsin ceded his prerogative to appoint these leaders in favour of direct elections (Zlotnik 1996; Busygina 1997).[1] By the turn of the millennium, with power transferred from Yel'tsin to Vladimir Putin, virtually all regions had popularly elected leaders.[2] The governors had also become a political force to be reckoned with at the federal level (Solnick 1999; Lussier 2002).[3]

Under Vladimir Putin, however, the pendulum swung back. Moscow tightened the reins anew over 'the executive vertical'[4] and began to scale back regional autonomy, including the power of the governors (Hyde 2001; Reddaway & Orttung 2004). During his first term, Putin deprived the governors of their federal platform by abolishing *ex officio* representation in the Federation Council, and established a limit on the number of consecutive terms they could serve (Ross 2003; Blakkisrud 2003). In his second term, Putin also stripped the governors of their independent regional power-base by

A first draft of this essay was presented at the annual convention of the AAASS, Boston 12–15 November 2009. The author would like to thank his fellow panellists as well as Pål Kolsto and Elana Wilson Rowe for valuable comments on earlier drafts.

[1]The heads of the regional executive branch have various names, including governor, president, head of administration and mayor. For simplicity, these will be referred to collectively here as 'governors'.

[2]The president of Karachaevo-Cherkessiya resisted elections until the spring of 1999. In Dagestan, the president was elected indirectly; in Udmurtiya, there was a parliamentary system until 2000.

[3]The clearest example of the new political ambitions of the gubernatorial corps was the emergence of a regionally based 'party of power', Fatherland–All Russia (*Otechestvo–Vsya Rossiya*), that attempted to challenge the Kremlin over the succession issue in 1999–2000.

[4]The vertical chain of command through which presidential policies are implemented is commonly referred to as 'the executive vertical' (*vertikal' vlasti*). A central goal of Putin's presidency was to restore the power vertical.

scrapping direct elections and reverting to the system of appointed governors (Goode 2007; Chebankova 2007).[5]

Medvedev's election as president was met with anticipation of new revisions of centre–periphery relations. Some regional leaders, expecting the new president to espouse a more liberal agenda than his predecessor, tested the waters by suggesting the reintroduction of popular elections as a way to legitimise regional executive power (Bocharova 2008).[6] However, Medvedev was quick to rule out yet another cycle of institutional reform, opting instead for fine-tuning the structure inherited from Putin. By mid-term, the only significant institutional reform of the 'executive vertical' was a modification of the nomination procedure whereby responsibility for identification of gubernatorial candidates was transferred from the presidential administration to the party in control of the legislature in the region in question (Medvedev 2008).

On the other hand, this does not imply that Medvedev has not been able to put his stamp on the gubernatorial corps: halfway through his term, he had already appointed governors to almost half of Russia's regions, and in the process, made far more active use of his right to replace the formerly elected governors than had Putin. According to Russian political analyst Evgenii Minchenko, Medvedev has yet to develop a coherent policy on the gubernatorial corps; 'decisions are made spontaneously, on a try-and-fail basis' (Bilevskaya 2009); others, however, hold that Medvedev has embarked on a 'cadre revolution' (Radzikhovskii 2010).

This essay discusses the transformation of the gubernatorial corps under Medvedev by drawing a collective portrait of the new governors as of Medvedev's mid-term (May 2010). Many of the first generation of Russian governors after 1991 had belonged to the old *nomenklatura*, and several former first secretaries made the successful transition to the governorship (Lane & Ross 1999; Rigby 2001). During Putin's presidency, it was argued that the Kremlin had introduced a 'militocracy' (Kryshtanovskaya & White 2003), drawing heavily on people with backgrounds in the FSB and other security structures to fill the top echelons of government and the bureaucracy, including the regional elite (Petrov & Slider 2005; Kryshtanovskaya & White 2009).

How do Medvedev's appointees differ from the Yel'tsin-era and Putin-era governors they replaced? Does the Kremlin seem to have a preference for a certain type of candidate?[7] Does the change in nomination procedures affect the kind of candidate put forward? And what can the appointments policy tell us about the current direction of centre–periphery relations in Russia?

[5]Officially, governors are not 'appointed', but 'empowered'; the relevant legislation speaks of the 'empowerment on the proposal of the President of the Russian Federation' (*nadelenie pol'nomochiyami po predstavleniyu Prezidenta Rossiiskoi Federatsii*). As pointed out by Aleksei Titkov, however, even Putin has referred to the procedure as 'appointment' (*naznachenie*) (Titkov 2007, p. 101).

[6]First to express an opinion was President Mintimer Shaimiev of Tatarstan in June 2008, soon followed by another prominent regional leader, Murtaza Rakhimov of Bashkortostan (Bocharova 2008).

[7]The focus here is on formal background characteristics such as age, gender, place of birth, ethnicity and professional background, and not on aspects of the governors' performance once in office such as their ability to act independently or their popularity. Moreover, the essay concentrates on who was actually appointed, rather than discussing the nature of the current Medvedev–Putin tandem or what influence Putin still wields over the final choice of candidates.

Medvedev's appointees: turnover in the gubernatorial corps[8]

By mid-term, Medvedev had appointed or reappointed close to half of Russia's gubernatorial corps—at the end of May 2010, 41 out of 83 regions had heads of executive power that had been selected by Medvedev.[9]

The most striking feature of Medvedev's gubernatorial cadre policy—and where it most clearly differs from Putin's approach—is the turnover among incumbents. Under Putin, incumbents were generally granted a new term. During the first year after reverting to presidentially appointed governors, the 'reappointment rate' among incumbents had been 72.7%: 32 out of 44 governors were reappointed.[10] Although the turnover increased somewhat over the next years (see Figure 1), Putin's second term ended with an overall reappointment rate of 65.8% for incumbents (54 reappointments out of a total of 82 nominations).[11]

Halfway through Medvedev's presidency, however, the picture looks quite different. For those who had expected the change in presidency would strengthen the governors' bargaining position in federal politics—assuming that the new president would be more dependent on the support of the entrenched governors to provide societal stability and electoral support than Putin had been—Medvedev started out with a very discouraging series of appointments. In 2008, not a single governor was reappointed (see Table 1). In 2009, and in the first half of 2010, incumbents have succeeded in gaining reappointment only in a little more than one third of the cases (15 out of 42, or 35.7%).[12] It should be added that, formally, Medvedev did not dismiss any governors during this period. The incumbents who left office had either failed to win the Kremlin's endorsement for a new term, or had asked to be relieved of their duties before their current term expired.[13] This latter practice of 'voluntary' resignations began to develop toward the end of Putin's presidency (Kynev 2008): to save face, governors were allowed to make the announcement about their retirement themselves.[14] That such requests do not necessarily originate with the incumbent in question can be illustrated by the response from the regional administration when Egor Stroev allegedly submitted his resignation in February 2009. When journalists

[8]Unless otherwise indicated, all data on the governors' tenure as well as age, birthplace and professional background are taken from the author's own database on Russian governors.

[9]Medvedev made a total of 42 appointments, but two of these have been to Irkutsk, as the first newly appointed Governor Igor' Esipovskii died in a helicopter accident in May 2009.

[10]Among the 12 incumbents who were not reappointed during this period there was at least one instance of job promotion: Sergei Sobyanin stepped down as governor of Tyumen in order to take up the highly influential position as Head of the Presidential Administration.

[11]Moreover, of the 28 new appointments, two came as the result of the death of an incumbent (Viktor Shershunov in Kostroma and Mikhail Evdokimov in Altai *Krai*).

[12]One of the incumbents, Governor Igor' Esipovskii of Irkutsk, had, as noted, died.

[13]Already in 2007, the Kremlin had developed a long list of criteria for evaluating gubernatorial performance. Initially, there were 82 different parameters. In April 2009, under the impact of the economic crisis, 102 new criteria were added, including unemployment rate, salary level and the share of small and medium-sized businesses in the regional economy. So far, however, these criteria have never actually been referred to when a governor has had to step down (Vorobeva 2009).

[14]According to Aleksei Titkov, the practice of 'voluntary' resignations commenced in the summer of 2007 when it became clear that Mikhail Prusak in Novgorod and Ivan Malakhov in Sakhalin would not be granted a new term if they appealed to the president for to be reappointed (Titkov 2007, p. 94).

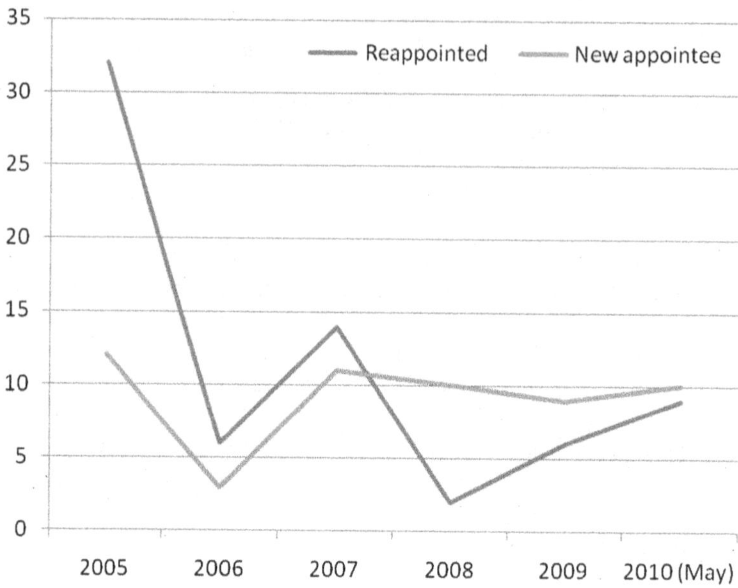

FIGURE 1. TURNOVER AMONG APPOINTED GOVERNORS (JANUARY 2005–MAY 2010).

tried to elicit a comment from Stroev's spokesperson, he replied that he could not make a statement as he had no written information about the resignation (Abdullaev & Krainova 2009).

Age and gender

Who are the new appointees? Do they differ in background (age/gender/origin/ ethnicity and professional experience) from the governors they replaced? Can we speak of a distinct 'Medvedev generation' of governors?

By the time Medvedev took office, the Russian gubernatorial corps was clearly ageing. In the early 1990s, Boris Yel'tsin had brought to power several young reformers: Mikhail Prusak in Novgorod was only 31 when he assumed office in 1991, and Boris Nemtsov in Nizhnii Novgorod was 32. In other regions, well established representatives of the *nomenklatura* made the successful transformation from *apparatchiki* to governors.[15] During the transition from appointed to elected governors, several Yel'tsin appointees were replaced (Zlotnik 1996; Busygina 1997), but overall, a large group of regional heads succeeded in developing power bases

[15]The degree to which the *nomenklatura* was able to reproduce itself in a post-Soviet setting is disputed (Lane & Ross 1999, pp. 143–66). Whereas Ol'ga Kryshtanovskaya and Stephen White have identified considerable continuity in personnel (Kryshtanovskaya & White 1996), Vladimir Gel'man has warned about drawing the conclusion that elite continuity means regime continuity: 'it would be incorrect to conclude ... that the old Communist *nomenklatura* was simply brought back to power' (Gel'man 2002, p. 155).

TABLE 1
MEDVEDEV'S APPOINTEES, MAY 2008–MAY 2010[a]

	Region	*Governor*	*New/ incumbent*	*Confirmed by regional parliament*
1	Stavropol	Valerii Gaevskii	New	23 May 2008
2	Chukotka Autonomous *Okrug*	Roman Kopin	New	13 July 2008
3	Karachaevo-Cherkessiya	Boris Ebzeev	New	5 August 2008
4	Amur	Oleg Kozhemyako	New	20 October 2008
5	Ingushetiya	Yunus-bek Evkurov	New	31 October 2008
6	Irkutsk	Igor' Esipovskii[b]	New	22 November 2008
7	Khakasiya	Viktor Zimin	New	10 December 2008
8	Kirov	Nikita Belykh	New	18 December 2008
9	Udmurtiya	Aleksandr Volkov	Incumbent	20 February 2009
10	Nenets Autonomous *Okrug*	Igor' Fedorov	New	24 February 2009
11	Voronezh	Aleksei Gordeev	New	26 February 2009
12	Pskov	Andrei Turchak	New	27 February 2009
13	Orel	Aleksandr Kozlov	New	27 February 2009
14	Vladimir	Nikolai Vinogradov	Incumbent	28 February 2009
15	Murmansk	Dmitrii Dmitrienko	New	25 March 2009
16	Khabarovsk	Vyacheslav Shport	New	6 May 2009
17	Irkutsk	Dmitrii Mezentsev	New	8 June 2009
18	Altai *Krai*	Aleksandr Karlin	Incumbent	29 July 2009
19	Sverdlovsk	Aleksandr Misharin	New	17 November 2009
20	Astrakhan	Aleksandr Zhilkin	Incumbent	9 December 2009
21	Kurgan	Oleg Bogomolov	Incumbent	29 December 2009
22	Volgograd	Anatolii Brovko	New	30 December 2009
23	Marii El	Leonid Markelov	Incumbent	31 December 2009
24	Primore	Sergei Dar'kin	Incumbent	11 January 2010
25	Altai Republic	Aleksandr Berdnikov	Incumbent	12 January 2010
26	Komi	Vyacheslav Gaizer	New	15 January 2010
27	Tatarstan	Rustam Minnikhanov	New	4 February 2010
28	Dagestan	Magomedsalam Magomedov	New	10 February 2010
29	Khanty-Mansi Autonomous *Okrug*	Natal'ya Komarova	New	15 February 2010
30	Jewish Autonomous *Oblast*	Aleksandr Vinnikov	New	17 February 2010
31	Krasnoyarsk	Lev Kuznetsov	New	17 February 2010
32	Kursk	Aleksandr Mikhailov	Incumbent	1 March 2010
33	Yamal-Nenets Autonomous *Okrug*	Dmitrii Kobylkin	New	3 March 2010
34	Kemerovo	Aman Tuleev	Incumbent	18 March 2010
35	Tula	Vyacheslav Dudka	Incumbent	18 March 2010
36	Chelyabinsk	Mikhail Yurevich	New	22 March 2010
37	Saratov	Pavel Ipatov	Incumbent	23 March 2010
38	Lipetsk	Oleg Korolev	Incumbent	26 April 2010
39	Penza	Vasilii Bochkarev	Incumbent	29 April 2010
40	North Osssetiya	Taimuraz Mamsurov	Incumbent	29 April 2010
41	Rostov	Vasilii Golubev	New	21 May 2010
42	Orenburg	Yurii Berg	New	22 May 2010

Notes: [a]Vyacheslav Shtyrov, the President of Sakha, resigned on 31 May 2010, but as his successor was not formally named until 9 June, he is not included here.
[b]Igor' Esipovskii had been acting governor since 15 April 2008, that is, since before Medvedev was inaugurated, but he was not officially appointed until November that year.

which allowed them to remain in office. As time passed, the average age of incumbents thus increased steadily. By 1999, it had reached 52.7 years, with the youngest governor being 35 and the oldest 69 years of age (Rigby 2001, p. 4). Putin's first term did not witness any change in this trend: on the eve of the return to appointed governors, the average age had increased to 54.2, with an age range from 36 to 74 years.[16]

When Putin first introduced the idea of resurrecting the practice of appointing governors, many observers expected that he planned to use his new prerogatives to renew the gubernatorial corps substantially; to replace 'red' governors and other political opponents, and to bring in a new generation of loyal managers. However, that did not happen. Putin did remove some of the oldest governors, and more than 40% of his new appointees were at least 15 years younger than the men they replaced.[17] In Tula, the new Putin appointee was 29 years younger than the incumbent he replaced,[18] and Putin was also responsible for installing the youngest governor ever, 30-year-old Ramzan Kadyrov, in Chechnya. However, due to the modest turnover, the average age of governors nevertheless continued to rise, although at a slow pace. Summing up the development of elite circulation during the Putin years, Ol'ga Kryshtanovskaya and Stephen White (2009, p. 302) find that no group within the ruling elite saw a lower turnover than the governors, and no group held a higher average age. By the end of Putin's second term, the average governor was 55 years old, and governors ranged in age from 32 to 74 years.

During Medvedev's presidency, however, the trend has been broken and a partial rejuvenation has taken place. Medvedev has quite consistently replaced outgoing incumbents with younger men—and in one case, a younger woman.[19] Some of the youngest members of the gubernatorial corps have stepped down—Mikhail Kuznetsov in Pskov (born 1968) and Roman Abramovich in Chukotka Autonomous *Okrug* (born 1966)—but these were replaced by even younger appointees. In 2010, the average age of the 26 governors appointed by Medvedev between May 2008 and May 2010 was 48.5 (the youngest new appointee being 35, the oldest 61).[20] On average these appointees were almost 12 years younger than the governors they replaced.[21] Not

[16]The data relate to governors in office at the end of 2004. The dataset does thus not include the last gubernatorial election, which took place parallel with the introduction of appointed governors in January and February 2005. If the 2005 results were included, this would push the average age even higher, as the new governor of Nenets Autonomous *Okrug*, Aleksei Barinov, was born in 1951, while the incumbent, Vladimir Butov, was born in 1958.

[17]This was the case in 12 out of 28 instances. Indeed, in six regions (Buryatiya, Kaliningrad, Kamchatka, North Ossetiya, Tula and Tuva) the new governors were more than 20 years younger than the incumbents.

[18]Vyacheslav Dudka (born 1960) replaced Vasilii Starodubstev (born 1931), who is best known for his participation in the August 1991 coup attempt to preserve the Soviet Union.

[19]The only exceptions were in Irkutsk, where Igor' Esipovskii (born 1960) was replaced by Dmitrii Mezentsev (born 1959), and in Stavropol, where Aleksandr Chernogorov (born 1959) was replaced by Valerii Gaevskii (born 1958).

[20]Igor' Esipovskii is not included here, as he died in 2009.

[21]This dataset consists of 25 outgoing governors. Esipovskii is again excluded, as is his predecessor as governor of Irkutsk, Aleksandr Tishanin. Although Esipovskii was appointed by Medvedev, Tishanin had resigned before Medvedev assumed office. The outgoing governors were on average 60.1 years old (with an age range from 42 to 73).

surprisingly, the incumbents who succeeded in winning reappointment pushed the average age up somewhat, but if we compare all Medvedev's appointees to the rest of the gubernatorial corps, the former are still a full four years younger (51.5 compared to 55.5 years of age).[22] As a result, over the course of Medvedev's first two years in office, the average age dropped to 53.5.

It is especially the oldest generation of governors, those 70 years and older—the pre-World War II generation—that has been hard hit by Medvedev's renewal of the gubernatorial corps. By mid-term, five out of eight governors in this age cohort had been replaced—and most observers considered it unlikely that the remaining three could continue in office for long (Samarina *et al.* 2009; Ivanov 2010).[23] So far, the oldest governor to have been reappointed by Medvedev is Kemerovo Governor Aman Tuleev, who at the age of 65 (born in 1944) was granted a new term in 2010. A closer look nevertheless reveals that the trend under Medvedev has more to do with turnover than with appointing a qualitatively different age group than Putin did. Medvedev's and Putin's new appointees took up the governorship at about the same age: the new Putin appointees were on average 48.8 years old when they first became governors, while the Medvedev appointees were 47.5.[24]

Figure 2 shows the age distribution of the gubernatorial corps as of May 2010. The new Medvedev appointees are concentrated in the age range from 46 to 57. Although Medvedev has intensified the process of rejuvenating the gubernatorial corps, governors are still generally older than in the late Yel'tsin years. Few governors come from the same age cohort as the president,[25] and the regional executives are still slightly older than the federal ones—in 2010, the average age of members of the federal government was 52.

As regards the gender balance within the gubernatorial corps, the description T.H. Rigby gave of this at the turn of the millennium still holds true: 'The gender story is brutally short' (Rigby 2001, p. 4). During the 1990s, only one woman was elected governor, and that was in one of the smallest and economically least developed regions of the federation: from 1996 to 2000, Valentina Bronevich served as governor of Koryak Autonomous *Okrug* on the Kamchatka Peninsula. During Putin's first term, Valentina Matvienko became the second female politician to break the glass ceiling of regional politics. Unlike Bronevich, Matvienko won the post in a politically and economically influential location, St Petersburg. She enjoyed strong backing from the Kremlin in her electoral campaign, but gender was not an issue here since Putin's main concern was to unseat the incumbent, Vladimir Yakovlev, and replace him with a

[22]For Medvedev's appointees ($N=41$) the median is 52, the youngest governor being 35 and the oldest 66. For Putin's appointees ($N=42$) the median is 55, with the youngest governor aged 34 and the oldest 76.

[23]Murtaza Rakhimov (born 1934) stepped down in July 2010, more than a year before the end of his term; in September the same year, after a vicious public showdown, Moscow Mayor Yurii Luzhkov (born 1936) was fired (he was the first governor Medvedev fired, and only the fourth governor to be publicly forced to leave office since 2005). The only remaining governor from this cohort is thus Leonid Polezhaev in Omsk (born 1940).

[24]Ramzan Kadyrov, who became governor at the age of 30, was an exception; the second youngest appointee in this group was 37-year-old Vladimir Yakushev in Tyumen.

[25]Medvedev himself was born in 1963.

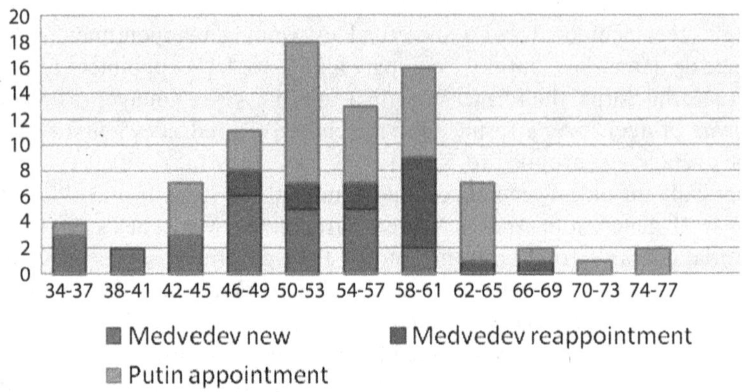

FIGURE 2. AGE DISTRIBUTION OF GOVERNORS IN OFFICE, MAY 2010.

member of his inner circle.[26] Besides Bronevich and Matvienko, no other woman won a governorship through elections, nor were there any women among the new names promoted by Putin after 2005.

Under Medvedev, the number of female governors has doubled—but only from one to two—as a result of Natal'ya Komarova being appointed to Khanty-Mansi Autonomous *Okrug*. Komarova's nomination was followed by one of the few cases of public protest against the Kremlin's appointment policy. The protest was not directed primarily against Komarova as a female governor but was more a result of local discontent with the removal of a well-entrenched and successful governor who had been at the helm of this wealthy oil-producing *okrug* ever since the introduction of the post of governor in 1991 (Whitmore 2010). The protests failed to sway the Khanty-Mansi legislature, however, and in due course Komarova's candidature was unanimously adopted.

Thus, neither the introduction of appointed governors nor the change of presidency has contributed to an improved gender balance among the governors. Women are under-represented in all positions of political power in Russia, but their share of the gubernatorial corps (2.4%) remains particularly low even compared to other institutions of executive and legislative power. In spring 2010, 14.2% of the members of the State *Duma* were women (64 out of 450), and 5.4% of Senators (nine out of 166) and 11.1% of the members of the federal government (three of 27) were female.[27]

[26]Putin was keen to replace Yakovlev. Not only had Yakovlev as deputy mayor of St Petersburg challenged and defeated Putin's old patron, Anatolii Sobchak, he had also been one of the leaders of the Fatherland–All Russia Bloc (*Otechestvo–Vsya Rossiya*), which had promoted itself as an alternative 'Party of Power' in the crucial 1999 State *Duma* elections. The Kremlin had tried to replace Yakovlev already in the 2000 gubernatorial election, but Matvienko had withdrawn from the race when it became clear that she stood no chance. This time Yakovlev had been 'promoted' to a new deputy premiership in Moscow in order to clear the field.

[27]For the State *Duma*, data on gender composition were retrieved from www.duma.gov.ru; for the Federation Council from www.council.gov.ru/staff/members/index.html; and for the government from www.government.ru/gov, accessed 28 June 2010.

Locals and outsiders

Despite recent centralisation, the Russian Federation still, in many respects, continues to resemble an archipelago where the regions function as isolated islands with their own local bureaucracy, local businesses and local mores. In the Soviet period, the Communist Party (*Kommunisticheskaya Partiya*, KPSS) served as a 'transmission belt', ensuring a certain rotation of cadre between the different parts of the union. The *nomenklatura* system provided the authorities with a pool of eligible candidates to fill key positions at various administrative levels (Hough 1969). According to Joel Moses, there was a 'Soviet bias that [viewed] natives [locals] as politically unreliable and more subject to corrupting influences' (Moses 1974, p. 144).

From the early 1970s, however, careers tended to become more regionally bound, with the first secretary frequently recruited among the regional party elite.[28] The Communist Party nevertheless continued to ensure vertical mobility, recruiting regional cadre to staff the party apparatus and state structures in Moscow. Then, with the end of party rule and the abolition of the *nomenklatura* system, career prospects for the new heads of the regional executive seemed limited to their respective regions. During the 1990s, there were very few examples of vertical as opposed to horizontal mobility within the executive branch. This meant strong incentives for the governors to entrench themselves in their gubernatorial seats, cultivating patron–client relations and warding off attempts at federal intervention in regional politics.

The introduction of presidentially appointed governors was seen as a mechanism for penetrating the regions and reintegrating them into a more tightly knit executive vertical—a process which had begun with Putin's initial thrust of federal reforms in 2000, when the presidential oversight function over the regions had been strengthened through the reorganisation of the institution of presidential representatives.[29] Although these reforms had helped the Kremlin to recapture the initiative in centre–regional relations (Hahn 2001),[30] Richard Sakwa has argued that they failed 'to transform the set of regional actors' or to 'significantly weaken traditional elite structures at the regional level' (Sakwa 2004, p. 154). Now, however, it became possible to 'parachute in' new leaders from the federal centre as a way of breaking a regional governor's monopoly on political power within a region. To what extent have Putin and Medvedev used their control over nominations to install outsiders—or *varyagi* as they are often referred to in the Russian debate—as governors?

Even with the limited mobility that has characterised regional political life in post-Soviet Russia, few politicians spend their entire careers in the same region. The

[28]At the 24th Party Congress in 1971, Secretary General Leonid Brezhnev stated that Moscow now assigned outsiders as first secretaries only in 'exceptional cases' (Moses 1974, p. 146), and there was a marked drop in the number of outsiders appointed to the position of *obkom* first secretaries from the Khrushchev to the early Brezhnev years (Moses 1974).

[29]Nikolai Petrov has noted that, in conjunction with the establishment of the federal *okruga* and the offices of the presidential plenipotentiaries, 'one undeniably positive feature of these extensive cadre reshufflings [was] the restoration of the national "elite space", which had been fragmented into 89 discrete pieces, with almost no horizontal elite exchanges' (Petrov 2002, p. 82).

[30]For a discussion on how Putin's first round of federal reforms affected the governors, see Blakkisrud (2003).

number of outsiders among the new appointees thus depends on the criteria applied for defining a person as a 'native' to a given region. One possible criterion of 'nativeness' could be being born in the region in question but such a definition would also include people who had then spent most of their professional careers outside the region and thus for all practical purposes were outsiders in relation to the local elite. One example is the new governor of Rostov, Vasilii Golubev. Although he grew up in Rostov, he left the region at age 18 and spent the next 35 years in Moscow and Moscow *Oblast'*. A better criterion therefore is having a professional track record in the region. Although a gubernatorial appointee may not be born and bred in the region, he may still have spent a substantial part, or perhaps all, of his professional career there. Such an approach was employed by Joel Moses in his study of the regional party leadership in the Soviet period, in which he defined a 'native' as someone 'either born or educated (secondary level or higher education) in the same region or contiguous regional area in which they held office' and 'served a minimum of 75 percent of their total careers in the same current region' (Moses 1974, p. 147). Table 2 therefore, includes different definitions of 'nativeness': being born in the region, whether the new governor spent the last 10 years immediately prior to his appointment working in the region, or alternatively, whether he had worked there for at least five of the last 10 years before their appointment. As shown in Table 2, the share of 'natives' among the new appointees appears remarkably similar under Putin and Medvedev, irrespective of which criterion we choose to apply.

The definition above excludes individuals who have represented the region at the federal level. It could well be argued that members of the State *Duma* elected from single-seat constituencies should be counted as members of the regional elite. These representatives have to maintain contact with the regional electorate and not least cultivate their relations with the incumbent governors.[31] Three more of Medvedev's appointees would qualify as natives if we include *Duma* representatives—Mikhail Yurevich representing Chelyabinsk from 1999 to 2005, and Vyacheslav Shport representing Khabarovsk from 1999 to 2007, who held single-seat constituencies, and Viktor Zimin who represented United Russia (*Edinaya Rossiya*) from 2007 to 2008 on

TABLE 2

NUMBER OF 'NATIVE' APPOINTEES UNDER PUTIN (JANUARY 2005–MAY 2008) AND MEDVEDEV (MAY 2008–MAY 2010)

	Born in the same region	*Worked in the same region the last 10 years*	*Worked in the same region at least five out of the last 10 years*
Putin's appointees (*N*=28)	10	8	11
Medvedev's appointees (*N*=27)	7	6	12

[31]On the governors' ability to influence the outcome of single-seat elections, see Lussier (2002). As regards the upper house, the Federation Council, many regions have chosen to appoint representatives with weak or no previous local affiliation (Remmington 2003).

a party list according to the reformed electoral system for State *Duma* elections from 2007. Yurevich and Shport were born and have spent their entire professional careers in their respective regions except for their terms in the State *Duma* and should therefore qualify as natives, and Zimin had worked in Khakasiya for 15 years prior to his short period in the State *Duma*. Adding the *Duma* representatives increases the number of Medvedev's appointed governors with over 10 years' affiliation to the region immediately prior to becoming governor to nine, and it increases those with at least five years' affiliation to 13. More than half the appointees would still fall into the category of 'outsiders'. Indeed, one in three of Medvedev's new appointees had no previous professional affiliation whatsoever with the region to which they were appointed, making them classical examples of the type of governors referred to as *varyagi*.

The high number of outsiders who have become governors under Putin and Medvedev clearly breaks with the trend in evidence during the period when governors were elected.[32] The appointment procedure has thus undoubtedly affected horizontal and vertical mobility.[33] The main difference between Putin's and Medvedev's presidency in this respect is related to turnover. While both presidents appointed the same number of new governors, the share of outsiders in the total number of appointments is significantly higher under Medvedev with 42.9% as compared to 23.1% under Putin.[34] Furthermore, an interesting pattern emerges when we break down Medvedev's new appointees into those who assumed office before and after the introduction of party-based nominations. Although Medvedev still has the final word when it comes to who is appointed,[35] the procedural change nevertheless seems to have spurred a greater acceptance of recruiting locally. Whereas seven out of nine of Medvedev's appointees with no previous links to the region in question were nominated before the changes took effect, all six appointees who had spent the last 10 years in the region were nominated after the changes (Table 2).[36] The dataset includes only 12 appointments according to the new procedure, and it is too early to conclude whether the pattern we see is the result of a deliberate policy change or is merely coincidental,

[32]The best-known cases of outsiders winning the governorship in electoral contests included some prominent generals-turned-politicians, like Aleksandr Lebed' in Krasnoyarsk (1998–2002), Boris Gromov in Moscow *Oblast'* (2000–present) and Georgii Shpak in Ryazan (2004–2008).

[33]Still, the only example of a governor moving horizontally during Medvedev's rule is Oleg Kozhemyako, who was appointed governor of Amur in 2008, having previously been governor in the now defunct Koryak Autonomous *Okrug* (2005–2007).

[34]This is based on the stricter definition of 'nativeness' but adding State *Duma* representatives to this category. Under Medvedev, 18 appointees out of 42 are defined as outsiders (of the remaining, nine were natives and 15 incumbents); under Putin 19 of 82 are defined as outsiders (nine were natives and 54 incumbents).

[35]In connection with the adoption of the new procedures for nominating governors, Andrei Isaev, First Deputy Secretary of the Presidium of the General Council of United Russia, confidently announced: 'The party system in Russia has developed to the point where parties can now bear full responsibility for the situation in the regions' (Sidorov 2008). This is of course an exaggeration. Not only is Medvedev free to reject the list of names proposed by the party and nominate a candidate of his own, he also has the right to dissolve the regional parliament and call early elections if the legislators should reject the president's candidate twice.

[36]If we include the *Duma* members in the latter category, the split becomes two before and seven after.

but the relatively abrupt change that occurred parallel to the implementation of the party-based nomination strengthens the former interpretation.[37]

One possible explanation for such a policy shift—besides formally delegating the nomination procedure to United Russia—could be the somewhat disappointing results of previous attempts at penetrating the closely knit ranks of the local elite by appointing an outsider to 'bring order'. One example is Nikolai Kolesov, who lasted only 16 months as governor of Amur. Kolesov, who made his career in Tatarstan, was appointed governor of Amur on the insistence of Far Eastern Presidential Plenipotentiary Kamil' Iskhakov, who also hailed from Tatarstan (Petrov 2008). Kolesov quickly came into conflict with the local elite, and when Iskhakov was subsequently promoted to Deputy Minister of Regional Affairs, he no longer had a patron in the region. In the end, Medvedev had no other choice than to relieve Kolesov of his duties. As argued by the Russian political scientist Rostislav Turovskii:

> The existing practice of appointing *varyagi* to the post of governors has proven its ineffectiveness. The new appointees are not good administrators able to rely on the local elites, but have to count solely on the resources of the lobbying forces which promoted them to the position as governors. As a result, they can hardly change the situation in the region for the better. (Bilevskaya 2009)

The ethnic factor

It can be hard for an 'outsider' to gain a firm foothold in any region, but it is generally even more difficult to penetrate the ethnically defined republics within the federation.[38] It is also politically a much more sensitive issue. A case in point concerns the Bashkortostani President Murtaza Rakhimov. In 2009, after having ruled the republic for close to two decades, he signalled that he was willing to step down at the end of his current term, but opposed the idea of an 'outsider' replacing him. According to Rakhimov, 'The republic will never accept someone from outside' (Rostovskii 2009). In discussing the question of 'nativeness' therefore, we should examine the ethnically defined republics within the Russian Federation.

Out of a current total of 83 regions, 21 have republic status on the basis of being defined as the homeland of an ethnic minority.[39] Both Putin and Medvedev seem to

[37]This change has taken place even though it is not the regional branch, but the party leadership in Moscow which decides on the final composition of the list of candidates to be forwarded to the Presidential Administration.

[38]As regards the lower-level autonomous regions, the Jewish Autonomous *Oblast'* and the autonomous *okruga*, ethnicity in general has been less politicised due to the weaker position of the titular ethnic groups in these regions. In relative terms, according to 2002 census data, the share of titular groups ranges from 2.1% of Jews in the Jewish Autonomous *Oblast'* to 23.4% of Chukchi in Chukotka Autonomous *Okrug* (the 2002 census, *Vserossiiskaya perepis' naseleniya 2002 goda*, is available at: www.perepis2002.ru/index.html?id=11; as for census data on the ethnic composition of the regions, these can be downloaded from www.perepis2002.ru/index.html?id=17, both sites accessed 12 January 2011).

[39]Three of the republics are official homelands to more than one ethnic group. These are Kabardino-Balkariya and Karachaevo-Cherkessiya, both of which include two distinct ethnic groups, and Dagestan, which is the home of more than a dozen different ethnic minorities.

have been sensitive to the ethnic dimension and the new republican appointees have predominantly been 'natives'. Five out of eight new republic heads nominated by Putin and four out of six of Medvedev's appointees had spent at least the last 10 years in the republics that they were tasked to govern. Compared to the rest of the gubernatorial corps, the difference is striking: among the newly appointed republic heads, the share of 'natives' was 64.3% as opposed to a share of 21.6% for the rest of the new appointees.[40]

In addition, the two Medvedev-appointed republic heads who had not spent at least the last 10 years in the republics they now govern, Boris Ebzeev in Karachaevo-Cherkessiya and Yunus-bek Evkurov in Ingushetiya, both belong to the titular groups of their respective republics. While the Kremlin opted for 'outsiders' to bring order to these volatile North Caucasian republics, it nevertheless attempted to assuage ethnic sensitivities by picking titulars with a federal career,[41] assuming that their ethnic affiliation would make them easier for the republic's elite to accept.[42] The same was the case with one of Putin's two 'outsiders', Arsen Kanokov, a Moscow-based businessman and an ethnic Kabardin—although he had arguably maintained closer ties with his native Kabardino-Balkariya, including serving as deputy permanent representative of the republic in Moscow. The only instance of a *varyag* being appointed to an ethnic republic was thus Putin's promotion of Vyacheslav Nagovitsyn, an ethnic Russian and first deputy governor of Tomsk, to head Buryatiya in 2007. Nagovitsyn had no previous affiliation with the republic whereas the incumbent he replaced, although he was an ethnic Russian, was a 'native' of the region who even spoke Buryat.[43]

During the 1990s, some of the ethnically defined republics had developed a reputation for cultivating authoritarian regimes (Hahn 2003). Henry E. Hale has argued that 'institutionalized ethnicity gave the "titular" leaders of the ethnic minority regions special will and ability to cultivate machine politics' (Hale 2003, p. 230). In various rankings of regional democratic development, the republics were consistently over-represented at the bottom end of the scale (McMann & Petrov 2000). Since 2005, both Putin and Medvedev have made active use of the appointment procedures to remove entrenched republican presidents. Under Putin the heads of republics had a lower-than-average reappointment rate, while under Medvedev they have scored slightly better.[44] Nevertheless, by May 2010, two-thirds

[40]Among new republic heads, nine out of 14 were 'natives', and among the remaining new appointees, nine out of 41 were 'natives'.

[41]Both men had spent their entire professional careers outside the republics. Ebzeev, a member of the Russian Constitutional Court, had made an unsuccessful attempt to be elected president of Karachaevo-Cherkessiya in 1999 (finishing in sixth place). Evkurov, a general in the airborne troops, had no previous political career.

[42]That all groups were not satisfied with Evkurov's appointment was demonstrated by an attack on Evkurov's motorcade in 2009, in which the new president was severely injured.

[43]The incumbent, Leonid Potapov, had grown up in Buryatiya and had ruled the republic since 1990, initially as a first secretary of the Communist Party, later as chair of the regional parliament and from 1994 as president.

[44]Under Putin nine out of 17 republican heads were reappointed (52.9% compared with a reappointment rate of 69.2% for the rest of the governors); under Medvedev four out of 10 were reappointed in the period covered here (40.0% compared with 34.4% for the rest of the governors).

of the republics had been given new chief executives since the change from elections to appointment.[45]

At the same time, it seems as if the Kremlin has given priority to avoid fuelling ethnic tensions. Partly this has been attempted by selecting members of the republic elite—and if necessary, by giving the incumbent a decisive say in the succession question.[46] Alternatively, the Kremlin has opted for 'federal titulars': individuals belonging to the titular group who have been tested through a federal career. Only one of Medvedev's new appointments involved a non-titular: Viktor Zimin in Khakasiya.[47] Zimin is an ethnic Russian, but has, as mentioned above, a long career that links him to the republic. Moreover, Khakasiya has the highest share of ethnic Russians of all the republics (80.3% according to the 2002 census),[48] and the ethnic issue is probably less acute there than in most of the other republics to which Medvedev appointed executive heads during this period.[49]

Professional background

A crucial criterion in the selection of governors is professional background. Studying the new appointees' professional career can give us not only a better understanding of what type of experience the Kremlin is currently looking for when recruiting new regional executives, but it can also provide insights into whether recruitment at this level appears guided by less formal criteria such as patron–client relationships. During Putin's presidency, considerable attention focused on Putin's practice of drawing on his old network connections in the FSB and other security structures—the so-called *siloviki*—when filling positions in the Kremlin, the government, and the federal bureaucracy (Kryshtanovskaya 2002; Petrov & Slider 2005). Ol'ga Kryshtanovskaya and Stephen White have estimated that the share of *siloviki* in the elite rose from 11.2% under Yel'tsin to 26.6% during Putin's first presidential term (Kryshtanovskaya & White 2003, p. 293).[50] Similarly, Putin was seen as filling the federal structures with people from his native St Petersburg—not only *siloviki*, but also people he had

[45]Five more republican heads were replaced during the summer of 2010. The only previously elected republican heads that seem to have weathered the storm are Aleksandr Volkov in Udmurtiya (whose current term expires in 2014), Leonid Markelov in Marii El (whose current term expires in 2015) and Nikolai Merkushkin in Mordoviya (whose current term also expires in 2015).

[46]In the case of Tatarstan, incumbent president Mintimer Shaimiev was, according to Aleksei Makarkin, able to handpick his successor (Makarkin 2010). The new president was Shaimiev's protégé and had served as his prime minister since 1998.

[47]Medvedev had appointed a Karachai to Karchaevo-Cherkessiya, an Ingush to Ingushetiya, a Komi to Komi, a Tatar to Tatarstan and a Dargin to Dagestan. (The Dargins are the second largest ethnic group in Dagestan.)

[48]*Vserossiiskaya perepis' naseleniya 2002 goda*, available at: www.perepis2002.ru/index.html?id=11, accessed 12 January 2011.

[49]Zimin replaced Aleksei Lebed' (1996–2009), who is of mixed Ukrainian and Cossack descent. The first head of the republic, Evgenii Smirnov (1992–1996), was also an ethnic Russian.

[50]'The elite' is here defined as members of the federal government, the Federal Assembly (both houses), the Security Council and the governors. The data represent the situation in 1993 and in 2002 (Kryshtanovskaya & White 2003, p. 293).

worked with under the liberal Mayor of St Petersburg, Anatolii Sobchak, in the early 1990s.[51]

At the regional level, the share of *siloviki* was particularly high among the new presidential plenipotentiaries and chief federal inspectors appointed in connection with the reform of the institution of presidential representatives in 2000 (Petrov 2002),[52] but it was also to some degree extended to Putin's appointment of new governors—although, arguably, there were more *siloviki* elected by popular vote between 2000 and 2004 than appointed by the president between 2005 and 2008.[53] According to data in their official CVs, six of Putin's new appointees, or around one fifth, had backgrounds in the KGB or FSB, the armed forces, the Ministry of the Interior, the police and the *prokuratora*. Is it possible to discern a similar recruitment pattern under Medvedev? Table 3 shows the professional backgrounds of the 27 persons in our dataset who were first appointed governor during Medvedev's presidency.

Examination of the professional background of Medvedev's appointees fails to reveal any proclivity for promoting either *siloviki* or St Petersburgers. None of his new appointees has officially been affiliated with the FSB; and among the incumbents, he has replaced two 'FSB governors'—Vladimir Potapenko in Nenets Autonomous *Okrug* and Vladimir Kulakov in Voronezh—with appointees from private business and the federal government, respectively (Arutunyan 2009). Medvedev has promoted three officers from the armed forces, but only one of these, Major General Yunus-bek Evkurov, progressed directly from active duty to becoming head of Ingushetiya. The other two had been decommissioned for almost 20 years at the time they were appointed.[54] If we apply the same criteria for who may qualify as *siloviki* as above, the share of *siloviki* among the appointees fell from 21.4% under Putin to 11.1% in the current dataset under Medvedev. Likewise, only two of the 'outsiders' recruited by Medvedev had a career background in St Petersburg: Andrei Turchak (appointed governor of Pskov) and Dmitrii Mezentsev (governor of Irkutsk).

In general, the new appointees appear to be drawn from a wide range of professional backgrounds. Many of them have in common a period of service in Moscow before their appointment to a governorship in the regions.[55] Experience in

[51]The practice of bringing regional clients to fill leading positions in Moscow was nothing new; previous examples included Brezhnev's 'Dnepropetrovsk mafia' and Yel'tsin's 'Sverdlovsk mafia'.

[52]According to Nikolai Petrov, 'some three-fourths' of the chief federal inspectors came 'from the military, the MVD, and the special services, including more than one-third from the FSB (many of whom were the chiefs of regional FSB departments)' (Petrov 2002, pp. 83–84).

[53]Only one of the appointees, Valerii Potapenko, the new governor of Nenets Autonomous *Okrug*, officially listed that he had served in the KGB and FSB. There has been considerable discussion on how to define the category of *silovik*. See for example Kryshtanovskaya and White (2003, 2009), and for dissenting views, Rivera and Rivera (2006) and Renz (2006).

[54]Dmitrii Mezentsev, the new governor of Irkutsk, was decommissioned in 1990, and Dmitrii Dmitrienko in Murmansk, in 1992.

[55]So far however, a governorship seldom has served as a springboard for a federal career. Many former governors have taken up seats in the Federation Council, but rather than a promotion, this is frequently seen as an honourable retirement position. The only governor to have been promoted by Medvedev to the federal government so far is Aleksandr Khloponin, former governor of Krasnoyarsk. In January 2010, he was named presidential plenipotentiary to the new North Caucasus Federal *Okrug* and simultaneously deputy prime minister in the federal government.

TABLE 3
PROFESSIONAL BACKGROUND OF NEW GOVERNORS APPOINTED BY MEDVEDEV, MAY 2008–MAY 2010

	Region	*Governor*	*Professional background*
1	Stavropol	Valerii Gaevskii	Various positions in *Komsomol* in Stavropol, and later Moscow, 1981–1991; businessman, Moscow, 1991–1996; Stavropol government (including first deputy prime minister) 1996–2005; deputy presidential representative, Southern Federal *Okrug*, 2006–2007; Deputy Minister of Regional Development from 2008 until appointed governor same year.
2	Chukotka Autonomous *Okrug*	Roman Kopin	Kostroma customs department 1995–1998; SBS-Agro Bank, Kostroma, 1998–1999; advisor to the governor of Chukotka Autonomous *Okrug* 1999–2001; head of local administration 2001–2008; deputy governor from 2008 until appointed governor same year.
3	Karachaevo-Cherkessiya	Boris Ebzeev	Various positions at the Saratov Juridical Institute 1977–1991 (professor from 1990); judge in the Constitutional Court of the Russian Federation from 1991 until appointed president 2008.
4	Amur	Oleg Kozhemyako	Businessman; member of the Primore *Duma* 2001–2002; the *Duma*'s representative in the Federation Council 2002–2004; advisor to chairman of the Federation Council 2004–2005; deputy governor of Koryak Autonomous *Okrug* 2005, governor 2005–2007; assistant to head of Presidential Administration from 2007 until appointed governor 2008.
5	Ingushetiya	Yunus-bek Evkurov	Officer in the airborne troops from 1989 until appointed president; took part in the First Chechen War, the Kosovo War, and the Second Chechen war. Attained the rank of major general. Appointed president in 2008.
6	Irkutsk	Igor' Esipovksii	Menatep 1988–1991; director general of Rossiiskii aviafond 1992–2000; director Rosoboroneksport 2001–2005; director general Avtovaz 2005–2006; member of the State *Duma* (United Russia) from 2007 until appointed governor 2008.
7	Kirov	Nikita Belykh	Working in investment and finance, Perm, 1993–2004; member of the Perm *Duma* 2001–2004; deputy governor of Perm 2004–2005; party leader of Union of Right Forces 2005–2008 and member of the Perm *Duma* from 2006 until appointed governor 2008.
8	Khakasiya	Viktor Zimin	Construction department of Krasnoyarsk Railways 1985–1992; deputy director of Abakan branch of Krasnoyarsk Railways 1992–2007; member of the upper house of Khakasiya *Duma* 2003–2007; member of the State *Duma* (United Russia) from 2007 until appointed president (chair of government) in 2008.
9	Nenets Autonomous *Okrug*	Igor' Fedorov	Various positions in Arkhenergo, Arkhangel'sk, 1995–2005; deputy mayor of Arkhangel'sk in 2005; director of Arkhenergo 2005–2008; deputy governor of Arkhangel'sk from 2008 until appointed governor in 2009.

(*continued*)

TABLE 3
(*Continued*)

	Region	*Governor*	*Professional background*
10	Voronezh	Aleksei Gordeev	Various positions in agricultural administration and business, 1981–1992; deputy head of local administration, Moscow *Oblast'*, 1992–1997; in Ministry of Agriculture 1997–1999, including first deputy minister 1998–1999; deputy leader of the Agrarian Party (*Agrarnaya Partiya Rossii*) 1999–2003; Minister of Agriculture from 1999 until appointed governor in 2009.
11	Pskov	Andrei Turchak	Various positions in St Petersburg-based businesses, most of which affiliated with holding company Leninets, 1996–2005; United Russia coordinator of youth policy from 2005 to 2009; member of the Pskov *Duma* 2007; representative of Pskov in the Federation Council 2007 until appointed governor in 2009.
12	Orel	Aleksandr Kozlov	Various positions in Tatarstan Ministry of Finance 1968–1984 and of the USSR 1984–1989; in Presidential Administration 1991–1992, in government apparatus 1992–1996; deputy head of apparatus 1996–1998 and 1999–2004; deputy CEO of TNK, 1998–1999; Deputy Minister of Agriculture from 2004 until appointed governor in 2009.
13	Murmansk	Dmitrii Dmitrienko	Served in the submarine forces 1980–1992; in business 1992–1999; advisor to governor of Krasnoyarsk 1999–2002; advisor, later assistant to the head of the Federal Agency for Sea and Inland Water Transport 2002–2006, deputy head 2006–2008; deputy head of Federal Agency for Fisheries from 2008 until appointed governor in 2009.
14	Khabarovsk	Vyacheslav Shport	Various positions in KnAAPO (*Komsomolsk-na-Amure aviatsionnoe proizvodsvennoe ob''edinenie*) (part of Sukhoi), Khabarovsk, 1979–1999, including head engineer 1997–1999; member of State *Duma* (first People's Deputy, then Unity (*Edinstvo*) and United Russia) 1999–2007; director, Sukhoi, 2007–2008; deputy prime minister of Khabarovsk from 2008 until appointed governor in 2009.
15	Irkutsk	Dmitrii Mezentsev	Officer (military press) 1984–1990; head of St Petersburg mayor's committee on press 1991–1996; deputy head of State Committee on Press 1996–1999; head of Centre for Strategic Research 1999–2002; representative of Irkutsk in Federation Council (deputy chair from 2004) from 2002 until appointed governor in 2009.
16	Sverdlovsk	Aleksandr Misharin	Various positions in Sverdlovsk Railways 1981–1998 except 1989–1991, when involved in Ekaterinburg metro construction; Deputy Minister of Transport 1998–2002 and 2004–2009; head of Sverdlovsk Railways 2002–2004; director of department of industry and infrastructure of the Russian government in 2009 until appointed governor same year.

(*continued*)

TABLE 3
(*Continued*)

	Region	*Governor*	*Professional background*
17	Volgograd	Anatolii Brovko	Deputy director and director of various enterprises (pipe plants and metallurgy), Volgograd, Rostov and Vladimir 1994–2005; head of Agency for Investments and Development of Volgograd *Oblast'* 2005–2006; deputy governor from 2006 until appointed governor in 2009.
18	Komi	Vyacheslav Gaizer	Various positions, Komibank and Komi Social Bank, 1993–2002; First Deputy Minister of Finance 2002, Minister of Finance from 2003 and simultaneously deputy head (from 2009 first deputy head) of republic from 2004 until appointed head of republic in 2010.
19	Tatarstan	Rustam Minnikhanov	Working in Sabinskii, then Arskii local consumer board, Tatarstan, 1983–1990; head of Arskii *raiispolkom*, later deputy head of administration 1990–1993; head of Vysokogorskii *Raion* 1993–1996; minister of finance, 1996–1998; prime minister from 1998 until appointed president in 2010.
20	Dagestan	Magomed-salam Magomedov	Various positions, including professor of economics, at Dagestan State University 1991–2001; head of governmental working group on the development of the Dagestani shelf 2001–2006; member of the Dagestan *Duma* 1999 (chair 2006–2007) until appointed president in 2010.
21	Khanty-Mansi Autonomous *Okrug*	Natal'ya Komarova	Economist, various positions in Novyi Urengoi *gorispolkom* (including first deputy head 1992–1994) 1980–1994; mayor 1994–2000; first deputy governor of Yamal-Nenets Autonomous *Okrug* 2000–2001; member of State *Duma* (United Russia) 2001 until appointed governor in 2010.
22	Jewish Autonomous *Oblast*	Aleksandr Vinnikov	Teacher, various positions in Leninsk *raikom* (including first secretary), Jewish Autonomous *Oblast*, 1978–1991; director of local branch of insurance company 1992–1996; head of department of state support and small business development, Jewish Autonomous *Oblast* government, 1996–1999; mayor of Birobidzhan 1999 until appointed governor in 2010.
23	Krasnoyarsk	Lev Kuznetsov	Economist, various positions, including first deputy CEO, Noril'skii Nikel' 1996–2001; first deputy governor of Taimyr Autonomous *Okrug* 2001–2002, first deputy governor of Krasnoyarsk 2002–2007 (except for five months as acting head of Norilsk in 2003); CEO of Kolmar, Sakha, from 2008 until appointed governor in 2010.
24	Yamal-Nenets Autonomous *Okrug*	Dmitrii Kobylkin	Geophysicist, in Purneftegazgeologiya, Yamal-Nenets Autonomous *Okrug*, 1996–2001; CEO of Khancheineftegaz 2001–2005, head of Pur *Raion* from 2005 until appointed governor in 2010.
25	Chelyabinsk	Mikhail Yurevich	Businessman; director of holding company Makfa, Chelyabinsk, 1995–2000; member of State *Duma* (People's Deputy, later United Russia) 1999–2005; mayor of Chelyabinsk from 2005 until appointed governor in 2010.

(*continued*)

TABLE 3
(Continued)

	Region	*Governor*	*Professional background*
26	Rostov	Vasilii Golubev	Party work, Moscow *Oblast'*, 1983–1990; head of Leninsk *Raion*, 1991–1999; deputy governor, 1999–2000; first deputy chair of Moscow *Oblast'* government 2000–2003; head of Leninsk *Raion* from 2003 until appointed governor in 2010.
27	Orenburg	Yurii Berg	Teacher, later school director, Orsk, Orenburg, 1976–1992; deputy head of Orsk 1996–1996; director in local business, 1997–2005; head of Orsk from 2005 until appointed governor in 2010.

the federal government, State *Duma* or Federation Council seems to be considered a valuable asset as regards gubernatorial candidates. For example, Putin nominated four former federal ministers or deputy ministers as governors and, similarly, during his first two years in office Medvedev chose four candidates from this category.[56] In addition, four of the new appointees had at some stage worked in the Presidential Administration,[57] and the same number had served as presidential plenipotentiaries.[58] About a fifth had previously been elected to the State *Duma*,[59] and a few had served in the Federation Council.[60]

There is a certain overlap in personnel between the categories listed above as some of the new governors had previously held more than one position at the federal level. For instance, Medvedev's first new appointee, Valerii Gaevskii, who became Governor of Stavropol in May 2008, had served both as deputy plenipotentiary to the Southern Federal *Okrug* and as federal deputy minister of regional development. But even if we correct for double entries, and also apply a narrower definition of federal experience, leaving out plenipotentiaries (who after all serve in the regions) and the pre-2000, part-time members of the Federation Council,[61] we find that 10 out of Putin's 28 new appointees (36%) and 12 out of Medvedev's 27 (44%) had a previous federal career position in either the executive or the legislative branches.

[56]Putin's appointees from this category were Georgii Boos, Aleksandr Karlin, Sergei Mitin and Igor' Slyunyaev; Medvedev's have been Valerii Gaevskii, Aleksei Gordeev, Aleksandr Kozlov and Aleksandr Misharin.

[57]Of Putin's appointees, Aleksandr Karlin and Vladimir Artyakov; and of Medvedev's, Oleg Khozemyako and Aleksandr Kozlov.

[58]Of Putin's appointees this applies to Aleksandr Berdnikov, Valerii Potapenko and Sergei Vakhrukov; and of Medvedev's, Valerii Gaevskii.

[59]Under Putin, these were Sergei Antuf'ev, Georgii Boos, Arsen Kanokov, Oleg Kovalev, Mikhail Men' and Sergei Mitin; under Medvedev these were Vyacheslav Shport, Igor' Esipovskii, Viktor Zimin, Natal'ya Komarova and Mikhail Yurevich.

[60]In this category there were two of Putin's nominees, Oleg Kozhemyako and Igor' Slyunyaev, and three of Medvedev's, the same Oleg Kozhemyako as well as Dmitrii Mezentsev and Andrei Turchak.

[61]Four of Putin's appointees—Mukhu Aliev, Sergei Antuf'ev, Sholban Kara-ool and Sergei Vakhrukov—had enjoyed *ex officio* representation in the Federation Council due to being elected chair of their respective regional parliaments.

Interestingly, Aleksandr Misharin, the first governor to be nominated according to the party-based procedure, was also the last of the new governors within this dataset to have served as a federal (deputy) minister—none of the subsequent 11 nominations included candidates from this category. Again, we can note an apparent shift in the trend taking place around the time of the implementation of the new nomination procedure: up to the Sverdlovsk nomination, nine out of 16 new appointees had either served as a member of the federal government or the Federal Assembly. In addition, both Boris Ebzeev, who had been a Constitutional Court judge since 1991, and Dmitrii Dmitrienko, whose last position before being appointed had been as a deputy head of the federal agency for fisheries, clearly had experience on the federal level. From Sverdlovsk onwards, however, only three out of 12 fall into this category. (Besides Misharin, these were the two State *Duma* deputies Natal'ya Komarova and Mikhail Yurevich.) The practice of identifying 'federal natives'—candidates with a regional affiliation but with federal experience—thus seems to have given way to selecting people with more narrowly local career backgrounds.

Another trend is the emergence of 'New Russian' governors (Radzikhovskii 2010)—governors with a mixed background from business and the bureaucracy. That individuals migrate between business and politics at the regional level is nothing new—already during Putin's first term there were several businessmen who ran for office (Söderlund 2005, p. 529). At the time, this was interpreted as an attempt by the companies to capture the region in question (Orttung 2004).[62] After the change to the practice of appointing governors however, it was no longer cost-effective for big business to invest in a governorship in this way. The economic influence of these companies had been sufficient to sway the electorate, especially in some of the more sparsely populated but resource-rich autonomous *okruga*, but the non-transparent nomination procedure, as well as the fact that the president now could remove the governor at will, made a long-term investment in a governorship a risky business. The new generation of businessmen-turned-politicians, the 'New Russian' governors, are therefore not primarily representatives of a given firm, but a product of changing dynamics in elite recruitment (Rivera & Rivera 2006), and of the changing nature of the elite itself. Typical examples of this new type of regional head include Anatolii Brovko (Volgograd) and Mikhail Yurevich (Chelyabinsk), but, as seen from Table 3, most of Medvedev's new appointees have some professional experience from working in private business.

The relationship between incumbency and gubernatorial turnover

Traditionally, incumbent governors have been seen as enjoying a great advantage due to their control over 'administrative resources'—their ability to mobilise organisational and financial resources within the state apparatus as well as the judiciary, law enforcement organs and the media.[63] During the 1990s, the Kremlin quietly accepted

[62]Examples include the election of a 'Yukos governor', Boris Zolotarev, in Evenk Autonomous *Okrug* and of a 'Noril'skii Nikel' governor', Oleg Budargin, in Taimyr Autonomous *Okrug*.

[63]Every year from when the first elections for regional executive heads were held in 1991 up to the introduction of appointed governors in 2005, a majority of the incumbents running for re-election won a new term. The only exceptions were in 1996 and 1998 (Blakkisrud 2005).

that some governors extended their powers and control far beyond what was prescribed by law, as long as they delivered the vote in federal elections (Hale 2003; Chebankova 2008). As a result, by the end of the decade, a group of powerful regional leaders had crystallised; these were leaders who, according to Richard Sakwa, had managed to transform their territories into 'separate fiefdoms where they ruled like the boyars of the old, apparently insulated from the writ of federal laws and the constitution' (Sakwa 2002, p. 16). When Yel'tsin stepped down on New Year's Eve 1999, he left behind no less than 15 governors who had been able to hold on to their positions ever since this institution (or, alternatively, the republican presidency) was first introduced.[64]

During Putin's first term (2000–2004), various institutional reforms were introduced to stimulate turnover in the regional elite: the maximum length for a gubernatorial term was set at five years, and no governor was to serve more than two consecutive terms. As the Constitutional Court ruled against applying the two-term limit retroactively in 2002, many incumbents were allowed to run for a third, or in some cases even a fourth term.[65] Nevertheless, some of Russia's most powerful regional leaders were approaching the end of their tenure as governors.[66] The 2004 decision to reintroduce presidentially appointed governors was therefore welcomed by many regional leaders as it offered some respite: with the switch from elected to appointed governors, the formal limit on the number of terms was no longer an obstacle, as this applied to elected offices only.

Those who had counted on the new procedure providing enhanced job security for the incumbents were initially proven right. For example, the old legislation had barred 10 of the governors currently serving a third term from seeking re-election. Only one of these stood down during Putin's presidency—and not because Putin dismissed him, but because his region was merged with another region (Irkutsk *Oblast'*). All the others were either reappointed or allowed to remain in office until the end of Putin's term. Overall, between 2005 and 2008 more incumbents secured an extension of their tenure than ever before, irrespective of whether the governors had been appointed or elected.[67] The low replacement rate led to speculation about a deal between the Kremlin and the governors—that they had been promised extended tenure in return for not opposing Putin's reform—as well as concerns about the lack of elite turnover.

[64]These were the governors of Astrakhan, Khabarovsk, Novgorod, Omsk, Samara, Tomsk, Rostov, Yaroslavl, the Jewish Autonomous *Oblast'*, Khanty-Mansi Autonomous *Okrug* and Taimyr Autonomous *Okrug*, as well as the republican heads of Bashkortostan, Dagestan, Sakha and Tatarstan.

[65]It has been argued that the concession on the term-issue was granted 'in return for regional abstention from obstructing the implementation of Putin's other federal reforms' (Hahn 2003, p. 126) and for support for the Kremlin in the 2003–2004 electoral cycle (Sakwa 2004, p. 153).

[66]The legislation had quite different consequences depending on the timing of regional electoral cycles. In 2004, there were 24 governors serving a third term. Of these, 14 were allowed to seek a fourth term due to loopholes in the legislation, including Murtaza Rakhimov, who, if he had been re-elected in 2008, would have been allowed to rule his republic until 2013 (a total of 23 years). It was less advantageous however, for another powerful figure, Yurii Luzhkov, who would have been forced to step down already in 2007 (Blakkisrud 2005).

[67]For the turnover rate from 1991 up to the introduction of appointed governors, see Blakkisrud (2005).

Elena Chebankova warned that the 'pre-existing pattern of poor cadre alteration, combined with the high reappointment rate, resulted in a serious stagnation of personnel in the regions' (Chebankova 2006, p. 471).

Consequently, when Medvedev assumed office in May 2008, the ranks of the governors were crowded with incumbents with long tenure: one in three had been in office for more than 10 years, and 11 had held on to their post for 15 years already. A partial renewal of the gubernatorial corps was thus long overdue, and Medvedev's first steps seemed to indicate that he was ready to take on the challenge.

During his first two years in office, Medvedev dramatically reduced the number of Yel'tsin-era governors (see Figure 3).[68] Especially hard hit was the very first generation of governors: the cohort which had come to power during Yel'tsin's first term in office (1991–1996) or before. Only one of them had his tenure prolonged,[69] which fuelled speculation that Medvedev was planning to remove the entire cohort.[70] This group included several regional leaders who had governed their regions ever since Russia became an independent state, as well as some key actors in the development of Russian federalism in the 1990s. They included President Mintimer Shaimiev of Tatarstan, a previously 'untouchable' regional leader who had been central in developing the form of federalism Russia embraced in the 1990s, including the bilateral power-sharing treaties between Moscow and the regions (Walker 1996); Governor Eduard Rossel' of Sverdlovsk, who had challenged the asymmetric federalism and championed the rights of the *oblasti* and *kraya* (Easter 1997); and Governor Egor Stroev of Orel, who as Chairman of the Federation Council had facilitated collective bargaining with the federal centre after the governors became popularly elected.

While lengthy tenure no longer seems to work to the advantage of the incumbents, not even Putin's handpicked men proved to be immune to replacement: Nikolai Kolesov enjoyed only 16 months as governor of Amur, and Vladimir Potapenko in Nenets Autonomous *Okrug* had his term cut short by 'voluntary' retirement. Mukhu Aliev in Dagestan served a full term, but failed to be rewarded with a second term in 2010 when power was returned to the powerful Magomedov clan.[71] Nevertheless, Putin's new appointees represented the only cohort where a majority of the incumbents were reappointed than dismissed (see Figure 3).

[68]Only six of the Yel'tsin era governors were reappointed during this period, whereas 14 were either asked to tender their resignation or failed to get endorsed for a new term when their term expired.

[69]The sole exception was Aleksandr Volkov of Udmurtiya, who was reappointed by Medvedev in February 2009. One could argue that he does not belong to this cohort, as his presidential term began to run only in 2000. In the capacity of elected chair of the Udmurt government, however, he had served as executive head of the republic since April 1995.

[70]As of May 2010, the remaining members of this cohort were Murtaza Rakhimov (Bashkortostan, in office since 1990), Leonid Polezhaev (Omsk, since 1991), Viktor Kress (Tomsk, since 1991), Yurii Luzhkov (Moscow, since 1992), Evgenii Savchenko (Belgorod, since 1993), Kirsan Ilyumzhinov (Kalmykiya, since 1993), Nikolai Fedorov (Chuvashiya, since 1994), Ravil' Geniatulin (Chita, now Zabaikalsk *Krai*, since 1996) and Vyacheslav Pozgalev (Vologda, since 1996). In the course of the summer, Medvedev went on to replace Rakhimov, Fedorov, Ilyumzhinov and Luzhkov.

[71]The new President of Dagestan, Magomedsalam Magomedov, is the son of Magomedali Magomedov, who had ruled the republic during the Soviet period and until 2006.

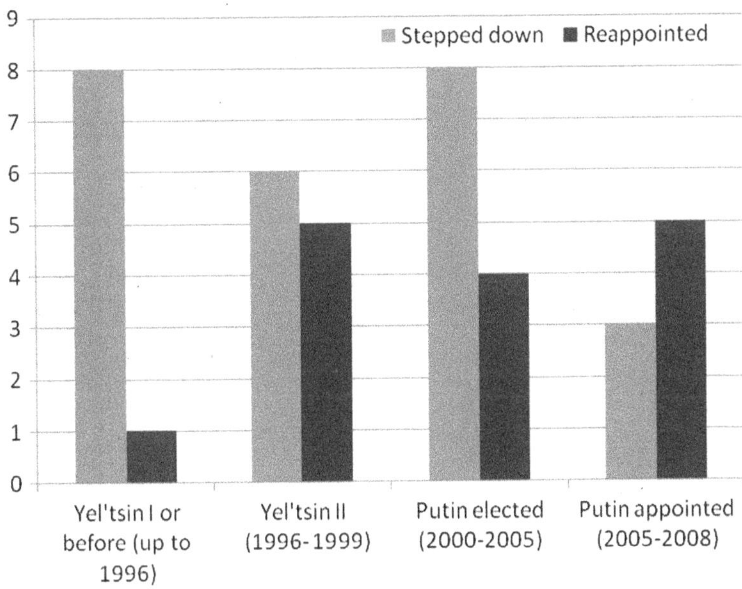

FIGURE 3. Turnover among Incumbents under Medvedev (May 2008–May 2010).
Note: Aleksandr Tishanin is not included in the dataset as he stepped down before Medvedev assumed office. His successor as governor of Irkutsk, Igor' Esipovskii, is also excluded since he was not removed but died in an accident (*N*=40).

While it is not surprising that the Putin-appointed governors fared better than the other cohorts, perhaps more unexpected is the relatively strong performance of the governors who came to power in the late 1990s. This group did much better than the subsequent cohort elected during Putin's first term,[72] and its success contradicts Medvedev's stated preference for greater turnover. Although formally there is no longer a limit on how many years an incumbent can remain in office, Medvedev has made it clear that governors should not expect to sit for more than three consecutive terms—a fourth term, according to Medvedev, might be granted only 'as an exception' (Medvedev 2009). In reality, however, fourth terms have proved far from exceptional: 'fourth-termers' have actually made up 40% of Medvedev's appointees.

Despite the concessions regarding some Yel'tsin-era governors, Medvedev has, in the course of two years, nonetheless come a long way in transforming the gubernatorial corps. Figure 4 gives a snapshot as of May 2010 of the distribution of governors according to when they first assumed office (that is, their 'generational cohort' according to presidency) and whether they were appointed by Putin or Medvedev. This indicates the magnitude of cadre reshuffling that Medvedev has been undertaking at the regional level.

[72]More than half of the incumbents who had to step down during Putin's second term belonged to this cohort. The low reappointment rate within this group gives rise to the question of whether—as has frequently been claimed (Petrov 2002)—the Kremlin in the early 2000s was able to determine the outcome of gubernatorial elections.

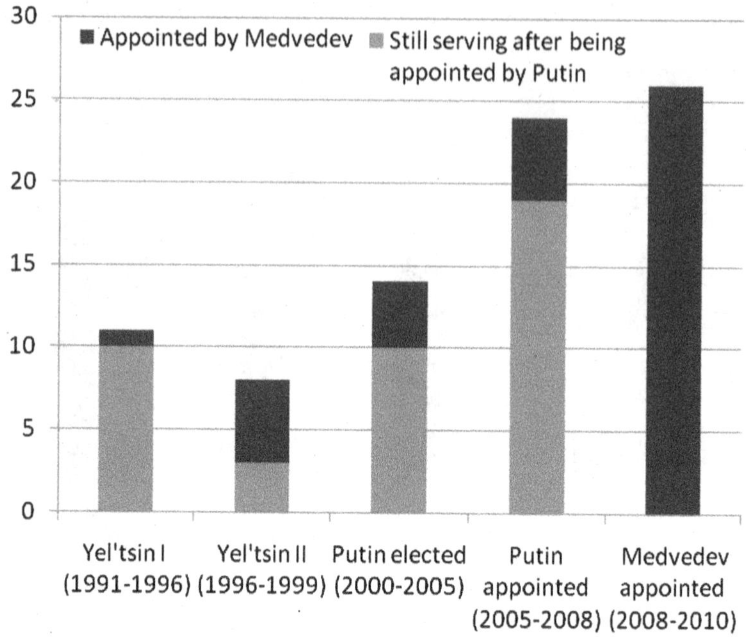

FIGURE 4. GOVERNORS IN OFFICE MAY 2010, GENERATIONAL COHORTS.

Patterns of regional elite recruitment under Medvedev

Overall, the main trend in regional elite recruitment over the two first years of Medvedev's presidency has been toward greater turnover among the incumbents. Limited renewal over an extended period has meant a steady influx of new governors with more than 10 years in office. While by the end of May 2010 Medvedev had replaced 14 incumbents who had been in office for more than a decade, the total number of such governors nevertheless only dropped from 29 to 21 over the same period. Medvedev has also failed to limit the fourth term to 'exceptional cases'. Still, his regional cadre policy represents a clear break from the far more accommodating line pursued by Putin. Where Putin seemed content to reappoint governors as long as they expressed loyalty to the Kremlin and delivered the vote, Medvedev has taken the reform of the executive vertical one step further and confronted many of the entrenched governors.

Who are these new governors? When we examine the professional background of Medvedev's new appointees, it is difficult to identify a clear pattern. At least according to their official CVs, there is no trace of the alleged 'FSB-isation' or militarisation of the regional elite. The new governors hail from a wide range of different professional backgrounds. One thing many of them have in common is that they have spent part of their careers in private business before turning (or returning) to elected or administrative positions. While only one of Medvedev's 27 new appointees, Lev Kuznetsov in Krasnoyarsk, was recruited directly from a position in a private company, a much more common career trajectory involves holding a position such as mayor of a regional capital or as local head of executive power *en route* from a business position to being appointed governor. A second common characteristic of the new appointees is that many have experience at the federal level—in positions in the federal executive or in the Federal Assembly—before being appointed. This latter trend seems, however, to have been weakened after the procedure for selecting gubernatorial candidates was changed in mid-2009.

The procedural change was formally implemented to ensure greater transparency in the nomination process. It was, however, also a way to address the shortage of available candidates on the roster of the Presidential Administration.[73] The lack of an institutionalised system for elite recruitment had been a recurrent problem since the dismantling of the *nomenklatura* system. Throughout the 1990s, most political parties were Moscow-centred, short-lived structures that failed to develop robust regional organisations.[74] Medvedev's predecessors therefore frequently turned to trusted former colleagues and acquaintances from their old power bases in Sverdlovsk and St Petersburg or from the FSB to fill strategic positions in the apparatus. Unlike Yel'tsin and Putin, however, Medvedev lacked his own network of clients to recruit from. As a member of Putin's inner circle, his network by and large coincided with the 'liberal' wing of Putin's entourage. After the initial redistribution of personnel in connection with Putin's relocation from the Kremlin to the White House, turnover in the Presidential Administration and the federal government has thus been limited. By mid-term, few members of the federal elite could be said to be unequivocally Medvedev protégés. At the regional level, however, Medvedev nevertheless embarked on a 'cadre revolution'. The high turnover rate among the incumbents put great pressure on the existing cadre reserve and led Medvedev to seek new mechanisms for identifying potential regional leaders.

In February 2009, the Kremlin published the first instalment of a new roster of eligible leaders and bureaucrats—100 names drawn from the federal and regional bureaucracy as well as business and science (often referred to as the 'Golden Hundred') (Prezident Rossii 2009). This new cadre reserve list was meant to serve as a pool of potential administrators from which the Kremlin could draw when seeking to replace inept and ineffective leaders. As yet, however, this reserve has not yielded many new governors: only three of Medvedev's appointees have been recruited from the list (Aleksandr Turchak in Pskov, Anatolii Brovko in Kaliningrad and Vyacheslav Gaizer in Komi).

Instead, United Russia has come to play a key role as a source of potential candidates. In November 2008, in his first annual address to the Federal Assembly, Medvedev proposed 'that nominations of heads of the executive authorities in the regions could be made only by the parties that have won the biggest number of votes in the regional elections, and by no one else' (Medvedev 2008). The necessary

[73]Ol'ga Kryshtanovskaya and Stephen White have previously indicated 'the lack of a pool of eligible candidates' to explain the mass influx of military personnel into state service (Kryshtanovskaya & White 2003, p. 291).

[74]At the regional level, parties were often merely 'political machines' set up by the governor to bring out the vote in regional elections (Hale 2003).

legislative amendments were adopted in April 2009, and the new procedure was implemented later that autumn. This reduced some of the pressure on the Presidential Administration, while the president remained in full control of the final outcome of the appointment process. Whereas the establishment of a federal cadre reserve seems to have played a minor role when it comes to identifying new candidates, the transfer of responsibility for finding suitable nominees to United Russia appears to have affected the kind of candidates that are brought forward: since November 2009, the new governors appointed by Medvedev have tended to be much more 'local' in their career pattern.

Even before the new nomination procedures went into effect, Medvedev had promoted candidates with strong ties to United Russia, beyond the formal membership that almost all governors rushed to acquire in connection with the shift from elected to appointed governors (Titkov 2007). Examples include Viktor Zimin in Khakasiya, a member of the State *Duma* representing United Russia, and Andrei Turchak in Pskov, the coordinator of United Russia's youth policy (Rozhkova 2009). But Medvedev had also made some surprise nominations, like Nikita Belykh, former leader of the Union of Right Forces (*Soyuz pravykh sil*), who was appointed governor of Kirov in December 2008. The idea of promoting a member of the opposition to the rank of governor clearly broke with the pattern established by Putin.[75] On the other hand, given United Russia's current total dominance of the regional legislatures, this experiment is not likely to be repeated in the near future.

Despite the focus on the removal of entrenched governors, a higher turnover and a partial rejuvenation, it is worth recalling that Putin's arrangement as such remains intact. The age of institutional revolutions seems to be over for now. Medvedev's cadre reshuffling is aimed more at fine-tuning the existing system and streamlining the executive vertical, than as a reform of centre–periphery relations as such. The main focus seems to be to bring to a logical conclusion the reform that Putin had launched in 2004 but had implemented only partially, due to his reluctance to further confront the governors once he had gained control over their appointment and dismissals.[76] In the period 2004–2005, the power base of the governors had already been seriously weakened, but some of the regional executives were still able to resist—or at least obstruct—a full recentralisation. By the time of Medvedev's ascendancy to power in 2008, however, the Kremlin had been gradually limiting gubernatorial powers for eight years. Despite the occasional call for a return to gubernatorial elections, the governors who had hung on to power for close to two decades realised that time was running out. Putin's reform had given most of them an additional term. Now, however, Medvedev was ready to tighten the screws.

[75]Although Putin extended the tenure of governors formerly associated with the Communist Party (KPRF), these were all incumbents who had won their office in popular elections, not candidates selected by the Kremlin.

[76]One could argue that Medvedev has changed existing practice and thus broken with the Putin tradition. The *modus operandi* during Putin's presidency was nevertheless one of gradually cutting back on gubernatorial powers. In order to avoid regional reactions, Putin from time to time was willing to compromise: in 2002, he agreed on a liberal interpretation of how to count gubernatorial terms, and after 2005 he was ready to grant the entrenched governors another term. According to this logic, Medvedev's policy brings Putin's reform project to completion.

Whereas Putin reformed the structure but generally refrained from changing the personnel, Medvedev has been systematically replacing the old incumbents. During Medvedev's first two years, he all but completed the transformation of the gubernatorial corps from powerful managers (*khozyaistvenniki*) and, at least to some extent, independent politicians, to federal appointees. The Kremlin continues to put on a show of regional involvement in the selection process, emphasising party involvement in the nomination procedure and encouraging the practice of 'voluntary' resignation of unwanted governors, but it is clear that Moscow has the final word. The data presented above nevertheless indicate that the Kremlin does not hire and fire governors at will: it focuses on finding candidates who can win the endorsement of the regional elites. At mid-term, the tendency seems to be moving in the direction not only of higher turnover, but also of fewer *varyagi* being dispatched from the centre. Increasingly, the Kremlin appears to be relying on local cadre.

Norwegian Institute of International Affairs

References

Abdullaev, N. & Krainova, N. (2009) 'Kremlin Fires 4 Governors, Gordeyev', *Moscow Times*, 17 February.

Arutunyan, A. (2009) 'Medvedev Reshuffle a Wake-up Call to Governors', *Moscow News*, 19 February.

Bilevskaya, E. (2009) 'Gubernatorskii kasting-2010', *Nezavisimaya gazeta*, 25 June.

Blakkisrud, H. (2003) 'The Rise and Fall of the Russian Governor: Institutional Design vs. Elite Bargaining as Explanatory Factors in Russian Politics', in Steen, A. & Gel'man, V. (eds) (2003) *Elites and Democratic Development in Russia* (London, Routledge).

Blakkisrud, H. (2005) 'The Appointed Governor: The End of Russian Federalism?', paper presented at the *ASN 2005 World Convention*, New York, 14–16 April.

Bocharova, S. (2008) 'Sub"ekty federatsii potrebovali ob"ektivnosti', *Gazeta.ru*, 20 June.

Busygina, I. M. (1997) 'Die Gouverneure im föderativen System Rußlands', *Osteuropa*, 47, 6.

Chebankova, E. (2006) 'The Unintended Consequences of Gubernatorial Appointments in Russia, 2005–6', *Journal of Communist Studies and Transition Politics*, 22, 4, December.

Chebankova, E. (2007) 'Putin's Struggle for Federalism: Structures, Operation, and the Commitment Problem', *Europe-Asia Studies*, 59, 2, March.

Chebankova, E. (2008) 'Adaptive Federalism and Federation in Putin's Russia', *Europe-Asia Studies*, 60, 6, August.

Easter, G. M. (1997) 'Redefining Centre–Regional Relations in the Russian Federation: Sverdlovsk Oblast'', *Europe-Asia Studies*, 49, 4, June.

Gel'man, V. (2002) 'Democratisation, Structural Pluralism and Fragile Bi-centrism: The Case of Volgograd Oblast', in Ross, C. (ed.) (2002).

Goode, J. P. (2007) 'The Puzzle of Putin's Gubernatorial Appointments', *Europe-Asia Studies*, 59, 3, May.

Hahn, G. M. (2001) 'Putin's "Federal Revolution": The Administrative and Judicial Reform of Russian Federalism', *East European Constitutional Review*, 10, 1, Winter.

Hahn, G. M. (2003) 'The Impact of Putin's Federative Reforms on Democratization in Russia', *Post-Soviet Affairs*, 19, 2, April–June.

Hale, H. E. (2003) 'Explaining Machine Politics in Russia's Regions: Economy, Ethnicity, and Legacy', *Post-Soviet Affairs*, 19, 3, July–September.

Hough, J. (1969) *The Soviet Prefects: The Local Party Organs in Industrial Decision-Making* (Cambridge, MA, Harvard University Press).

Hyde, M. (2001) 'Putin's Federal Reforms and their Implications for Presidential Power in Russia', *Europe-Asia Studies*, 53, 5, July.

Ivanov, V. (2010) 'Gubernatory i reitingi', *Izvestiya*, 6 September.

Kahn, J. (2002) *Federalism, Democratization, and the Rule of Law in Russia* (Oxford, Oxford University Press).

Kryshtanovskaya, O. (2002) 'Rezhim Putina: liberal'naya militokratiya?', *Pro et Contra*, 7, 4.

Kryshtanovskaya, O. & White, S. (1996) 'From Soviet Nomenklatura to Russian Elite', *Europe-Asia Studies*, 48, 5, July.

Kryshtanovskaya, O. & White, S. (2003) 'Putin's Militocracy', *Post-Soviet Affairs*, 19, 4, October–December.

Kryshtanovskaya, O. & White, S. (2009) 'The Sovietization of Russian Politics', *Post-Soviet Affairs*, 25, 4, October–December.

Kynev, A. (2008) 'Federatsiya krugovoi poruki', *Gazeta.ru*, 17 March.

Lane, D. & Ross, C. (1999) *From Communism to Capitalism: Ruling Elites from Gorbachev to Yeltsin* (New York, St. Martin's Press).

Lapidus, G. W. & Walker, E. W. (1996) 'Nationalism, Regionalism, and Federalism: Center–Periphery Relations in Post-Communist Russia', in Lapidus, G. W. (ed.) (1996) *The New Russia: Troubled Transformation* (Boulder, CO, Westview Press).

Lussier, D. N. (2002) 'The Role of Russia's Governors in the 1999–2000 Federal Elections', in Ross, C. (ed.) (2002).

Makarkin, A. (2010) 'Unikal'nyi ukhod', *Ezhednevnyi zhurnal*, 23 January.

McMann, K. M. & Petrov, N. V. (2000) 'A Survey of Democracy in Russia's Regions', *Post-Soviet Geography and Economics*, 41, 3, April–May.

Medvedev, D. (2008) 'Poslanie Federal'nomu Sobraniyu Rossiiskoi Federatsii', available at: www.kremlin.ru/transcripts/1968, accessed 20 May 2010.

Medvedev, D. (2009) 'Beseda s prezidentom Respubliki Marii El Leonidom Markelovym', available at: www.kremlin.ru/news/6535, accessed 9 March 2010.

Moses, J. C. (1974) *Regional Party Leadership and Policy Making in the USSR*, Vol. 1 (New York, Praeger).

Orttung, R. W. (2004) 'Business and Politics in the Russian Regions', *Problems of Post-Communism*, 51, 2, March–April.

Petrov, N. (2002) 'Seven Faces of Putin's Russia: Federal Districts as the New Level of State–Territorial Composition', *Security Dialogue*, 33, 1, March.

Petrov, N. (2008) 'Moscow Losing Clout in the Regions', *Moscow Times*, 28 October.

Petrov, N. & Slider, S. (2005) 'Putin and the Regions', in Herspring, D. R. (ed.) (2005) *Putin's Russia. Past Imperfect, Future Uncertain* (Lanham, MD, Rowman & Littlefield).

Prezident Rossii (2009) '"Pervaya sotnya" rezerva upravlencheskikh kadrov, nakhodyashchikhsya pod patronazhem Prezidenta Rossii', 17 February, available at: http://news.kremlin.ru/news/3212, accessed 16 January 2010.

Radzikhovskii, L. (2010) 'Smena vekh', *Rossiiskaya gazeta*, 10 August.

Reddaway, P. & Orttung, R. W. (eds) (2004) *The Dynamics of Russian Politics. Putin's Reform of Federal Relations*, Vol. 1 (Lanham, MD, Rowman & Littlefield).

Remmington, T. F. (2003) 'Majorities without Mandates: The Russian Federal Council since 2000', *Europe-Asia Studies*, 55, 5, July.

Renz, B. (2006) 'Putin's Militocracy? An Alternative Interpretation of the Role of Siloviki in Contemporary Russian Politics', *Europe-Asia Studies*, 58, 6, September.

Rigby, T. H. (2001) 'Russia's Provincial Bosses: A Collective Career Profile', *Journal of Communist Studies and Transition Politics*, 17, 1, December.

Rivera, S. W. & Rivera, D. W. (2006) 'The Russian Elite under Putin: Militocratic or Bourgeois?', *Post-Soviet Affairs*, 22, 2, April–June.

Ross, C. (ed.) (2002) *Regional Politics in Russia* (Manchester, Manchester University Press).

Ross, C. (2003) 'Putin's Federal Reforms and the Consolidation of Federalism in Russia: One Step Forward, Two Steps Back!', *Communist and Post-Communist Studies*, 36, 1, March.

Ross, C. (2005) 'Federalism and Electoral Authoritarianism under Putin', *Demokratizatsiya*, 13, 3, Summer.

Rostovskii, M. (2009) 'Dissident respubliki Bashkortostan', *Moskovskii komsomolets*, 5 June.

Rozhkova, N. (2009) 'Korol' khodit peshkami. Politologi o kadrevoi politike prezidenta', *Vremya novostei*, 18 February.

Sakwa, R. (2002) 'Federalism, Sovereignty and Democracy', in Ross, C. (ed.) (2002).

Sakwa, R. (2004) *Putin: Russia's Choice* (London, Routledge).

Samarina, A., Rodin, I. & Bilevskaya, E. (2009) 'Kresla na vyvos. Medvedev formiruet sobstvennyi gubernatorskii korpus', *Nezavisimaya gazeta*, 19 Febraury.

Sidorov, V. (2008) 'Prezident prezyvaet partiinykh kandidatov', *Nezavisimaya gazeta*, 24 December.

Söderlund, P. J. (2005) 'Electoral Success and Federal-level Influence of Russian Regional Executives', *Europe-Asia Studies*, 57, 4, June.

Solnick, S. L. (1995) 'Federal Bargaining in Russia', *East European Constitutional Review*, 4, 4, Fall.

Solnick, S. L. (1999) 'Methods of Central Control over Russia's Provinces, and Prospects for the Future', *PONARS Policy Memo* 97, available at: http://csis.org/files/media/csis/pubs/pm_0097.pdf, accessed 21 May 2010.

Solnick, S. L. (2000) 'Is the Center Too Weak or Too Strong in the Russian Federation?', in Sperling, V. (ed.) (2000) *Building the Russian State: Institutional Crisis and the Quest for Democratic Governance* (Boulder, CO, Westview Press).

Teague, E. (1994) 'Center–Periphery Relations in the Russian Federation', in Sporzluk, R. (ed.) (1994) *National Identity and Ethnicity in Russia and the New States of Eurasia* (Armonk, NY, M.E. Sharpe).

Titkov, A. (2007) 'Krizis naznachenii', *Pro et Contra*, 11, 4–5, July–October.

Vorobeva, I. (2009) 'Gubernatory otvetyat za vse', *RBK Daily*, 24 April.

Walker, E. W. (1996) 'The Dog That Didn't Bark: Tatarstan and Asymmetrical Federalism in Russia', *The Harriman Review*, 9, 4.

Whitmore, B. (2010) 'Kremlin Stumbles in Regions as Unrest Mounts', *RFE/RL*, 16 February, available at: www.rferl.org/content/Kremlin_Stumbles_In_Regions_As_Unrest_Mounts/1959861.html, accessed 3 August 2010.

Zlotnik, M. (1996) 'Russia's Governors: All the President's Men?', *Problems of Post-Communism*, 43, 6, November–December.

Russia's Regional Legislative Elections, 2003–2007: Authoritarianism Incorporated

GRIGORII V. GOLOSOV

THE TRANSFORMATION OF RUSSIA'S POLITICAL LIFE IN 2003–2007 was profound, and it did not remain unnoticed by international democracy observers. Freedom House downgraded Russia's status from 'partly free' in 2003 to 'not free' in 2007; the Polity IV DEMOC score for Russia decreased from six in 2003 to five in 2007, which corresponds with crossing a major dividing line between an imperfect democracy and outright authoritarianism.[1] From such scores, one might conclude, what we have observed is a period of regime change. Indeed, several scholars and analysts have invested their efforts into the study of a set of incentives and strategies that led Russia's leadership to an abrupt authoritarian turn (Gill 2006; Hassner 2008; McFaul & Stoner-Weiss 2008). What is often missing in such analyses, however, is the process of transformation. Perhaps because they have concentrated on the national level of politics, the students of regime change in Russia seem to have missed empirical indicators that could have allowed them to trace the phases of transformation. As a result, the picture becomes blurred: we have the relatively free 2003 *Duma* elections, the obviously not-free 2007 *Duma* elections, and a black box in between.

The purpose of this essay is to unpack the black box by concentrating on an essential but often neglected element of contemporary Russian politics, regional legislative elections. This approach is expected to result in two kinds of gains, substantive and methodological. At the substantive level, I will demonstrate that contemporary Russia's authoritarianism, rather than being solely a product of nation-level politics, has emerged to a large extent as a continuation of the sub-national authoritarianism of the previous period of the country's political development—hence the subtitle of the essay, 'authoritarianism incorporated'. At the methodological level, my concentration on region-level politics will make it possible, first, to employ the richness of data from regional elections, and second, to subject these data to an analysis more rigorous than could be the case with a narrative exposition of major political developments. The major tool in this study is multiple regression analysis.

In the first section of the essay, I will establish my major expectations in the form of hypotheses, which will require a narrative exposition of most important political

[1]The Freedom House and Polity IV scores are available online at http://www.freedomhouse.org and http://www.systemicpeace.org/polity/polity4.htm, respectively.

trends during the period under observation. In the second section, the operationalisation of independent variables will be provided. Then I report and discuss the results of multiple regression analysis.

The data and hypotheses

The data for this analysis are derived from regional legislative elections held in Russia from December 2003, in which case the regional races were concurrent with the national *Duma* campaign, to April 2007, when Krasnoyarsk territory elected its first legislature after formal unification with its former autonomous districts.[2] There was also a very solid reason for taking December 2003 as a starting point. One of the most sweeping political reforms implemented during Vladimir Putin's first term in office was the transition to mixed electoral systems in regional legislative elections. In 2002, the law 'On the basic guarantees of citizens' electoral rights and the right to vote in referenda'[3] was amended to provide for the election of no less than a half of the deputies in the regional legislature, or one of its chambers, by party-list (PR). The adoption of the amendment was difficult, as it was obviously viewed with anxiety by the regional elites (Golosov 2004, pp. 263–66). Partly as a result of regional resistance, the implementation of the new rules was delayed to December 2003. Mixed electoral systems changed the patterns of competition in regional legislative elections profoundly, even if not comprehensively. The most salient change was, of course, the arrival of political parties as principal competitors. Before 2003, the rates of participation and the levels of success of party-nominated candidates in regional legislative elections were not only negligibly low but also tended to decrease over time. While, in December 1995–April 1999, the average share of party representatives in regional assemblies was 21.8%, in December 1999–May 2003 it fell to 14.2% (Golosov 2003a; Golosov 2003b; Hale 2006). For the period under observation in this study, it rose dramatically to 85.5%.

Overall, there were 77 elections to the single or lower chambers of Russia's regional legislatures in December 2003–April 2007. Of these, five were held by purely proportional systems, and the remaining 72 by mixed systems involving proportional components and majoritarian formulas, single-member plurality (first-past-the-post), multimember plurality, two-round majority, or single non-transferable vote.[4] In most cases, the shares of deputies elected by proportional and majoritarian formulas were equal or roughly equal, even though there were occasional discrepancies in favour of the proportional system, such as in Volgograd *Oblast'* (where 22 were proportional compared to 16 majoritarian) and Moscow (20 proportional compared to 15 majoritarian). Proportional seats were filled both by closed list and open list systems, with the use of several different seat allocation principles, mostly the simple (Hare) quota and largest remainders, but also, in a few cases, d'Hondt and Imperiali divisors. These institutional variations exerted some weight on the resulting seat distributions. Their impact is, however, of

[2]The December 2007 elections were not included for the obvious reason that they were held in entirely different, much more restrictive, political environments than was the case previously.

[3]See http://www.cikrf.ru/law/federal_law/zakon_02_67fz_n.html, accessed 5 January 2011.

[4]For a description of these electoral formulas and a discussion of their effects, see Golosov (2003b).

marginal importance for this analysis. This explains why, for constructing the dependent variable, I concentrate solely on one empirical indicator that is straightforwardly comparable across the regions: the vote shares of an individual party. The choice of this party was not problematic. Since the process under investigation manifested itself in regional elections as the formation of political monopoly, I had to choose the party that, as a result of the process, had become monopolistic, United Russia (*Edinaya Rossiya*).

The United Russia party was formed in 2002 by merging the successors of the principal 'parties of power' in the December 1999 national legislative elections: the Unity party (*Partiya Edinstvo*), the Fatherland party (*Partiya Otechestvo*) and the All Russia movement (*Dvizhenie Vsya Rossiya*) (Colton & McFaul 2000; Hale 2004). Its first experiences in regional legislative elections, starting with September 2002, brought about a mixed record of stunning successes (73.1% of seats in Bashkortostan) and miserable failures (8.0% in St Petersburg).[5] However, already in the December 2003 national legislative elections it emerged as the leading political party of Russia, taking 37.6% of the vote and 49.9% of seats in the *Duma*, and then greatly extending its majority by recruiting into its faction most of the independent deputies, as well as the nominees of many minor parties. Most observers estimated that the 2003 national elections, while marred by minor violations, were generally free and fair (Sakwa 2005). This means that quite a significant share of Russians cast their votes for United Russia sincerely, without any significant involvement of coercion, fraud, or other malpractices. Of course, the principal source of United Russia's success was its endorsement by the popular President of Russia, Vladimir Putin. Since the regional legislative elections investigated in this study took place in the same regions and within a brief chronological distance from the 2003 *Duma* elections, the first hypothesis in this study is self-evident:

> *the vote in regional elections was simply determined by the levels of success already gained by United Russia in the same regions in the 2003 national elections.*

Indeed, in most national settings one would assume that it simply could not be otherwise, and there is no apparent reason to expect that Russia would have completely defied this common-sense expectation.

However, even a preliminary inspection of the data reveals that discrepancies between the shares of the vote gained by United Russia in national and regional elections were significant. Paradoxically, this is true even with regard to concurrent elections held in December 2003. For instance, the national vote for United Russia in Ulyanovsk province was 34.0%, while the regional vote was 27.4%; in Ingushetiya, United Russia gained 57.0% of the national vote and 36.3% regionally. Therefore there must be an intervening variable, or a set of such variables. In search of such variables, I turned to regional political settings. The main body of research on Russia's regional politics in the 1990s and early 2000s has firmly established that the principal actors in Russia's regions were the heads of regional executives (Ross 2002). Despite

[5]All numerical data used in this study, unless otherwise stated, are taken directly or calculated by the author from the Russian Electoral Statistics Database, available online at http://db.irena.org.ru/.

the multiplicity of self-denominations (such as heads of administrations, presidents, heads of republics and the like), these officeholders are often jointly referred to as governors, and throughout this essay I will follow this convention.

The development of Russia's regions heavily depended on the choices made by Boris Yel'tsin when he exercised the right, delegated to him by the Congress of People's Deputies in November 1991, to appoint the heads of administrations (Moses 1992). In some of the regions, the appointees were taken from the old *nomenklatura* ranks. In other regions, Yel'tsin appointed his loyalists from the democratic movement who often lacked any significant political capital of their own. In most cases (with a few exceptions such as in Nizhny Novgorod and Novgorod provinces) this led to conflicts between the new power-holders and the majorities in the regional soviets, often supported by the municipal authorities (Gel'man *et al.* 2003). These conflicts were resolved, normally according to a 'winner takes all' model, in direct gubernatorial elections that took place in the second half of the 1990s (Solnick 1998). As a result of these elections, the vast majority of regions witnessed the emergence of consolidated regional political regimes. Most often, these regimes were authoritarian and fully controlled by governors as monopolistic political actors. Regional legislative assemblies were deprived of any political influence. At the same time, both regional and federal political parties were ultimately sidelined at the regional level (Hutcheson 2003; Golosov 2004). The outcome was the same in the ethnic republics of Russia, where no gubernatorial appointments took place throughout the period, except that it occurred even faster than in other regions (Hale 2003).

The principal aspects of regional authoritarian regimes were closely inter-related. The residual autonomy of the regional legislatures from the executive was largely based on the presence of groups of deputies representing federal political parties, most often but not necessarily the KPRF (Golosov 1999). This was a situation inherited by the regions from the relatively competitive electoral politics of the mid-1990s. Yet in the regional legislative elections of the early 2000s, loyalty to the governor became the predominant, if not the only, factor of electoral success. Party affiliations, in contrast, were not helpful in any possible sense. Indeed, the governors themselves were not affiliated to a party. But this did not hinder their electoral success. Of the 88 gubernatorial elections held in 1999–2003, incumbents won in 59, did not run in 13, and lost only in 16.

At the same time, while avoiding party affiliations, the governors proved to be capable of significantly enhancing, if not determining, the electoral chances of whatever party they chose to support in national legislative elections. The most clear proof of that came as a result of the 1999 national legislative elections, in which the relative success of the two 'parties of power', Unity and Fatherland–All Russia, was contingent upon the support of the governors (Konitzer-Smirnov 2003). In the first half of the 2000s, the governors emerged as decisive actors in regional electoral politics. The relative success of the United Russia party in December 2003 was to a large extent a product of the efforts of governors who joined the list of the 'party of power', thus accepting political responsibility for its performance at the polls. Yet the critical test of the efficiency of the new model was to come with its implementation in regional politics. Hence my second hypothesis in this study is:

the performance of United Russia in regional legislative elections stemmed from the governors' ability to supply it with the regional vote.

The second hypothesis, however defined in operational terms (which will be discussed in detail below), does not cover the whole spectrum of expectations regarding the possible impact of regional political settings on the performance of United Russia. Obviously missing, in the first instance, are the institutional determinants of the governors' ability to deliver the vote. While the political regimes of Russia's regions became less diverse in the 2000s than they were in the 1990s, some fundamental differences continued to shape governors' political capacity, and one of them was the differentiation of regions into ethnic-based (republics and autonomous districts) and those without a constitutionally defined ethnic component. As already mentioned, the political trajectories of the republics in the 1990s were such that the consolidated regional regimes emerged earlier than in other regions. Typically, they also assumed better articulated authoritarian characteristics (Matsuzato 2004). The autonomous districts were closer to other regions with regards to their political trajectories, but it is also true that their small populations, dense ethnic networks of societal control, and distant locations often contributed to the lack of competitive political structures. While in the 1990s this manifested itself mostly in the complete absence of political parties, in the period of regime transformation one would expect this constellation of circumstances to be conducive to political monopoly. Hence my third hypothesis is:

the ability of governors to deliver the vote to United Russia was greater in ethnic-based regions than in other regions.

In the second instance, the governors' ability to deliver the vote is, quite clearly, the function not only of their own political resources but also of their willingness to do so. The preliminary inspection of the data shows that during the early phase of the period under observation, the most significant threat to United Russia was posed not by other parties but by electoral blocs, especially if they were created with the support of the governors (Golosov 2006). In Amur *Oblast'* United Russia lost regional legislative elections to the bloc named 'We Are For the Development of Amur Province' (*My–Za Razvitie Amurskoi Oblasti*); in Sakhalin *Oblast'*, to the bloc 'Our Motherland Is Sakhalin and Kuril Islands' (*Nasha Rodina–Sakhalin i Kurily*); and in Khakasiya it only marginally outperformed the bloc 'Khakasiya'. In accordance with the federal legal requirements, the formal founders of such blocs were the local branches of national small parties, but the regional populations often remained unaware of their very existence. The important facts about the blocs were that they appealed to local sentiment, often received direct endorsement from the governors, used the political resources of the governors in their campaigns, and therefore effectively operated as local 'parties of power'. For the governors themselves, sponsoring the blocs did not necessarily mean challenging United Russia. Rather, they simply did not want to commit completely to UR. An outright majority for United Russia in the regional assembly was unproblematic only to those regional leaders who, like Mintimer Shaimiev in Tatarstan and Murtaza

Rakhimov in Bashkortostan, kept the regional branches of the party under their own unrestricted control. But many governors lacked such political resources, and for them, it was more expedient to deal with fragmented legislatures, and thus to be able to arbitrate between a variety of rival factions none of which was ultimately in control of the legislative agenda.

While it is true that the 'winner takes all' model prevailed in the political conflicts of the 1990s, it is also true that in some of the regions, elements of political competition survived into the second half of the 2000s. Such cases were not numerous, yet their presence in statistical analysis needs to be accounted for in the construction of independent variables. For instance, Tuva is an ethnic-based region in which both the incumbent office-holder in the gubernatorial contests and United Russia used to perform very well in national elections, which would lead us to expect its successful performance in regional elections too. Yet this expectation has to be moderated by the fact that the governor of the region failed to appease rival elite groups, as a result of which many important local politicians joined the lists of a rival party. There is a methodological difficulty with incorporating this aspect into our research design: namely, it is empirically almost indistinguishable from the previous issue. While Tuva is a clear-cut instance of intra-elite struggles acting as an obstacle to the delivery of the vote to United Russia, in many cases the governors, while making deals with minor parties, invested additional effort into making these parties appear as true competitors, much in the same way as they created 'governor blocs'. Quite often, this was the case with the Agrarian Party of Russia and the Pensioners' Party. Therefore my fourth hypothesis applies to both aspects identified above:

> *the ability of governors to deliver the vote to United Russia was smaller in those regions where no significant actors, whether independent of the governor or supported by him, challenged the 'party of power'.*

Finally, concerning the governors' ability to deliver the vote, we have to take into account the practice of poster candidates. The poster candidates are figures of regional significance who head party lists in regional elections, not with the goal of taking seats, but rather to provide additional salience to the list itself and clearly manifest their support for it. In particular, this practice was a powerful tool in counteracting governors' attempts to diversify their support in regional legislative elections, for example by creating blocs. Thus my fifth hypothesis is:

> *the governors who ran in legislative elections as poster candidates were better disposed to deliver the vote to United Russia than those who did not.*

The process under investigation in this study is two-sided. On the one hand, the resources of the (mostly) authoritarian regional regimes were used to enhance the performance of United Russia. On the other hand, in order to achieve that, the federal centre undertook a systematic effort that developed over time. Thus the purpose, to better United Russia's performance, was achieved to varying extents depending on whether elections took place in the beginning or at the end of the period. The corresponding explanatory variables are therefore not region-specific but time-specific.

Thus the sixth hypothesis, even if, as mentioned before, there were discrepancies between the results of United Russia in the concurrent national and regional elections, in general is that there are reasons to expect that

> *the party's performance in concurrent elections was better than in the non-concurrent ones.*

This applies not only to the December 2003 campaign, but also to the March 2004 presidential elections. The reason is that concurrent elections, even if to a different office, resulted in an increased turnout. This, in turn, led to a greater share of voters willing to support Vladimir Putin in the national presidential election and, by implication, United Russia in the regional legislative one.

My other expectations stem from the specific policy measures taken by the national authorities in order to create United Russia's political monopoly. By far, the most important of these measures was the abolition of direct gubernatorial elections in December 2004. By this, the federal authorities greatly enhanced their political control over the governors, deprived them of any incentives to support parties other than United Russia, and strongly stimulated them to join United Russia. Therefore, the abolition of direct gubernatorial elections resolved the problems confronted by the federal centre after the imposition of mixed electoral systems upon the regions. But the Kremlin moved further to eliminate not only the problem itself but also its manifestations of the period from 2003 to early 2005. This resulted in the deterioration of electoral legislation, and in several political measures. Below, these actions of the Kremlin are discussed not in their chronological order of implementation (Lyubarev 2007), but rather in relation to the political tasks they were intended to achieve. First, electoral blocs were prohibited from running in regional legislative elections. Second, a new version of the law on political parties was adopted, according to which the membership requirement was raised from 10,000 to 50,000, and this requirement was extended both to the already existing parties and to new parties in the process of formation. As a result, of the 46 parties that were registered by December 2003, only 15 were still active by December 2007, and no new parties emerged between 2004 and 2007. Third, minor parties were seriously damaged by a legal provision, introduced in July 2005, according to which the legal thresholds of representation in regional legislative elections were to be set at no more than 7% of the valid votes. While formally intended to arrest the unrestricted rise of the thresholds, in effect this provision led to the rapid shift of the regions from the 5% thresholds that were most widespread in 2003–2005 to 7%, a level scarcely achievable by the minor parties. Fourth, two political parties that posed a significant threat to United Russia between 2003 and the spring of 2005, Motherland (*Rodina*) and the Pensioners' Party (*Partiya Pensionerov*), were effectively dismantled by the Kremlin by systematically disqualifying them from regional elections, mostly on technical pretexts. All measures listed above took effect in regional elections starting with the autumn of 2005. Thus my seventh hypothesis is that even if other factors are controlled,

> *the performance of United Russia in non-concurrent elections in 2004 and the spring of 2005 was worse than in later elections.*

This expectation, however, has to be moderated by taking into account that in the run-up to the 2007 national elections, the Kremlin carried out a political manoeuvre that temporarily hindered United Russia. A new party, named A Just Russia (*Spravedlivaya Rossiya*), was forged by merging the previously insignificant Russian Party of Life (*Rossiiskaya Partiya Zhizni*), led by Sergei Mironov, with what remained of Motherland and the Pensioners' Party. There were expectations that the new entity would be able to split the voters of the KPRF (*Kommunisticheskaya Partiya Rossiiskoi Federatsii*), and even to replace it as the second largest party in the country without causing any serious harm to United Russia. Ideologically, therefore, A Just Russia committed itself to the left. At the same time, the process of building A Just Russia into a nationwide organisation included an important regional component, because in order to make it viable, Mironov was allowed to recruit into his party those members of regional elites who, while possessing significant personal political resources, for this or that reason did not want to join United Russia or were rejected by it. This strategy, while obviously beneficial for the new party itself, proved to be risky for the ruling group as a whole. The March and April 2007 regional elections, generally viewed as a wide-scale experiment with two parties of power, not only did not bring better results to United Russia, but also resulted in a number of its spectacular failures, most visibly in Stavropol territory. As a result, the strategy of building A Just Russia into a new party of power was abandoned. For my analysis, however, this twist in the Kremlin's strategy made it necessary to formulate the eighth hypothesis, also time-related:

> *the performance of United Russia in the March 2007 regional legislative elections was worse than in earlier elections.*

Finally, I introduce the ninth hypothesis derived from my previous research on regional legislative elections in Russia. This research, while narrow in its chronological scope, as it covered only elections held between December 2003 and May 2005, has convincingly demonstrated that United Russia's performance depended on the number of party lists in regional legislative elections (Golosov 2006). Specifically then, the hypothesis is:

> *with the larger number of lists, the performance of United Russia can be expected to deteriorate.*

Of course, the number of lists was a function of many factors already introduced above, from the governors' ability to control the electoral arena, thus preventing the emergence of undesirable competitors or facilitating the emergence of desirable ones, to the federal centre's manipulations of the number of registered parties. There is, however, an additional component—voters' behaviour—which makes me expect that even if these factors are controlled, the number of lists may survive as an independent variable. In the conditions where party identifications in the electorate are weak, every new competitor, if allowed to run, may reasonably expect to take votes from major parties.

The operational definitions of variables

The dependent variable in this analysis is simply the percentage share of the vote received by United Russia in the proportional sections of elections to the single or lower chambers of regional legislatures. Given that the method used in this study is ordinary least-squares linear regression (OLS), an obvious difficulty with such an approach is that for dependent variables defined as percentage shares, it is often desirable either to use different models, or to redefine the dependent variable, normally by means of logit-transformation (Collins *et al.* 1992). When trying the second of these options, I arrived at results that did not bring anything new to the OLS yet, quite naturally, made the resulting coefficients much more difficult for substantive interpretation. That is why below I report the results of the OLS performed on percentage shares, not on logit-transformed values. The overall number of observations is 66, which corresponds to the same number of elections held in 64 regions. I had to omit 11 elections because one or another independent variable of crucial importance for my study was unavailable. There is no apparent reason to believe that the omitted regions, if introduced into the analysis, would have profoundly influenced the results. The average share of the vote received by United Russia in the 66 elections selected for this analysis was 40.78%, with the range from 16.26% in Amur *Oblast'* (March 2005) to 76.23% in Mordoviya (December 2003), and a standard deviation of 13.69.

My operationalisation of the first independent variable was not problematic, as it obviously had to be defined as 'the share of the vote received by United Russia in the proportional section of the December 2003 national legislative elections'. Measuring the ability of the governors to deliver the vote, which was necessary for testing the second hypothesis, was not prohibitively difficult either. During the period under observation, the vast majority of the governors had been, at one time or another, directly elected. While this is obviously true for the period between December 2003 and the spring of 2005, the number of governors who lost their positions soon after the abolition of direct elections was small. Many of them asked Vladimir Putin to express his confidence in them by subjecting their candidacies to approval by regional assemblies, which was normally granted by Putin and invariably provided by the assemblies. Of the 66 elections in this analysis, 43 were held in regions where directly elected governors remained in place, and 23 in regions where the elected governors were reappointed before the legislative elections. When running preliminary analyses for this study, I checked whether the reappointments influenced the performance of United Russia in the respective regions, but found no sizeable effects. Then I chose to treat all governors, irrespective of this circumstance, equally on the basis of their most recent performance in gubernatorial elections. The second independent variable is therefore defined as 'the percentage share of the vote received by the acting governor in the most recent gubernatorial election in which he participated'. For the sake of data comparability, I used the results of single or first rounds of voting, but not those of the run-offs. The average share of thus defined governors' vote was 56.94%, ranging from 91.50% in Orel *Oblast'* to 18.3% in Pskov *Oblast'*, with a standard deviation of 20.44. Chronologically, the included gubernatorial elections range from March 2000 to December 2004.

The third hypothesis was not confirmed by my preliminary analysis when the independent variable was operationalised as an 'ethnic region/non-ethnic region dummy'. Then I tried to split it into two variables, one including autonomous districts and the autonomous province, and the other, only the republics. While the former fitted into the multivariate analysis from the beginning, the latter continued to resist my efforts. Upon additional consideration, I came to the conclusion that the expected effect was still there, but it was partial and interactive. Namely, the republics stood out in contrast to the other regions only in early regional elections, and only in those held concurrently with the national ones. Based on this reasoning, I constructed an interactive variable by multiplying the dummy variable in which republics were coded as 1 and all other regions 0, by a time variable in which concurrent elections were coded as 1 and all other elections 0.

The independent variable for testing the fourth hypothesis was probably most difficult to build, yet the result was rewarding. The problem was how to operationalise the notion of 'intra-elite struggle' in a compact numerical form, and to do that without taking into account actual election results. When answering this question, I turned to a well established tradition of analysing the professional composition of competitors in regional legislative elections. Clearly, regional political arenas include certain positions of importance. If people occupying such positions run on the lists of parties other than United Russia, then we can establish the fact of an intra-elite struggle with a reasonable degree of certainty. The problem is which of the positions are to be included. Based on my previous research (Golosov 2004, pp. 138–49), I selected the following: chairpersons and deputy chairpersons of regional legislatures; deputy heads of regional governments/administrations; Federation Council members; and mayors of the regional administrative centres. In all those cases when the lists of parties other than United Russia were headed by people occupying these positions, the variable assumed the value of 1; otherwise, it was 0. As a compensation for these difficulties, the independent variable necessary for testing the fifth hypothesis was quite easy to operationalise: if the governor headed the list of United Russia, the value is 1, and it is 0 otherwise. Yet, when thus constructed, the variable failed on my preliminary analysis. This was not surprising. One of the effects of the increased pressure exerted by the federal centre on governors was that starting with March 2006, they almost invariably, with few largely random exceptions, led the lists of United Russia. That is why the variable lost its explanatory power. During the earlier period, however, the governor's position at the head of United Russia's list was a matter of choice, and a highly consequential one. Then again, I had to bring the time component into the construction of the variable. The resulting interactive variable was therefore defined by multiplying 1, if the governor led the list (or 0 if not) by 1, if this happened earlier than in March 2006 (or 0 if in March 2006 or later).

My sixth hypothesis did not survive preliminary tests in a pure form and therefore entered the statistical analysis only as a component of the interactive variable with the republic status. The seventh and eighth hypotheses, in contrast, received full confirmation even when operationalised in the most straightforward form. As follows from the narrative exposition in the previous section of the essay, the two periods for which we can reasonably expect the performance of United Russia to deviate from the mainstream are from the autumn of 2004 to the spring of 2005, when the advantages of concurrency had already vanished but no additional pressures from the federal centre had taken effect, and throughout the autumn of 2006, when these pressures achieved their apex and the formation of A Just Russia party was still only in project. The first of these variables is a dummy that codes 'all elections held from October 2004 to May 2005' as 1, and the second is a dummy with the value of 1 for 'all elections held in October 2006'. The last independent variable in this analysis, the number of competitors in regional legislative elections, was operationalised in a self-evident way, as 'the actual number of party lists on the ballot on the day of elections'. The average value of this variable in my analysis is 7.11, with a range from 2 (Chukotka autonomous district) to 11 (Sakhalin, Tambov and Tula *Oblasti*), with a standard deviation of 2.10. While I do not provide descriptive statistics for dummy variables, it is worth mentioning that the overall number of the non-zero values is 8 for the interactive variable ethnic region/non-ethnic region by concurrent elections, 6 for the interactive variable republic by time, 18 for the intra-elite split, 10 for the interactive variable governor leads UR list by time, 16 for elections held from October 2004 to May 2005, and 9 for the October 2006 elections. Descriptive data for individual cases and variable values are provided in Table 1.

Before turning to the substantive results, I should note that I have experimented with all three control variables that are standard in the multivariate analyses using Russia's regions as principal units: population size, the share of ethnic Russians, and the share of urban population. None of them proved to fit well into the model. I also unsuccessfully tried several variables related to the specificities of the political arenas of the regions. In particular, I vested much hope into a variable designed to measure the organisational strength of United Russia. The related hypothesis was, of course, that the stronger the organisational capacity of the party, the better its performance. When constructing the variable, I acted on the assumption that an organisationally strong party is able to contest as many seats, particularly in the majoritarian sections of the elections, as available. Correspondingly, the variable was operationalised as the share of seats contested by United Russia. However, no significant effects occurred. I believe that this finding is substantive, as it reveals the secondary role played by the organisational structures of United Russia in regional elections during the period under observation.

Multivariate analysis

The OLS model reported in Table 2 includes only the effects statistically significant at the 0.05 level or better. One might not be surprised by the huge explanatory power of the model, given that the national election results, some of them concurrent with the regional results under study, are entered into the analysis. In this case, however, the lack of surprise would be premature. In fact, the United Russia's vote share in the proportional section of the December 2003 national legislative elections is a relatively weak explanatory factor. When we regress the dependent variable on this variable alone, the R-squared falls to 0.37, even if the statistical significance of the variable rises quite visibly, as testified by the increase of the T-value from 3.32 in the overall model to 6.12 in a model including it as the only independent variable. This provides us with a clue to the apparently small explanatory power of the percentage share of the vote

TABLE 1

REGIONAL LEGISLATIVE ELECTIONS, 2003–2007: THE DATA AND VARIABLES

Region	*Date of legislative elections*	*Share of UR vote in regional elections*	*United Russia's vote share in the 2003 Duma elections*	*The percentage share of the vote received by the acting governor in the most recent gubernatorial election in which he participated*	*Interactive variable ethnic region/non-ethnic region by concurrent elections*	*Interactive variable republic by time*	*Intra-elite split*	*Interactive variable governor leads UR list by time*	*Elections held from October 2004 to May 2005*	*Elections held in October 2006*	*Number of lists in regional legislative elections*
Adygea	12 March 2006	33.74	49.65	68.9	0	0	1	0	0	0	8
Aginski Buryat Autonomous *Okrug*	30 October 2005	66.64	58.08	89.3	1	0	0	0	0	0	3
Altai Territory	14 March 2004	24.43	29.63	47.5	0	0	1	0	0	0	6
Amur	27 March 2005	16.26	32.34	18.7	0	0	1	0	1	0	9
Arkhangelsk	19 December 2004	23.62	37.94	45.0	0	0	0	0	1	0	9
Astrakhan	8 October 2006	38.73	31.69	65.3	0	0	0	0	0	1	10
Belgorod	16 October 2005	52.78	33.06	61.2	0	0	0	1	0	0	7
Chechnya	27 November 2005	60.65	80.91	73.7	0	0	0	0	0	0	8
Chelyabinsk	25 December 2005	51.98	33.79	58.7	0	0	0	1	0	0	7
Chita	24 October 2004	35.61	38.09	68.2	0	0	0	0	1	0	5
Chukotka Autonomous *Okrug*	25 December 2005	69.21	54.41	90.6	1	0	0	0	0	0	2
Chuvashiya	8 October 2006	51.89	37.32	40.7	0	0	0	0	0	1	5
Ingushetiya	7 December 2003	36.31	57.02	19.2	0	1	1	0	0	0	5
Irkutsk	10 October 2004	30.19	32.79	45.5	0	0	0	0	1	0	9
Jewish Autonomous *Okrug*	8 October 2006	55.32	42.21	56.8	1	0	0	0	0	1	6
Kabardino-Balkariya	7 December 2003	71.42	74.78	87.2	0	1	0	0	0	0	6
Kalmykiya	7 December 2003	41.75	50.63	47.3	0	1	0	0	0	0	10
Kaluga	14 November 2004	40.03	35.36	66.9	0	0	0	1	1	0	6
Karachaevo-Cherkessiya	14 March 2004	55.69	49.59	41.7	0	1	0	0	0	0	7
Kareliya	8 October 2006	38.92	37.87	53.5	0	0	0	0	0	1	7
Khabarovsk	11 December 2005	40.99	34.31	85.3	0	0	0	0	0	0	6
Khakassiya	26 December 2004	23.17	30.36	59.2	0	0	1	0	1	0	8
Khanty-Mansi Autonomous *Okrug*	12 March 2006	54.63	41.25	90.8	1	0	0	0	0	0	5
Kirov	12 March 2006	28.54	32.89	33.8	0	0	0	0	0	0	9
Komi	11 March 2007	36.18	32.96	39.9	0	0	0	0	0	0	7
Koryak Autonomous *Okrug*	19 December 2004	22.24	47.35	37.4	1	0	1	0	1	0	4
Kostroma	4 December 2005	29.99	34.12	43.7	0	0	1	0	0	0	8
Krasnoyarsk	15 April 2007	42.52	29.90	25.3	0	0	0	0	0	0	7

(continued)

TABLE 1
(*Continued*)

Region	*Date of legislative elections*	*Share of UR vote in regional elections*	*United Russia's vote share in the 2003 Duma elections*	*The percentage share of the vote received by the acting governor in the most recent gubernatorial election in which he participated*	*Interactive variable ethnic region/non-ethnic region by concurrent elections*	*Interactive variable republic by time*	*Intra-elite split*	*Interactive variable governor leads UR list by time*	*Elections held from October 2004 to May 2005*	*Elections held in October 2006*	*Number of lists in regional legislative elections*
Kurgan	21 November 2004	25.74	33.58	35.3	0	0	0	0	1	0	8
Kursk	12 March 2006	37.36	30.11	39.5	0	0	0	0	0	0	9
Leningrad *Oblast'*	11 March 2007	35.24	38.11	56.9	0	0	0	0	0	0	6
Lipetsk	8 October 2006	50.65	28.21	73.1	0	0	0	0	0	1	8
Magadan	22 May 2005	28.76	34.36	26.0	0	0	0	0	1	0	4
Marii El	10 October 2004	32.25	34.57	29.2	0	0	0	0	1	0	5
Mordoviya	7 December 2003	76.23	76.06	87.3	0	1	0	0	0	0	4
Moscow	4 December 2005	47.25	34.44	74.8	0	0	0	1	0	0	9
Moscow *Oblast'*	11 March 2007	49.57	33.85	83.0	0	0	0	0	0	0	7
Murmansk	11 March 2007	42.19	39.20	77.1	0	0	0	0	0	0	6
Novgorod	8 October 2006	43.75	37.08	78.7	0	0	0	0	0	1	9
Novosibirsk	11 December 2005	33.12	28.92	57.7	0	0	0	0	0	0	7
Omsk	11 March 2007	55.65	32.74	56.0	0	0	0	0	0	0	7
Orenburg	12 March 2006	40.44	27.59	63.5	0	0	0	0	0	0	8
Oryol	11 March 2007	39.02	44.62	91.5	0	0	0	0	0	0	8
Primorsky	8 October 2006	48.27	27.88	23.9	0	0	0	0	0	1	10
Pskov	11 March 2007	45.42	37.15	18.3	0	0	1	0	0	0	7
Sakhalin	10 October 2004	17.74	30.13	35.2	0	0	1	0	1	0	11
St Petersburg	11 March 2007	37.37	30.67	48.7	0	0	0	0	0	0	6
Stavropol	11 March 2007	23.87	32 01	28.6	0	0	1	0	0	0	5
Sverdlovsk *Oblast'*	11 March 2004	38.24	34 14	42.9	0	0	0	1	0	0	10
Sverdlovsk *Oblast'*	8 October 2006	40.54	34 14	42.9	0	0	0	0	0	1	9
Taimyr Autonomous *Okrug*	23 January 2005	31.28	48 1	69.1	1	0	1	0	1	0	4
Tambov	18 December 2005	40.49	28 98	71.1	0	0	0	1	0	0	11
Tatarstan	14 March 2004	69.2	59 53	79.5	0	1	0	0	0	0	9
Tomsk	11 March 2007	46.79	34 04	70.1	0	0	0	0	0	0	8
Tula	3 October 2004	22.31	29 86	49.1	0	0	1	0	1	0	11
Tver	18 December 2005	33.23	34 53	42.1	0	0	0	1	0	0	8
Tuva	8 October 2006	46.38	66 83	53.6	0	0	1	0	0	1	6
Ulyanovsk	7 December 2003	27.38	34 00	56.3	0	0	1	0	0	0	10

(*continued*)

TABLE 1
(Continued)

Region	*Date of legislative elections*	*Share of UR vote in regional elections*	*United Russia's vote share in the 2003* Duma *elections*	*The percentage share of the vote received by the acting governor in the most recent gubernatorial election in which he participated*	*Interactive variable ethnic region/ non-ethnic region by concurrent elections*	*Interactive variable republic by time*	*Intra-elite split*	*Interactive variable governor leads UR list by time*	*Elections held from October 2004 to May 2005*	*Elections held in October 2006*	*Number of lists in regional legislative elections*
Ust-Ordynsky Buryat Autonomous *Okrug*	14 March 2004	58.81	46.37	53.7	1	0	1	1	0	0	3
Vladimir	20 March 2005	20.53	30.37	65.6	0	0	1	0	1	0	7
Volgograd	7 December 2003	36.69	28.89	36.7	0	0	0	0	0	0	6
Vologda	7 December 2003	38.79	38.94	82.9	0	0	0	0	0	0	6
Vologda	11 March 2007	41.90	38.94	82.9	0	0	1	0	0	0	5
Voronezh	20 March 2005	29.12	25.86	52.5	0	0	0	1	1	0	9
Yamalo-Nenets Autonomous *Okrug*	27 March 2005	60.69	45.83	88.1	1	0	0	1	1	0	4
Yaroslavl	14 March 2004	25.98	35.65	73.2	0	0	1	0	0	0	10

TABLE 2

MULTIPLE REGRESSION STATISTICS (DEPENDENT VARIABLE IS THE SHARE OF THE VOTE RECEIVED BY UNITED RUSSIA IN THE PROPORTIONAL SECTIONS OF REGIONAL LEGISLATIVE ELECTIONS)

	Unstandardised coefficients				
Independent variables	*B*	*Standard error*	*Standardised coefficients*	*t*	*Significance*
United Russia's vote share in the 2003 *Duma* elections	0.34	0.10	0.30	3.32	0.00
The percentage share of the vote received by the acting governor in the most recent gubernatorial election in which he participated	0.12	0.05	0.18	2.59	0.01
Interactive variable ethnic region/ non-ethnic region by concurrent elections	6.66	3.26	0.16	2.04	0.05
Interactive variable republic by time	9.33	3.86	0.20	2.42	0.02
Intra-elite split	–9.61	1.99	–0.31	–4.84	0.00
Interactive variable governor leads UR list by time	6.60	2.40	0.17	2.75	0.01
Elections held from October 2004 to May 2005	–9.79	2.05	–0.31	–4.77	0.00
Elections held in October 2006	5.39	2.58	0.14	2.09	0.04
Number of lists in regional legislative elections	–1.06	0.50	–0.16	–2.12	0.04
Intercept	29.48	5.87		5.02	0.00

Number of cases=66; R-squared=0.81; Adjusted R-squared=0.78.

received by the acting governor in the most recent gubernatorial election in which he participated. When standing against the dependent variable alone, it explains as much as 28% of the variation. But it is highly correlated with United Russia's *Duma* vote share as well (Pearson's $r = 0.36$, significant at 0.01), which is not surprising given the role played by the governors in delivering the vote to United Russia in the 2003 national elections. Yet taking the overall model as it is, the strongest explanatory variables are intra-elite split and the time variable singling out elections held from October 2004 to May 2005, followed by the United Russia's *Duma* vote and the interactive variable governor leads the UR list by time. The weakest explanatory factors are the time variable for elections held in October 2006 and the interactive variable ethnic region/non-ethnic region by concurrent elections.

Of course, the potential issues of endogeneity in the results should not be overlooked. In particular, one would argue that the governors could have refused to lead the UR lists if they had reasons to believe they would not achieve a good result, rather than a bad result stemming from their refusal to run. Also, it cannot be excluded that the Kremlin, on its side, prevented electorally weak governors from running at the top of the UR lists. I have to recognise that such explanations may be viable. The problem is that, empirically, we cannot distinguish them from the second hypothesis of this study as formulated above. Then the question is, which of the explanations—that the performance of United Russia in regional legislative elections stemmed from the governors' ability to supply it with the regional vote, or that the governors refused or were prohibited from running in elections if the prospects of United Russia were discouraging—is more encompassing in substantive terms? I think the first alternative is the correct choice. It does not make much difference whether the governors actually ran as poster candidates and failed to deliver the vote, or whether they did not run because they (or the Kremlin) knew that they would fail on that. Either way, what matters is the governor's ability to deliver the vote, not his individual strategies.

Turning to a more general interpretation of the coefficients, it is particularly interesting to look at the effects of the dummy variables. Here, the effects of the federal centre's efforts to promote the success of United Russia in regional elections are especially salient. In the beginning, the levels of success of the 'party of power' were close to those achieved in national elections, which was apparently acceptable for the centre. At that time, the republics stood out as the hubs of United Russia's influence, as testified by the fact that the non-zero values of the interactive variable republic by time variable promised an addition of 9.33% to the vote for United Russia. During the period of October 2004–May 2005, the electoral demise of United Russia was in progress, so that its share of the vote fell by 9.79%, as indicated by the corresponding time variable. Then, after the federal centre intervened into the regional electoral arenas with a number of institutional and political measures, the standing of United Russia improved again, and it reached its apex in October 2006 when it was likely to perform at a level of 5.39% better than before. In the spring of 2007, however, it temporarily moderated its appetite for political monopoly as a result of the federal centre's experimentation with A Just Russia. The analysis demonstrates that United Russia suffered heavily from intra-elite conflicts, as it was likely to lose 9.61% in those cases when influential regional figures joined opposition parties, yet it was likely to perform 6.60% better if the governor led its list before this had become a nearly universal practice.

Conclusion

Authoritarian breakdowns are often viewed as top-down processes but, from the analysis developed here, it is clear that the picture of Putin's Russia transition to authoritarianism is more complex. In 1999–2003, Russia remained to a large extent an electoral democracy, even though at that time, its failure on certain aspects of democratic consolidation was quite apparent, especially with regards to the under-development of its party system (McFaul 2001). At the sub-national level, however, most of Russia's regional regimes were overtly authoritarian, with the political monopoly of the governors being matched by the weakness of regional assemblies and the lack of meaningful oppositions. A democratic exit from his situation was possible by means of institutional engineering, and in fact, the introduction of mixed electoral systems in regional elections was potentially beneficial. In 2004, however, Russia's national political leadership drastically changed its strategy by seeking a political monopoly for its new 'party of power', United Russia. This was achieved by a set of policies that included the abolition of direct gubernatorial elections, institutional deteriorations and political restrictions. Yet, as follows from my analysis, it would be misleading to understand these policies as targeted against regional political regimes. The real purpose was to incorporate these regimes into the emerging national authoritarian order, euphemistically referred to as the 'vertical of power', and to bring them to the service of the political monopoly in the making. While it is true that the political monopoly was not feasible without the federal centre's effort, it is also true that this effort probably would have been fruitless without the co-optation of resources and mechanisms of regional authoritarianism. As suggested by my analysis, the effects of the two components of contemporary Russian authoritarianism are empirically distinguishable, and the ultimate breakdown of Russia's electoral democracy was a product of their joint operation.

European University at St Petersburg

References

Collins, J. J., Fanciulli, M., Hohlfeld, R. G., Finch, D. C., Sandri, G. V. H. & Shtatland, E. S. (1992) 'A Random Number Generator Based on the Logit Transform of the Logistic Variable', *Computers in Physics*, 6, 6, November/December.

Colton, T. (2005) 'Putin and the Attenuation of Russian Democracy', in Pravda, A. (ed.) (2005) *Leading Russia: Putin in Perspective, Essays in Honour of Archie Brown* (Oxford, Oxford University Press).

Colton, T. & McFaul, M. (2000) 'Reinventing Russia's Party of Power: Unity and the 1999 Duma Election', *Post-Soviet Affairs*, 16, 3, Summer.

Gel'man, V., Ryzhenkov, S. & Brie, M. (2003) *Making and Breaking Democratic Transitions: The Comparative Politics of Russia's Regions* (2005) (Lanham, MD, Rowman and Littlefield).

Gill, G. (2006) 'A New Turn to Authoritarian Rule in Russia?', *Democratization*, 13, 1, February.

Golosov, G. V. (1999) 'From Adygeya to Yaroslavl: Factors of Party Development in the Regions of Russia, 1995–1998', *Europe-Asia Studies*, 51, 8, December.

Golosov, G. V. (2003a) 'The Vicious Circle of Party Underdevelopment in Russia: The Regional Connection', *International Political Science Review*, 24, 4, October.

Golosov, G. V. (2003b) 'Electoral Systems and Party Formation in Russia: A Cross-Regional Analysis', *Comparative Political Studies*, 36, 8, October.

Golosov, G. V. (2004) *Political Parties in the Regions of Russia: Democracy Unclaimed* (Boulder, CO, Lynne Rienner).

Golosov, G. V. (2006) 'The Structure of Party Alternatives and Voter Choice in Russia: Evidence from the 2003–2004 Regional Legislative Elections', *Party Politics*, 12, 6, November.

Hale, H. (2003) 'Explaining Machine Politics in Russia's Regions: Economy, Ethnicity, and Legacy', *Post-Soviet Affairs*, 19, 3, July–September.

Hale, H. (2004) 'The Origins of United Russia and the Putin Presidency: The Role of Contingency in Party-System Development', *Demokratizatsiya: The Journal of Post-Soviet Democratization*, 12, 2, Spring.

Hale, H. (2006) *Why Not Parties in Russia? Democracy, Federalism, and the State* (Cambridge, Cambridge University Press).

Hassner, P. (2008) 'Russia's Transition to Autocracy', *Journal of Democracy*, 19, 2, April.

Hutcheson, D. (2003) *Political Parties in the Russian Regions* (London, RoutledgeCurzon).

Konitzer-Smirnov, A. (2003) 'Jurisdictional Voting in Russia's Regions: Initial Results from Individual-Level Analyses', *Europe-Asia Studies*, 55, 1, January.

Lyubarev, A. (2007) 'Izmeneniya izbiratel'nogo zakonodatel'stva v 2004–2007 godakh', *Rossiiskoe Elektoral'noe Obozrenie*, 1, available at: http://www.irena.org.ru/index.php?option=content&task=view&id=339, accessed 1 August 2010.

Matsuzato, K. (2004) 'Authoritarian Transformations of the Mid-Volga National Republics: An Attempt at Macro-Regionology', *Journal of Communist Studies and Transition Politics*, 20, 2, June.

McFaul, M. (2001) 'Explaining Party Formation and Nonformation in Russia: Actors, Institutions, and Chance', *Comparative Political Studies*, 34, 10, December.

McFaul, M. & Stoner-Weiss, K. (2008) 'The Myth of the Authoritarian Model: How Putin's Crackdown Holds Russia Back', *Foreign Affairs*, 87, 1, January/February.

Moses, J. (1992) 'Soviet Provincial Politics in an Era of Transition and Revolution, 1989–91', *Soviet Studies*, 44, 3, May–June.

Ross, C. (2002) *Regional Politics in Russia* (Manchester, Manchester University Press).

Sakwa, R. (2005) 'The 2003–2004 Russian Elections and Prospects for Democracy', *Europe-Asia Studies*, 57, 3, May.

Solnick, S. L. (1998) 'The 1996–97 Gubernatorial Elections in Russia: Outcomes and Implications', *Post-Soviet Affairs*, 14, 1, January–March.

Electoral Legislation in Russian Regions

ARKADY LYUBAREV

RUSSIAN ELECTORAL LEGISLATION IS BASED ON a Federal Law 'On the Basic Guarantees of Electoral Rights and the Right of Russian Federation Citizens to Participate in a Referendum',[1] which provides a framework for all elections across the country (hereafter, the Federal Law 'On the Basic Guarantees of Electoral Rights', or the 'framework law'). This law takes priority over regional electoral legislation. Therefore, ever since this framework legislation was first enacted in 1995, the development dynamics of regional electoral legislation have been shaped by the changes to this law. However, while in the past this framework law had only been amended once or twice over a four-year election cycle, since 2004 it has been continually amended (Lyubarev 2009a). Thus, for example, over the four years of its mandate, the fourth State *Duma* of 2003–2007 amended the 'Law on the Basic Guarantees' 17 times, whilst the fifth *Duma* amended it 14 times in its first two years (2007–2009).

What impact have these amendments to the framework legislation had on regional electoral legislation? Theoretically, regional assemblies are supposed to bring their respective electoral laws into line with the framework law as soon as the latter changes. In practice however, different regions do so in their own ways: whereas some regions constantly keep their laws updated, others only review their regional electoral laws before regional elections. It should be noted also that the structure of regional electoral legislation is rather diverse. In some regions all regional and municipal elections (and often regional and local referenda) within the territory of a region are regulated by codified acts while in others there are separate pieces of legislation on electing regional deputies, municipal deputies and officials, as well as on the electoral commission of the region (plus laws on regional and local referenda). There are yet other regions where some kinds of elections are regulated together as a group by one law (for example, all municipal elections). Thus, currently there are several hundred regional laws on elections and referenda.

Bringing regional electoral legislation into accord with the federal law is achieved in various ways. One way is to introduce amendments into existing laws. However, after

Translated by Andrey R. Gladkov.

[1]For example, see the 2002 edition of the Law: Federal Law No. 67, 12 June 2002, 'Ob osnovnykh garantiyakh izbiratel'nykh prav i prava na uchastie v referendume grazhdan Rossiiskoi Federatsii', *Sobranie Zakondatel'stva Rossiiskoi Federatsii*, 24, 2002, article 2253.

major changes of the framework law it is often easier to enact a revised version of the relevant regional law or to adopt a new law altogether, and many regions follow this path. For example, among the regions where electoral laws were amended most often in 2005–2009 are the Republic of Kabardino-Balkariya, and Saratov, Samara and Vladimir *oblasti.* Thus, the Kabardino-Balkariya Republic Law 'On Electing Kabardino-Balkariya Republic Parliament Deputies',[2] was changed 12 times, including the enactment of a new law. In Saratov *Oblast'* in the period between two regional election campaigns (2003 and 2007) a new law 'On Electing Saratov *Oblast' Duma* Deputies' was adopted twice, first in May 2006 and then in June 2007, whilst other laws were reviewed and amended a total of 12 times over these five years. During the same period, the Samara *Oblast'* law, 'On Electing Samara *Duma*', was changed 14 times. A record number of changes to the Election Code, however, were observed in Vladimir *Oblast'*, where it was reviewed and amended 20 times.

As far as the content of regional electoral legislation is concerned, two points need to be considered. On the one hand, the Federal Law 'On the Basic Guarantee of Electoral Rights' provides a detailed description of most electoral procedures, and most regional laws largely duplicate federal norms (Astafichev 1999, pp. 137–38; Lyubarev 2004). On the other hand, the framework law leaves some major issues to regional legislatures' discretion. Among those are the limit on maximum spending from the Electoral Fund (and the size of the election deposit, which before 2009 was linked to it) and the structure of the electoral system. This study discusses how these issues are dealt with in Russian regions.

Electoral deposits

Until it was abolished by the federal law at the beginning of 2009, there was a requirement for an election deposit.[3] Prior to that however, although it was in place for a long time, regulations concerning the deposit underwent a range of different changes.

In 2002, the Federal Law 'On the Basic Guarantees of Electoral Rights' linked the size of the election deposit to the maximum limit on spending from the Electoral Fund (henceforth referred to as the 'electoral fund ceiling')—the election deposit was set at 15% of the electoral fund ceiling. From 2005, it could vary within a narrow range of between 10% and 15% of the 'ceiling'. Thus, a rising ceiling would automatically lead to a larger deposit. One would have thought that setting a higher ceiling was aimed at achieving the noble objective of allowing candidates and parties to legally fund election campaigns. According to our analysis, however, in many regions electoral fund ceilings were too high so that hardly any party had an electoral fund that was large enough, and often all the parties' funds combined were very much below the ceiling.

At the October 2006 election to the Legislative Chamber of Tuva Republic's parliament (the Great *Khural*), for example, the six competing parties combined failed,

[2]All laws of the regions are quoted as per the *Konsultant Plus* legislative database, available at: http://www.consultant.ru/online/.

[3]*Sobranie Zakondatel'stva Rossiiskoi Federatsii*, 2009, 7, article 771.

or were unwilling, to have funds with more than half of the maximum size allowed by regional legislation (Monitoring 2006, pp. 65–67). Similarly, at the March 2007 election in St Petersburg and Leningrad *Oblast'* the combined electoral funds of all competing parties were significantly below the ceiling set for one regional fund alone, whilst in Vologda *Oblast'* the combined funds of the contesting parties were barely able to reach the permitted limit. Notably, the party with the largest fund in Vologda *Oblast'* raised just over half of the maximum allowed amount, whereas its counterpart in St Petersburg and Leningrad *Oblast'* raised barely a third (Monitoring 2007, pp. 72–74).This leads us to the conclusion that the real reason for raising the electoral fund 'ceiling' was to increase the size of the election deposit which was linked to it.

Table 1 shows the regions with the highest absolute or relative electoral fund ceilings and election deposits for political parties. St Petersburg has by far the highest (in both absolute and relative terms) election deposit, with a deposit that was 1.5 times larger than that required for elections to the State *Duma*. However, proportionate to the number of voters, deposits and 'ceilings' are also high in smaller regions such as Tuva Republic, Kamchatka *Krai* and Nenets Autonomous *Okrug*.[4]

Table 2 ranks the regions in terms of the size of their deposits (absolute and relative) for candidates standing in single-mandate constituencies. The record in absolute terms is held by Rostov *Oblast'* and in relative terms by Karachaevo-Cherkess Republic.

TABLE 1

MAXIMUM ABSOLUTE AND RELATIVE LIMITS ON SPENDING FROM ELECTORAL FUNDS AND THE SIZE OF THE ELECTION DEPOSIT FOR POLITICAL PARTIES

		Maximum limit of spending from the electoral fund		*Election deposit*	
Region	*Year and month of elections*	*Size, millions of rubles*	*Proportionate to number of voters (rubles)*	*Size, millions of rubles*	*Proportionate to number of voters (rubles)*
Tuva Republic	October 2006	25	146.3	3.75	21.9
Tomsk *Oblast'*	March 2007	60	79.4	9	11.9
St Petersburg City	March 2007	600	162.0	90	24.3
Krasnoyarsk *Krai*	April 2007	100	46.5	15	7.0
Krasnodar *Krai*	December 2007	200	52.9	30	7.9
Kamchatka *Krai*	December 2007	60	223.5	6	22.4
Penza *Oblast'*	December 2007	50	44.1	7.5	6.6
Rostov *Oblast'*	March 2008	150	45.5	22.5	6.8
Karachaevo-Cherkess Republic	March 2009	15	48.3	2.25	7.3
Vladimir *Oblast'*	March 2009	82	67.5	12.3	10.1
Nenets Autonomous *Okrug*	March 2009	5	157.8	0.75	23.7

[4]However, high 'ceilings' in scarcely populated but territorially vast northern and eastern parts of Russia could be explained by the higher transport costs for running election campaigns.

TABLE 2
MAXIMUM ABSOLUTE AND RELATIVE LIMITS ON SPENDING FROM ELECTORAL FUNDS AND THE SIZE OF THE ELECTION DEPOSIT FOR CANDIDATES IN SINGLE-MANDATE CONSTITUENCIES

Region	*Year and month of elections*	*Maximum limit of spending from the electoral fund*		*Election deposit*	
		Size, millions of rubles	*Proportionate to number of voters (rubles)*	*Size, millions of rubles*	*Proportionate to number of voters (rubles)*
Tuva Republic	October 2006	1.5	140.5	0.225	21.1
Lipetsk *Oblast'*	October 2006	10	304.8	1.5	45.7
Tomsk *Oblast'*	March 2007	6	166.7	0.9	25.0
Komi Republic	March 2007	10	201.9	1.5	30.3
Krasnoyarsk *Krai*	April 2007	5	60.5	0.75	9.1
Kamchatka *Krai*	December 2007	3	257.1	0.3	25.7
Bashkortostan Republic	March 2008	3.5	71.9	0.525	10.8
Rostov *Oblast'*	March 2008	15	113.8	2.25	17.1
Karachaevo-Cherkess Republic	March 2009	5	580.1	0.75	87.0
Vladimir *Oblast'*	March 2009	4.3	67.5	0.648	10.1

After the election deposit was abolished, the tendency to raise the 'ceiling' of electoral funds was also weakened, which also proves that high ceilings had been caused by a desire to set larger deposits. In those parts of the Russian Federation where regional elections took place in October 2009 there is evidence of some inertia: the 'ceiling' in the Mari-El Republic was set at R50 million (R92 per voter) for parties and R1 million (R47.8 per voter) for candidates; in Moscow City the figures were R300 million (R42.8 per voter) and R20 million (R48.5 per voter), respectively. Where regional elections were held in March 2010 the highest 'ceiling' for parties was set in Yamalo-Nenets Autonomous *Okrug* (R50 million, or R143.5 per voter). A high relative 'ceiling' was also adopted in Altay Republic (R113.7 per voter), whereas in the other six regions the 'ceiling' did not exceed R40 per elector. These two regions also had high relative 'ceilings' for candidates (R157.8 and R113.7 per voter, respectively), whereas in the other regions the 'ceiling' hardly reached R55 per elector.

Proportional electoral system

Special attention should be given to changes in the electoral system with regard to those laws which regulate the election of deputies to regional assemblies. This is due to the special importance of these electoral norms, as well as the fact that federal legislators have provided the regions with considerable leeway over the specifics of such legislation. Thus, any changes to the electoral system (unlike most other changes) in this area have not been dictated by the requirement to bring regional laws into line with federal legislation, but rather are the result of the free choice of regional assemblies.

The most important norms (or groups of norms) regulating the electoral systems of elections to regional assemblies concern a choice between a mixed and a fully proportional system; the size of the electoral threshold; the type of party list (open, closed divided into groups, or simple closed without division into groups); and the method of distributing seats between lists. All of these norms have recently been amended, and such changes usually have taken place just before regional assembly elections.

Since 2003 the Federal Law 'On the Basic Guarantees of Electoral Rights' has required that the share of proportionally elected deputies should be at least half of the total number of legislators. Until 2005, most regions had an equal number of majority and party-list deputies, or there was one extra party-list deputy in assemblies with an uneven number of seats. The proportion was different in only five regions, but even there the largest share of party-list deputies was 58%. Sverdlovsk *Oblast'* was an exception, where a two-chamber regional assembly was established as early as 1996, and a proportional system was adopted for one of the chambers. In this region one chamber is still fully elected on a proportional principle, while the other chamber is formed by majority vote.

The first region to move over to a fully proportional electoral system for its regional legislature was St Petersburg, where a law to that effect was passed in 2005. By March 2010, 11 regions had held elections based on a fully proportional representation party list electoral system.

As shown in Table 3, it was only in St Petersburg that the law on adopting the proportional system was passed in good time before the elections in this region. In the Republic of Kabardino-Balkariya and in Kaluga and Tula *Oblasti* such laws were enacted from four to eight months before the start of election campaigns. The remaining seven regions adopted such laws immediately before campaigning.

The switchover to a fully proportional system of elections to regional assemblies took place in the wake of the adoption of a full proportional representation party list system by the State *Duma* in 2007. The major disadvantage of the fully proportional party list electoral system is the denial of the right of self-nomination to non-party citizens, which means that candidates are prevented from competing for a seat as an

TABLE 3

INTRODUCTION OF FULLY PROPORTIONAL ELECTORAL SYSTEMS IN RUSSIAN REGIONS

Region	*Year and month of elections*	*Year and month of adopting legislation*
St Petersburg City	March 2007	June 2005
Moscow *Oblast'*	March 2007	October 2006
Dagestan Republic	March 2007	November 2006
Ingush Republic	March 2008	November 2007
Kalmyk Republic	March 2008	December 2007
Amur *Oblast'*	March 2008	December 2007
Chechen Republic	October 2008	June 2008
Kabardino-Balkar Republic	March 2009	August 2008
Nenets Autonomous *Okrug*	March 2009	November 2008
Tula *Oblast'*	October 2009	December 2008
Kaluga *Oblast'*	March 2010	April 2009

individual and not as a representative of one of the few political parties that currently exist. Moreover, since independents were able to play a more significant role at the regional level than at the federal level, due to the smaller size of the regional assemblies and the more localised scale of the issues which are covered by the legislatures, abandoning single mandate elections was a significant limitation of electoral rights.

Electoral thresholds

As far as the electoral threshold is concerned, in most of the original regional laws which introduced the proportional system, the majority of which were passed in 2003, the electoral barrier was set at the level of 5%, whilst in others it was 4% or even 3%. In a small number of regions it was higher, at 7%. Only five regions decided to put in place a barrier above 7% (and three of those set a 10% threshold) (Kynev & Lyubarev 2003; Lugovskaya 2003). In 2005 a federal law mandated a maximum limit of 7%, but this novelty, officially aimed at curbing high regional barriers, in practice led to a universal increase of the threshold to its maximum permitted level of 7%.

Table 4 shows the rising dynamics of the electoral threshold. In 2006 it was raised in 22 regions, in 2007 in 13, in 2008 in eight, and in 2009 in three more, totalling 46 regions, which is more than half of Russia's current 83 regions. The threshold was predictably raised on the eve of election campaigns in these regions.

To date, out of 62 regional campaigns that have taken place since October 2006, only seven have employed a barrier below 7%, and three of these were newly created merged regions where elections were held in accordance with the norms set by Presidential Decrees. However, as frequently noted by scholars of elections, a 7% threshold is considered excessive, depriving a large section of the electorate of proper representation (Ivanchenko & Lyubarev 2005, pp. 53–55, 245–63).

There is enough reason to believe that the universal increase of the threshold to 7% in so many regions was hardly by chance. For example, a new Law 'On Electing People's Deputies in the Republic of Sakha (Yakutiya)', which was adopted on 18 October 2007, among other things, set a 4% barrier. However, just three weeks later, on 8 November, another law was passed with the sole purpose of bringing the barrier up to 7%. What prompted the legislators to amend a recently enacted piece of

TABLE 4
DYNAMICS OF RAISING THE ELECTORAL BARRIER TO 7%

Year	*Regions*
2006	Ingush, Kareliya, Komi, Nothern Osetiya-Alaniya, Tuva, Chuvash Republics; Primorsk *Krai*; Astrakhan, Kurgan, Lipetsk, Moscow, Murmansk, Novgorod, Orlov, Pskov, Samara, Sverdlovsk, Tver, Tomsk, Tyumen, Chita *Oblasti*; Jewish Autonomous *Oblast'*
2007	Buryat, Mordova, Sakha (Yakutiya), and Udmurt Republics; Krasnodar *Krai*; Amur, Irkutsk, Kemerovo, Penza, Rostov, Saratov, Smolensk, Ulyanovsk *Oblasti*
2008	Kabardino-Balkar, Marii-El, Khakasiya, Chechen Republics; Khabarovsk *Krai*; Arkhangel'sk, Bryansk, Tula *Oblasti*
2009	Voronezh, Kaluga *Oblasti*, Yamalo-Nenets Autonomous *Okrug*

legislation? It should be noted that electoral thresholds were raised in a similar fashion in many other regions.

Further evidence in favour of the assertion that the raising of the barrier did not take place sporadically can be found from Kostroma *Oblast'* where a 4% barrier had been set in the region's law. As mentioned above, there were quite a few regions where the barrier was originally set below 5%, but only in three regions, including Kostroma *Oblast'*, did it remain unchanged. According to a former Kostroma *Oblast' Duma* deputy and Chair of the State *Duma*'s Legislation Committee, Svetlana Shakelina, this was despite pressure from the Presidential Administration. Svetlana Shakelina confessed: 'We were literally being terrorised by representatives of the Presidential Administration; I myself received four calls' (Ivanchenko & Lyubarev 2005, pp. 191–93). Undoubtedly, the Presidential Administration acted in a similar fashion and put pressure on other regions and it is this that explains the universal rise of the barrier.

The trend to adopting higher thresholds did not change even after the Russian President, in his November 2008 Address to the Federal Assembly, expressed the view that it was unfair to deny representation to those who voted for parties which received over 5% of the ballot but did not meet the minimum threshold of 7%.[5] Immediately afterwards the electoral barrier was raised in the Republic of Khakassiya, in Yamalo-Nenets Autonomous *Okrug*, and in Arkhangelsk, Voronezh, Kaluga and Tula *Oblasti*. However, in November 2009 in his annual Address to the Federal Assembly, the president was more specific: 'Parties which win over 5% of the vote in regional elections must receive guarantees of representation in the regional legislature of the region',[6] and this did change the tide slightly. Plans to raise the electoral barrier in Altai Republic and Ryazan *Oblast'* were abandoned, and in a similar way to the law on electing State *Duma* deputies, a norm was introduced in Voronezh *Oblast'* which stated that those parties which secured between 5% and 7% of the vote should receive one seat in the regional assembly.[7] At the same time however, the remaining five regions where elections were scheduled to take place in March 2010 did not reduce their thresholds. In Kaluga and Sverdlovsk *Oblasti*, opposition parties suggested lowering the barrier but failed to gain the support of a majority of deputies.[8]

[5]See the official site of the President of the Russian Federation, available at: http://www.kremlin.ru/text/appears/2008/11/208749.shtml, accessed 18 February 2010.

[6]See the official site of the President of the Russian Federation, available at: http://www.kremlin.ru/text/appears/2008/11/208749.shtml; http://www.kremlin.ru/transcripts/5979, accessed 18 February 2010.

[7]The Federal Law of 12 May 2009 (*Sobranie Zakondatel'stva Rossiiskoi Federatsii*, 2009, 20, article 2391) stipulates that a party which captures between 5% and 6% of the vote in State *Duma* elections receives one seat, and two seats if it wins between 6% and 7%. Thus, such parties secure representation in the State *Duma*, but not proportionally to the votes they receive. (Proportionally, they should receive approximately 30 seats.) Adopting such a norm for elections to smaller regional assemblies will often differ little from bringing the electoral barrier down to 5%, since regional parties with 5%–7% of the vote will usually win one or two seats.

[8]*Nezavisimaya Gazeta*, 1 December 2009, p. 11.

The type of party list

As far as types of party lists are concerned, the Central Electoral Commission of the Russian Federation issued a set of guidelines in 2002 in which it recommended that regions should either set up open lists or divide closed lists into geographical groups.[9] Few regions followed these guidelines, however. Whereas 10 regions initially introduced open lists, only four actually conducted elections (in the period 2003–2005) using this system: the Kalmyk Republic, Tver *Oblast'*, and Koryak and Yamalo-Nenets Autonomous *Okrugi* (Ivanchenko *et al.* 2005, pp. 253–62; Butaev & Titov 2006; Kynev 2009, pp. 47–50). Subsequently, this system was dropped by all the regions which had adopted it.[10] There is strong reason to believe that such decisions were also made in response to pressure from the federal centre. Thus, the system which allowed voters to influence the choice of deputies elected on party lists was abolished.

Dividing party lists into geographical groups is practised in State *Duma* elections. At the election of the first *Duma* in 1993 such a breakdown was optional for the party, but from the second *Duma* (1995) it became compulsory. Unlike most other countries using the proportional system, national elections in Russia are held within a single constituency covering the whole territory of the country. The geographical breakdown of party lists is designed to compensate for the lack of a single list and to bring candidates and elected deputies closer to the electorate.

At the elections to regional legislatures that were held before 2003, dividing party lists into geographical groups was never practised. During 2003–2005, this practice was adopted in a small minority of regions. However, from 2006 it has been practised more widely (Kynev 2009, pp. 44–47).

As seen in Table 5, as far as dividing lists into groups is concerned both tendencies have been evident. More instances of a transition from simple lists to divided lists than the opposite have been observed. It should be added that in 2008–2009 there were no

TABLE 5
CHANGES IN REGIONAL LEGISLATION IN 2006–2009 AS REGARDS DIVIDING PARTY LISTS INTO GEOGRAPHICAL GROUPS

Nature of change	*Regions*
From simple lists to lists divided into groups	Bashkir, Udmurt Republics; Khabarovsk *Krai*; Astrakhan, Volgograd, Vologda, Voronezh, Kaluga, Penza, Pskov, Ryazan, Sverdlovsk and Tulsk *Oblasti*
From open lists to lists divided into groups	Tuva Republic; Lipetsk, Orel and Smolensk *Oblasti*
From lists divided into groups to simple lists	Komi, Sakha (Yakutiya) Republics; Krasnodar *Krai*; Moscow and Saratov *Oblasti*

[9] *Vestnik Tsentral'noi Izbiratel'noi Komissii Rossiiskoi Federatsii*, 2002, 11, pp. 159–92.

[10] In 2006 the open party list system was abandoned by Tuva Republic, Primorsk *Krai*, Lipetsk, Orel and Tver *Oblasti*; in 2007 by the Buryat and Kalmyk Republics, as well as Smolensk *Oblast'*; and in 2009 by Yamalo-Nenets Autonomous *Okrug*.

instances of abandoning divided lists. Whilst dividing lists into geographical groups should be practised in those regions which either cover a large territory, have a large population or heterogeneous electorate, in practice, the opposite has often been the case. For example, party lists in Moscow *Oblast'* (the second largest region in terms of the population) were not divided, neither were those in such large and diverse regions as Krasnodar *Krai*, Rostov *Oblast'* and the Komi Republic with its vast territory and heterogeneous electorate. At the same time, geographical divisions were adopted in smaller regions such as Kurgan, Orlov and Pskov *Oblasti*.

When dividing lists into geographical groups, account is taken of the following norms concerning the core of the list (those candidates who would have priority in seat allocation) and the maximum number of candidates; the rules of dividing the territory of the region into segments assigned to groups (clearly stipulated by the law and uniform for all parties, or a possibility for parties to choose their own divisions); the highest and lowest limit to the number of geographical groups; the highest and lowest limit to the number of candidates in a group; and the methodology for working out the distribution of seats between geographical groups.

In this connection, two interesting cases are worth considering. In Kurgan *Oblast'* the party lists were originally broken down into groups, but subsequently the parties were told to include 10 core candidates. Since no party won, nor was able to capture, more than 10 seats at the November 2004 regional election, the grouping was a pointless exercise (Ivanchenko *et al.* 2005, pp. 248–50). Orlov *Oblast'* legislators, having introduced the compulsory division of lists, 'forgot' to include the seat distribution methodology in the law. Hence, the seats at the March 2007 regional legislature election were distributed irrespective of the votes for the groups (Monitoring 2007, p. 154). These two incidents can be regarded as attempts by regional legislators to outwit the federal centre that had been putting pressure on them.

Norms regulating how lists are divided into geographical groups are often used to restrict citizens' electoral rights and to create advantages for the 'party of power', United Russia. Thus, in some regions—the Republic of Mordoviya, in 2003 and 2008, Kaliningrad *Oblast'* in 2006, the Republic of Bashkortostan in 2008, and Kurgan *Oblast'* in 2010—party lists did not identify the core candidates, and as a result most voters were not presented with the names of the regional party leaders on their ballot papers.

Unlike the case for State *Duma* elections, in most of the regions which use geographically divided lists, the territorial partitioning is the same for all parties and is rigidly prescribed by law. It usually sets a very high minimum number of groups, often equal to the number of single-mandate constituencies formed for the second half of the legislature (which is either equal or nearly equal to the number of seats allocated proportionally). Such legal requirements lead to a situation whereby a significant number of groups from all parties, except that of United Russia (and occasionally including United Russia) end up with no chance of winning seats, thus discouraging candidates from campaigning for votes. In a number of regions, the elections result in some territories having no representation in the party list seats in the legislature (or in the legislature as a whole, if all seats are allocated by proportional representation) (Lyubarev 2007).

Yet another superfluous and burdensome requirement for parties in such positions is the prescribed minimum number of candidates in a group. This norm forces parties to put more candidates on lists (occasionally several times over) than the number of proportionally allocated seats while most parties can realistically expect to win very few seats. Such excessive requirements have been put in place in the Republic of Mordoviya, and in Vologda, Leningrad, Orel and Smolensk *Oblasti* (Kynev 2009, p. 52).

There is also a legislative norm, in a number of regions, which states that parties may be denied registration of their lists if, following candidate withdrawals, the number of groups on the list is fewer than that set in the law. Such a requirement was used to deny registration of party lists submitted for the March 2007 elections by the Union of Right Forces (*Soyuz Pravykh Sil*) in the Dagestan Republic, and in Pskov and Vologda *Oblasti* where, in the latter *Oblast'*, only two candidates had dropped out. In Dagestan Republic a Communist Party list was initially rejected but later reinstated following a court decision that two candidates had withdrawn because of administrative pressure and had not personally submitted their letters of withdrawal to the electoral commission (Monitoring 2007, pp. 53–59). Subsequently, on 11 March 2008, the Russian Constitutional Court upheld an appeal by the Union of Right Forces as concerned the registration of its candidates in Vologda *Oblast'*.[11]

The methodology of seat distribution

As far as the methodology of seat distribution between lists is concerned, until November 2006 the same methodology was applied for State *Duma* and regional legislature elections—the Hare–Neimeyer method. The only exception to the rule was in the Kalmyk Republic where the D'Hondt method was used.

Our analysis shows that not only is the Hare–Neimeyer method the simplest, it is also best suited for distributing seats under proportional representation. The D'Hondt method favours a large party and using this method will usually give it one extra seat over that of the Hare–Neimeyer method. The most favourable formula for the leading party is the Imperiali divisor method which has hardly ever been adopted (the only example was in Belgian municipal elections). This method always allocates one or two extra seats to the dominant party (Taagepera & Shugart 1989; Ivanchenko *et al.* 2005, pp. 178–82).

With these factors in mind, United Russia launched a review of the methodology used to distribute seats in the regions. The first step towards revising the system was taken in St Petersburg in 2006. First, there was a call for the Hare–Neimeyer method to be used in favour of the D'Hondt formula, but subsequently a more radical decision was made: to introduce the Imperiali divisor method in the city's electoral legislation. Following St Petersburg, the Imperiali method was adopted in Moscow and Samara *Oblasti*. Similarly, Tyumen *Oblast'* tried to introduce the Imperiali divisor method, but the formula was later modified in a way that in essence it was turned into the D'Hondt method since it has a slight deviation from the classic D'Hondt formula, but this is not visible under a system with a high electoral barrier (Shalaev 2009). We therefore call it the 'Tyumen method', or the modified D'Hondt method (Lyubarev 2009b).

The introduction of these new 'divisor systems' came under fierce criticism,[12] and for about a year and a half they (predominantly the modified D'Hondt method) were

[11] *Sobranie Zakondatel'stva Rossiiskoi Federatsii*, 2008, 11, article 1073.

[12] *Argumenty Nedeli*, 2006, 20, 33, p. 4; *Politicheskii Zhurnal*, 2007, pp. 13–14; *Nezavisimaya Gazeta*, 28 June 2007, p. 9.

used in only a handful of regions. At the end of 2008, however, this tendency changed as there were fears over United Russia's election prospects and they were used in nine out of 12 regions at the March and October 2009 elections (see Table 6). Once again, the Imperiali formula was used even though there are questions about how fair it is in distributing seats (Lyubarev & Shalaev 2009).

Changing laws before the beginning of election campaigns

Let us return to the dynamics of regional legislation. In 2002 the European Commission for Democracy through Law (the Venice Commission) recommended that any modifications to electoral systems which entered into force less than a year before an election should be prohibited.[13] Russian legislators, however, continue to introduce amendments to electoral laws as close to the start of election campaigns as possible.

Thus, out of the 65 regions which held elections over the period October 2006–March 2010, only six made no changes to their electoral legislation less than a year before campaigning started. Consequently, changing electoral legislation on the eve of elections is not an exception but a rule. Moreover, 27 regions reviewed their electoral laws less than a month before the beginning of campaigning. It should be emphasised that these changes were not prompted by the requirement to comply with federal laws; they were clearly the result of the creative spirit of regional legislators (see Table 7).

Moscow, Tyumen and Rostov *Oblasti* are especially noteworthy, as electoral changes were enacted literally on the eve of campaigning, thus flouting a federal law that stipulates that any law or regulation by a region on protecting civil and human rights and liberties must be published at least 10 days before it comes into force.[14]

TABLE 6
DYNAMICS OF INTRODUCING DIVISOR METHODS IN RUSSIAN REGIONS

Year and month of elections	*Imperiali divisor method*	*Modified D'Hondt method*
March 2007	St Petersburg City, Moscow and Samara *Oblasti*	Tyumen *Oblast'*
December 2007	Saratov *Oblast'*	Krasnodar *Krai*
March 2008	–	Sverdlovsk *Oblast'*
October 2008	–	Sakhalin *Oblast'*
March 2009	Nenets Autonomous *Okrug*, Arkhangelsk and Bryansk *Oblasti*	Karachaevo-Cherkess Republic; Vladimir and Volgograd *Oblasti*
October 2009	–	Moscow City, Marii-El Republic, Tula *Oblast'*
March 2010	Kurgan *Oblast'*	Voronezh and Ryazan *Oblasti*

[13] *Code of Good Practice in Electoral Matters: Guidelines and Explanatory Report*, 2002, available at: http://www.venice.coe.int/docs/2002/CDL-AD%282002%29023rev-e.pdf, accessed 18 February 2010.

[14] Paragraph 5, article 8 of the Federal Law of 6 October 1999, No. 184, 'On the General Principles of Organising Legislative (Representative) and Executive Bodies of State Power in the Subjects of the Russian Federation' (*Sobranie Zakondatel'stva Rossiiskoi Federatsii*, 1999, 42, article 5005).

TABLE 7
LAWS OF RUSSIAN REGIONS ENACTED LESS THAN A MONTH BEFORE THE START OF AN ELECTION CAMPAIGN

Region	*Change*	*Year adopted*	*Days*[a]
Astrakhan *Oblast'*	Raised the barrier from 5% to 7% and divided party lists into groups	2006	29
Samara *Oblast'*	Divided lists into groups and changed the methodology of seat allocation	2006	28
St. Petersburg City	Changed the methodology of seat allocation	2006	24
Moscow City	Changed the methodology of seat allocation	2009	24
Ryazan *Oblast'*	Changed the methodology of seat allocation	2009	23
Kareliya Republic	Raised the barrier from 5% to 7%	2006	23
Krasnodar *Krai*	Raised the barrier from 5% to 7%, cancelled the division of party lists into groups, changed the methodology of seat allocation	2007	22
Sakha (Yakutiya) Republic	Raised the barrier from 4% to 7%	2007	22
Vladimir *Oblast'*	Changed the methodology of seat allocation	2008	22
Bryansk *Oblast'*	Changed the methodology of seat allocation	2008	20
Nenets Autonomous *Okrug*	Adopted a fully proportional system and changed the methodology of seat allocation	2008	19
Sakhalin *Oblast'*	Changed the methodology of seat allocation	2008	18
Arkhangel'sk *Oblast'*	Raised the barrier to 7% and changed the methodology of seat allocation	2008	18
Ingush Republic	Adopted a fully proportional system	2007	17
Kurgan *Oblast'*	Changed the methodology of dividing party list into groups	2009	15
Murmansk *Oblast'*	Raised the barrier from 5% to 7%	2006	15
Tuva Republic	Raised the barrier from 5% to 7% and moved from open to closed lists	2006	14
Orel *Oblast'*	Raised the barrier from 5% to 7%	2006	14
Bashkir Republic	Divided lists into groups	2007	14
Sverdlovsk *Oblast'*	Changed the methodology of seat allocation	2007	14
Sverdlovsk *Oblast'*	Divided lists into groups	2009	14
Kalmyk Republic	Adopted a fully proportional system, abandoned open lists	2007	13
Amur *Oblast'*	Adopted a fully proportional system, raised the barrier from 5% to 7%	2007	13
Karachaevo-Cherkess Republic	Changed the methodology of seat allocation	2008	13
Tyumen *Oblast'*	Changed the methodology of seat allocation	2006	5
Rostov *Oblast'*	Raised the barrier from 5% to 7%	2007	5
Moscow *Oblast'*	Changed the methodology of seat allocation	2006	3

Note: [a]Number of days from enacting the law until the start of an election campaign.

In one instance, however, such an amendment did not bring about the intended outcome. In 2008, the leader of the Khakasiya Republic Alexey Lebed refused to ratify a law which raised the electoral threshold to 7% and this led to a situation whereby the law did not come into effect before the start of the election campaign and therefore was not implemented. This, however, is an exception.

Conclusion

Over the last few years Russian regional electoral legislation has been consistently mimicking the tendencies of the federal electoral laws aimed at restricting electoral rights of citizens and creating advantages for the 'party of power', United Russia. As a whole therefore, the present state of Russian electoral legislation and legislation on political parties appears utterly unsatisfactory. A group of experts, independent of the authorities, has recently started work on drafting a comprehensive package of proposed reforms to this part of the legislation.[15] This work presupposes abolishing the anti-democratic novelties enacted in recent years and codifying electoral legislation, and aims, ultimately, at the drafting of an Electoral Code of the Russian Federation, new laws on political parties and on an all-Russia referendum, as well as amendments to a number of other federal laws.

Association of Non-profit Organizations 'In Defense of Voters' Rights "GOLOS"'

References

Astafichev, P. A. (1999) *Izbiratel'noe Pravo Rossii: Sovremennoe Sostoyanie i Perspektivy Razvitiya* (Orel, Izdatel'stvo ORAGS).

Butaev, V. I. & Titov, M. V. (2006) 'Proportsional'naya Sistema s Ispol'zovaniem Otkrytykh Spiskov: Opyt Tverskoi Oblasti', *Zhurnal o Vyborakh*, 3, pp. 39–47.

Ivanchenko, A. V., Kynev, A. V. & Lyubarev, A. E. (2005) *Proportsional'naya Izbiratel'naya Sistema v Rossii: Istoriya, Sovremennoe Sostoyanie, Perspectivy* (Moscow, Aspekt Press).

Ivanchenko, A. V. & Lyubarev, A. E. (eds) (2005) *Rossiiskie Vybory v Kontekste Mezhdunarodnykh Izbiratel'nykh Standartov: Materialy Mezhdunarodnoi Konferentsii* (Moscow, Aspekt Press).

Kynev A. (2009) *Vybory Parlamentov Rossiiskikh Regionov 2003–2009: Pervyi Tsikl Vnedreniya Proportsional'noi Izbiratel'noi Sistemy* (Moscow, Tsentr 'Panorama').

Kynev, A. & Lyubarev, A. (2003) 'Novye Regional'nye Zakony o Vyborakh: Problemy Vvedeniya Smeshannoi Izbiratel'noi Sistemy', *Pravo i Zhizn'*, 61, 9, pp. 166–84.

Lugovskaya, M. L. (2003) 'Vvedenie Proportsional'noi Izbiratel'noi Sistemy v Regional'noe Zakonodatel'stvo o Vyborakh', *Zhurnal o Vyborakh*, 4, pp. 2–10.

Lyubarev, A. (2004) 'Puti Sovershenstvovaniya Zakonodatel'stva, Reguliruyushchevo Regional'nye i Mestnye Vybory', *Pravo i Zhizn'*, 65, 1, pp. 176–98.

Lyubarev, A. (2007) 'Razbienie Partiinogo Spiska na Regional'nye Gruppy: Problemy Territorial'novo Predstavitel'stva', *Zhurnal o Vyborakh*, 5, pp. 37–42.

Lyubarev, A. (2009a) 'Khronologiya Izmenenii Rossiiskovo Izbiratel'novo Zakonodatel'stva, 1989–2009', *Rossiiskoe Electoral'noe Obozrenie*, 2, pp. 4–22.

Lyubarev A. (2009b) 'Izpol'zovanie Metodov Delitelei na Rossiiskikh Vyborakh', *Rossiiskoe Electoral'noe Obozrenie*, 2, pp. 34–42.

Lyubarev, A. E. & Shalaev, N. E. (2009) 'O Kriteriyakh Proportsional'nosti pri Raspredelenii Mandatov mezhdu Partiinymi Spiskami', *Konstitutsionnoe i Munitsipal'noe Pravo*, 23, pp. 23–27.

Monitoring (2006) 'Monitoring Regional'nyh Izbiratel'nyh Kampanii 8 Oktyabrya 2006 goda', *Byulleten' Natsional'novo Tsentra Demokraticheskikh Protsedur*, 1, December.

Monitoring (2007) 'Monitoring Regional'nyh Izbiratel'nykh Kampanii 11 Marta 2007', *Byulleten' Natsional'novo Tsentra Demokraticheskikh Protsedur*, 3, May.

Shalaev, N. (2009) 'Opyt Izpol'zovaniya Sistemy Delitelei Imperiali v Regionakh Rossii', *Rossiiskoe Electoral'noe Obozrenie*, 1, pp. 4–11.

Taagepera, R. & Shugart, M. S. (1989) *Seats and Votes: The Effects and Determinants of Electoral Systems* (New Haven, CT, Yale University Press).

[15]Association of Non-profit Organizations 'In Defence of Voters' Rights "GOLOS"', available at: http://www.golos.org/r84.html, accessed 18 February 2010.

The Rise and Fall of Political Parties in Russia's Regional Assemblies

CAMERON ROSS

IN THIS ESSAY I EXAMINE THE PROBLEMS OF institutionalising and nationalising parties in Russia's regions and I trace the development of the party system from the period of fragmentation and high levels of volatility under Yel'tsin, to the monopolisation of power under Putin and Medvedev. In particular, I examine the party saturation and non-saturation of regional assemblies.

Parties and party systems

Whilst there is some debate about the importance of parties in contemporary industrial societies, it is still the case, as McFaul notes, that 'a party system is an essential attribute of a democratic polity. No parties, no democracy' (2000, p. 3). Parties are particularly important during regime transitions and the consolidation of democracy where they play a vital role in bolstering system legitimacy at a time of political uncertainty (Pridham & Lewis 1996, p. 5).

Scholars in the field have traditionally been divided over which prerequisites are necessary for the creation of a strong party system. One group stresses the external environment in which parties operate, the political culture and the strength of civil society. From this perspective, parties are seen as dependent variables and their ability to develop successfully is determined by these external cultural factors. As Karen Dawisha notes, 'a strong civil society is a necessary but not sufficient condition for a strong party and system and it is difficult to find examples where parties have been established in states with weak civil cultures' (1997, p. 55). In contrast, a second group of scholars focus on the internal structures, leadership and operational behaviour of parties. In this second approach, parties are seen as independent variables whose actions can positively or negatively shape civil society and culture. Here as Webb and Lewis observe, 'parties are far more than passive victims of the vicissitudes of public opinion, and it is widely recognised in the West that they can do much to shape political agendas, voter perceptions and electoral choices' (1998, p. 256). From this perspective institutions matter: change the institutions, change the culture. Strong cohesive parties can bring about consolidated democracies even in hostile cultural environments. Democratic parties can create democrats. On the other hand, weakly institutionalised parties and party systems can allow authoritarianism to take root.

Hence, before parties can play their vital role in the process of consolidating democracy, parties themselves must be institutionalised and consolidated.

The institutionalisation of parties

According to Mainwaring, institutionalisation (1998, p. 69) 'means the process by which a practice or organisation becomes well established and widely known, if not universally accepted'. Strongly institutionalised party systems exhibit the following characteristics. First, they have high degrees of stability of interparty competition and low electoral volatility. Secondly, parties have strong roots in society and most voters, conversely, have strong attachments to parties. Thirdly, political actors accord legitimacy to parties, they see parties as a necessary part of democratic politics. Fourthly, parties possess strong, disciplined and territorially comprehensive organisations with well established structures and procedures, significant material and human resources and an independent status which is not overshadowed by a personalistic leader or coterie (Mainwaring 1998, pp. 70–71; Mainwaring & Torcal 2006, p. 206).

Mainwaring contrasts the highly institutionalised parties largely to be found in Western Europe and North America with the weakly institutionalised inchoate parties of the third wave democracies in Eastern Europe and Russia. According to Enyedi, polities with low levels of party system institutionalism display the following key features: 'high electoral volatility, low popularity of parties, relatively low turnout, small party membership, weak partisan identities, weak grounding of parties in civil society, their financial dependence on the state, and low level of organisational loyalty among politicians' (2006, p. 229). As will be demonstrated below, regional party systems in the Russian Federation suffer badly from all of these negative features.

Nationalisation of parties and party systems

Another important factor in the development of party systems is the nationalisation of parties. According to Kasuya and Moenius (2008, p. 136), nationalisation

> refers to the extent to which parties compete with equal strength across various geographic units within a nation. Strongly nationalised party systems are systems where the vote share of each party is similar across geographic units (e.g. districts, provinces, and regions), while weakly nationalised party systems exhibit large variation in the vote shares of parties across sub-national units.

Strong and cohesive national parties have an important integrative function in federal states binding together the diverse subjects of the federation. As Lago and Montero note, 'the transformation of clientelistic, fragmented local organizations dominated by social or political elites, into disciplined, competitive national parties has contributed significantly to the responsiveness of party officials, the accountability of party politicians, and the nationwide representation of citizens' (2010, p. 2). For Jones and Mainwaring, 'the nationalisation of some major parties' is particularly important in 'new democracies where pronounced ethnic, national or religious cleavages coincide with territory' (2003, p. 144). In strongly nationalised party systems, 'the highly localised and territorialized politics is replaced by national electoral alignments and oppositions. Peripheral and regional specificities disappear, and sectional cleavages progressively transform into nationwide functional alignments' (Lago & Montero 2010, p. 5).

Federalism and parties

As Hopkin and Van Houten (2009, p. 131) note,

> the existing literature on political parties and party systems has paid only limited attention to the territorial organization of parties and their activities in multi-level political systems. Territorial, or centre–periphery, cleavages have been acknowledged as important factors shaping the nature of party systems, but the impact of such cleavages on the organization and strategies of state-wide parties has mostly been ignored.

Parties in federal systems face very different challenges from those in unitary systems. Gibson (2004, p. 21), in his study of federalism in Latin America, stresses the 'bidirectional nature' of the causal relations between party systems and federal institutions:

> Party systems, through the incentives they provide to political actors and the institutional mechanisms they set in motion, can exert centralizing or decentralizing influences on federal systems. However, federal systems, through the powers and political resources they impart to political actors located at different points in the federal structure, can also shape the nature of party competition, the structures of incentives for politicians, and the decentralization of parties and party systems.

Moreover, Thorlakson (2009, p. 158) makes the important point that, by 'creating multiple important sites for political organisation and competition, each with constitutionally guaranteed autonomy … federalism gives parties the opportunity to compete and capture significant rewards of office in both arenas, and use their organisational and electoral strength within each state to build a strong federal party'. However, as is the case in the Russian Federation, sharp variations 'in the economic and social conditions and priorities across the units of the federation … may make it difficult for a state-level party to respond to their local electoral base without bringing it into conflict with the federal level of the party organisation' (Thorlakson 2009, p. 158).

Factors explaining Russia's low levels of party institutionalisation and party-system nationalisation

Scholars of Russian politics have stressed the following key factors as major determinants of Russia's weak party system and its chronically poor levels of party system institutionalisation and nationalisation: the weakness of civil society and the legacy of an authoritarian political culture; the absence in the early years of the transition of strong and stable political and economic cleavages around which nationwide parties could coalesce; the excessive powers of Russia's super-presidential system and the dominance of the executive over the legislative and judicial branches; and the impact of the original choice of electoral systems at the national (up until 2007) and regional levels (up until 2003).

In this essay, I argue that parties in the regions continue to be weak because, as McFaul notes, 'powerful politicians in Russia have made choices to make them weak. Cultural, historical and socio-economic factors play a role in impeding party emergence, but individual decisions—especially decisions about institutional design—are the more proximate and more salient causes of poor party development' (2000, p. 4). Under both Yel'tsin and his successors, laws on elections and parties have been deliberately designed to prevent the creation of strong nationwide parties that could pose a challenge to the dominant position of the president and the 'party of power'.

Under Putin and Medvedev we have witnessed a massive reduction in the number of parties at the national and regional levels. To a large degree only those parties which are sanctioned by the Kremlin are allowed to register and compete in elections. This has been especially the case since 2005 when the president was granted the power to directly appoint regional governors (subject to the consent of the regional assemblies). Since that date we have witnessed a marked increase in the role of regional governors in bringing home the votes for United Russia (*Edinaya Rossiya*) and a sharp decline in the number of parties contesting regional elections. Moreover, scores of opposition parties have been denied participation in regional assembly elections (see discussion below).

Following the work of Gel'man *et al.* (2003), I also stress that the degree of contestation in the regions is closely linked to the specific form of elite rule. Where regional elites are unified (such as in many of the ethnic republics) we see more autocratic forms of rule and low levels of competition: where elites are divided we have witnessed higher levels of contestation. This was particularly the case in the 1990s when regional parties and blocs were prolific in many regions (Panov 2009).

Finally, I argue that the nature of Russia's quasi-federal system has had a negative impact on party institutionalisation and party system nationalisation. With a population of 142 million citizens incorporating 182 nationalities and an area covering 170 million square kilometres, Russia is one of the largest and most ethnically diverse multinational federations in the world. Moreover, the Russian Federation is highly asymmetrical. The current 83 regions vary widely in the size of their territories and populations, and their socio-economic status and ethnic composition. Such factors make it very difficult for parties to nationalise and create strong unified structures.

The fragmentation of regional assemblies in the 1990s

Russia's party system up until the early 2000s was 'excessively fragmented and excessively volatile'. As Gel'man notes (2006, pp. 545–46), it was fragmented first because,

> all segments of Russia's electoral market were over-supplied. Second, the high level of electoral volatility demonstrated great uncertainty and elasticity in voter demand .... Third, non-partisan politicians who possessed resources other than party support (mainly backed by regional and/or sectoral interest groups) also played a major role in national and, especially, sub-national electoral markets.

Thus, for example, up until changes to the electoral system in 2003 Russia's regional assemblies were dominated by non-party independents, members of regional parties and electoral blocks. Of the 3,481 deputies elected to 83 of Russia's 89 republics and regions, in post as of January 1998, only 635 (18.4%) were members of national political parties. A study of individual legislatures shows that party representation was very weak, with 17 of Russia's regional assemblies having no party representation at all (Ross 2009, p. 139).[1] Moreover, in only five assemblies did party members comprise a majority: Krasnoyarsk *Krai* (80.4%), Novosibirsk *Oblast'* (55.1%), Kemerovo *Oblast'* (57.1%), Ryazan *Oblast'* (50.0%) and Sverdlovsk *Oblast'* (69.3%). No party held a majority of the seats in any of Russia's 89 regional assemblies, and there were only 10 chairs of assemblies with a party affiliation (Ross 2009).

During this period it was common practice for candidates belonging to political parties to stand as independents and to only reveal their party affiliation after the conclusion of the elections. Such concealment of one's party affiliation shows that, for most candidates, party membership was seen as more of a liability than an asset. Thus, for example, data collected by Kynev and Glubotskii (2003) for regional elections held over the period 1993–2003 show that the actual number of party members was on average twice the number of officially declared party candidates.

Of those deputies with a national party affiliation in January 1998 by far the largest group were members of the Communist Party (*Kommunisticheskaya Partiya Rossiiskoi Federatsiya*, KPRF) which comprised 44.0% of all party deputies. However, overall the Communists won only 8.0% of the total number of seats in regional assemblies. All of the other political parties had a minimal presence, none comprising even as much as 1% of the total number of deputies. It was only in the regions of the so called 'red belt' (for example, Stavropol' *Krai*, Belgorod, Volgograd, Ryazan, Smolensk, Tambov, Bryansk and Penza *Oblasti*), where there were higher levels of party saturation, that the Communists were able to achieve a plurality, if not a majority, in coalition with other parties such as the Agrarian Party of Russia (*Agrarnaya Partiya Rossii*) and the National Patriotic Union of Russia (*Narodno Patrioticheskii Soyuz Rossii*) (Ross 2009, p. 139).[2]

Party membership was also much higher in the few regions where there was an element of proportional representation in the electoral system. Thus, for example, as Panov (2009, p. 163) notes, 'elections to the Sverdlovsk *Oblast' Duma* (the lower house of the regional legislature) were based on party lists alone. In Pskov *Oblast'* one third of the regional assembly deputies (11 out of 33) were elected in a similar fashion'. The Krasnoyarsk *Krai* Legislature was formed on the basis of a mixed PR and majoritarian system and in 1998 over 80% of the deputies were members of political parties. However, it should be stressed that these assemblies were dominated by regional parties and local 'clienteles' of the governors rather than by strong and cohesive national parties with strong programmatic policies.

A key feature of parties in the 1990s was their poor levels of party nationalisation. As Table 1 demonstrates, none of the parties had branches in all regions. In fact, none

[1]No parties were officially represented in the republics of Bashkortostan, Buryatiya, Dagestan; Primorskii *Krai*; Amur, Chel'yabinsk, Chita, Kostroma, Magadan, Novgorod and Perm *Oblasti*; Komi-Permiyak, Nenetsk, Taimyr, Khanty-Mansi, Chukotka and Evenk autonomous *okrugi*.

[2]Golosov found that of the 3,420 deputies elected to regional assemblies over the period August 1995–July 1999, 636 (18.6%) were members of political parties. Communists comprised 67% of party members (Golosov 2004, p. 150).

of the parties competed in all of the electoral districts in parliamentary elections. Thus, for example, in the 1999 elections for the State *Duma* even the KPRF could only field candidates in 62.2% of the single member election districts. *Yabloko* and Our Home is Russia (*Nash Dom–Rossiya*, NDR) fielded candidates in approximately 60%; Fatherland–All Russia (*Otechestvo–Vsya Rossiya*, OVR) and Union of Right Forces (*Soyuz Pravykh Sil*, SPS) in about half, and *Yedinstvo* ('Unity') in just 18%. Zhirinovsky's block failed to contest a single seat (Ross 2002, p. 110). Turning to the party lists, even here, none of the parties fielded candidates in all of the regions in 1999; NDR's candidates competed in 84 of Russia's 89 regions; the KPRF in 84 regions, OVR in 68, SPS in 63, *Yabloko* in 57 and Unity in 53 (Ross 2002, p. 110).

As Table 1 shows, the territorial distribution of parties in regional assemblies was also very low. The Communist Party had by far the greatest geographical spread, but even it had only 279 seats in less than half of Russia's regions (42 of 89). The situation for all the remaining parties was much worse. Thus, for example, The Agrarian Party of Russia won a mere 28 seats in seven assemblies; the National Patriotic Union of Russia (*Narodno Patrioticheskii Soyuz Rossii*), 26 seats in three assemblies; *Yabloko*, 22 seats in eight assemblies; Our Home is Russia, 18 seats in 12 assemblies; and the Liberal Democratic Party of Russia (*Liberal'no Demokraticheskaya Partiya Rossii*, LDPR), 15 seats in just six assemblies. Moreover, six parties had representation in only one assembly (Ross 2002, p. 99).

TABLE 1

INDICATORS OF PARTY NATIONALISATION: NUMBER OF SEATS WON BY CANDIDATES OF NATIONAL PARTIES IN REGIONAL ASSEMBLIES AND NUMBER OF ASSEMBLIES IN WHICH PARTIES HAVE SEATS IN JANUARY 1998

Name of party	*Total number of seats*	*Number of assemblies where parties won seats*
Communist Party of the Russian Federation	279	42
Agrarian Party of Russia	28	7
Russian Ecological Party 'The Greens', (*Rossiiskaya Ekologicheskaya Partiya 'Zelenye'*)	1	1
Russia's Democratic Choice (*Demokraticheskii Vybor Rossii*)	2	1
Honour and Fatherland (*Chesti i Ochestvo*)	11	4
Republican Party (*Respublikanskaya Partiya*)	1	1
Russian Communist Workers' Party (*Rossiiskaya Kommunisticheskaya Rabochaya Partiya*)	9	5
Liberal Democratic Party of Russia	15	6
National Patriotic Union of Russia	26	3
Our Home is Russia	18	12
Yabloko	22	8
Party of Independent Workers (*Partiya Samoupravleniya Trudyashchikhsya*)	1	1
People's Party of Russia (*Narodnaya Partiya Rossii*)	1	1
Congress of Russian Communities (*Kongress Russkikh Obshchin*)	2	1

Source: 'National Parties in Regional Assemblies', special report prepared for the author by the Russian Central Electoral Commission, no author, January 1998.

If party affiliation in regional assemblies was weak, in the governors' corps it was even more inchoate and transient. As Golosov notes, of the 459 candidates who stood in the gubernatorial elections over the period 1995–1999, only 16.1% were party members, and this fell to just 8.3% of deputies elected in the period 1999–2003 (2006, p. 66). Rather than governors joining parties in order to promote their election prospects, it was more often the case that parties were forced to turn to governors to help them bring home the regional votes. Regional governors had considerable control over electoral finances, the local media, courts, and electoral commissions. As Fleron *et al.* (1998, p. 231) note, the regional bosses, acted 'as functional equivalents to political parties, creating a wedge between the national party elites and the masses and acting as a break upon the creation of national parties with nation-wide appeals and constituencies'.

Summing up the situation in the early 2000s, Golosov (2004, p. 19) noted that candidates for executive posts and seats in regional assemblies simply did not need a party affiliation to be successful, and there 'were numerous and easily available alternatives to the services which parties could offer'. Administrative resources, social capital, and 'high status in key political hierarchies or superior financial resources substitute for party affiliations' (2004, p. 156). Hale (2006) also stresses the dominance of 'party substitutes' such as 'the powerful political machines of provincial governors ... and politicised financial–industrial groups ...'.

Thus, the main feature of regional politics in the 1990s was that competition primarily took place between informal interest groups (clans, clienteles, business groups), rather than between parties. Consequently, as Panov notes, although regional assemblies were formerly made up of non-party deputies they 'were not amorphous packs of independent deputies. On the contrary, they were structured into informal groups reflecting the makeup of regional elites' (2009, p. 162). A majority of the regional assemblies were dominated by entrepreneurs and state officials.

From fragmentation in the 1990s to a monopoly of power in the 2000s

Whilst the 1990s was a period of party fragmentation, low party nationalisation and high electoral volatility, the past decade has been epitomised by a sharp decline in the number of parties, and in the levels of party contestation. In place of highly fragmented regional assemblies dominated by regional parties, independents and governor's blocks, we have a monopoly of power by one party—United Russia.

In 2003 a major positive change was made to electoral legislation which stipulated that regional assembly elections henceforth would be conducted using a mixed electoral system whereby half of the deputies would be elected in PR party list contests and the remaining half in first-past-the-post majoritarian contests.[3] At present there is a 7% electoral threshold in most regions and there is also a trend towards creating

[3]Federal Law of the Russian Federation, 12 June 2002, No. 67, 'Ob osnovnykh garantiyakh izbiratel'nykh prav i prava na uchastie v referendume grazhdan Rossiiskoi Federtatsii', *Sobranie Zakonodatel'stva Rossiiskoi Federatsii*, no. 24, item 2253, 2002. This law came into force in July 2003.

100% PR party list systems in regional assemblies. Kaluga *Oblast'* is the 11th region to become fully proportional.[4]

However, whilst this injection of proportionality into regional assembly elections has naturally led to much higher levels of party saturation, it has not led to the development of a vibrant pluralistic party system. This positive change in the electoral system has been offset by a series of other laws on parties and elections which have made it far more difficult for parties to be legally registered and to participate in regional elections.

First, according to amendments made to the 2001 Law 'On Political Parties' in December 2004,[5] in order to be legally registered, parties (from 1 January 2006) were required to have a total of not less than 50,000 members (while previously according to the original 2001 law it was 10,000). Moreover they were required to have regional branches in over half of the regions, each with a minimum of 500 members (previously 100 members), and the number of members of other regional branches had to number not less than 250 members (previously 50).[6] The authorities at the federal and regional levels have been highly selective in their application of the law on parties. As Kynev (2009, p. 21) notes, a typical regional branch of a political party usually only numbered several dozen members. Thus, the law actually 'forced parties to falsify their documents and accept fake members (friends, neighbours, employees etc.)'. The only new party that was able to pass through all the legal hurdles instigated by the Law on Parties was Right Cause (*Pravoe Delo*) which has close links to the Kremlin. Other parties such as 'Great Russia' (*Velikaya Rossiya*), the 'National-Bolshevik Party' (*Natsional-Bolshevistskaya Partiya*), and 'The People's Democratic Union' (*Rossiiskii Narodno-Demokraticheskii Soyuz*), were denied registration for purely political reasons (Kynev 2009). Moreover, the law was also used by the Kremlin

> to enforce the replacement of the leaders of some parties: a split in the party was provoked and then the authorities approved only the group loyal to the Kremlin or they declared that the official protocols of a party convention were in violation of the law, thereby making the legal status of the leaders of the parties invalid. With the removal of the party leadership, the subsequent dissolution of the party was inevitable. The Russian Pensioners' Party [*Rossiiskaya Partiya Pensionerov*], *Rodina*, the Republican Party, the United Socialist Party of Russia [*Sotsialisticheskaya Edinaya Partiya Rossii*] and others went through this type of imposed reorganisation. (Kynev 2009, p. 22)

Second, even although Russia is supposedly a Federal State, the Law 'On Parties' prohibits regional parties from competing in elections. This policy was clearly designed to prevent regional governors from building local political machines, which would be powerful enough to mount a challenge to United Russia. For example, in Kemerovo *Oblast'* assembly elections in 2003, 34 of the 35 deputies were members of the

[4]The other regions which have adopted full proportional systems are: St Petersburg, Dagestan, Chechnya, Ingushetiya, Kabardino-Balkariya, Kalmykiya, Amur, Moscow, Tula *Oblasti* and the Nenetskii Autonomous *Okrug*.

[5]Federal Law, 11 July 2001, No. 95, 'O politicheskikh partiyakh', *Sobranie Zakonodatel'stva Rossiiskoi Federatsii*, no. 29, 16 July 2001, article 2950.

[6]Federal Law, 20 December 2004, No. 168, 'O vnesenii izmeneni v Federal'nyi zakon "O politicheskikh partiyakh"', *Rossiiskaya Gazeta*, 24 December 2004.

Governors' Bloc (*Blok Gubernatorov*). Third, in July 2005 electoral blocs were banned. Having earlier benefited from being able to form an electoral alliance, United Russia has now denied the same rights to other parties. Electoral blocks had enjoyed significant electoral support in regional elections held over the period 2004–2005.

Fourth, up until 2005 a candidate's registration could be refused if 25% of their nomination signatures were declared invalid. Under new legislation adopted in 2005 this was reduced to 10% for regional and local elections. These changes have made it far easier for opposition candidates to be denied registration for regional and municipal elections. Moreover, according to legislation adopted in July 2005 the size of the electoral deposit was set at 10% of regional electoral campaign funds. The deposit required for elections to the State *Duma* was raised from R37.5 to R60 million. For elections to Moscow City *Duma* the deposit was R20 million. The record sum was set in St Petersburg, where in elections to the City Assembly in March 2007, the deposit was an incredible R90 million or $3,360,000! It should also be stressed that there was no level playing field in the rules governing the registration process, as the 2005 legislation granted those parties with seats in the State *Duma* automatic registration for elections (Ross 2010, p. 176).

Fifth, in 2005, changes were made which raised the maximum electoral threshold set for regional assembly elections to 7%, and a majority of regions immediately raised their thresholds from 5% to 7%, a factor that made it much more difficult for many small parties to gain seats in the assemblies.[7] Sixth, as noted above, in December 2004 the *Duma* adopted legislation which gave the president the right (from January 2005) to directly appoint regional governors (with the approval of the regional assemblies). By the end of 2009 all 83 governors had been appointed. These Kremlin appointed governors have been anxious to show their loyalty to the president by ensuring victory for United Russia in their regions. As discussed below United Russia currently dominates all regional assemblies.

Seventh, on 27 July 2006 the *Duma* adopted a new 'Law on Combating Extremist Activity'[8] which gives the government new powers to ban parties from elections if any of their members are charged with extremist activities. There are fears that this law could be used to ban opposition parties on political grounds under a very broad interpretation of what exactly constitutes 'extremist activities'. These strict rules governing the registration process have made it much easier for opposition parties to be ousted from elections. Over the period 2003–2009 just under a quarter of all party lists were denied registration in regional assembly elections and in some regions the

[7]Federal Law, 21 July 2005, No. 93, 'O vnesenii izmenenii v zakonodatel'nye akty Rossiiskoi Federatsii, "O vyborakh i referendymakh i inye zakondatel'nye akty Rossiiskii Federatsii"', *Rossiiskaya Gazeta*, 26 July 2005. This law limited the electoral threshold to 7%. In line with the new legislation, Moscow *Oblast'* and Samara raised their electoral thresholds from 4% to 7%; Ingushetiya, Kareliya, Komi, Tuva, Chuvashiya, Primorskii *Krai*, Astrakhan, Kurgan, Lipetsk, Murmansk, Novgorod, Orel, Pskov, Sverdlovsk, Tver', Tomsk, Tyumen, Chita and the Jewish Autonomous *Oblast'*, raised their barriers from 5% to 7%. Saratov raised its barrier from 4% to 5%. In 2006 the republics of Dagestan, Kalmykiya, and Moscow City lowered their barriers from 10% to 7% (Ivanchenko & Lyubarev 2006, p. 17).

[8]Federal Law, 27 July 2006, No. 148, 'O vnesenii izmenenii v stat'i 1 i 15 Federal'novo Zakona, N. 114, 25 Iyulya 2002, "O protivodeistvii ekstremistskoi deyatel'nosti"', *Rossiskaya gazeta*, 9 July 2006.

percentage was much higher. In March 2006 in Nizhegorod *Oblast'* over half of the party lists were denied registration (53.8%) and in Krasnodar *Krai* the figure was 46.15%. In March 2007 in St Petersburg 45.4% were denied registration, in Volgograd the figure was 44.4%, in Leningrad and Tyumen *Oblasti* 40%, and in December 2007 in the Republic of Buryatiya, 55.6% (Kynev 2008, p. 5).

Eighth, new legislation governing the provision of free advertising during election campaigns has bankrupted a number of opposition parties. According to the legislation governing party finances those parties which do not receive 3% of the votes in State *Duma* elections are obliged to pay for their free campaign advertising. According to Kynev, in the December 2007 elections to the State *Duma* parties ran up a debt of over R1 billion. *Yabloko* had a bill of R170, Civil Power (*Grazhdanskaya Sila*) approximately R168 million, Patriots of Russia (*Patrioty Rossii*) approximately R168 million, the Agrarian Party of Russia approximately R161 million, the Democratic Party (*Demokraticheskaya Partiya Rossii*) approximately R161 million, Union of Right Forces R159 million, and the Party of Social Justice (*Partiya Sotsial'noi Spravedlivosti*) R146 million. Such huge debts led to the voluntary self-liquidation of the Agrarian Party, the Party of Social Justice, the People's Union (*Narodnyi Soyuz*), the Union of Right Forces, Civil Power, and the Democratic Party of Russia (Kynev 2009, p. 13). In 2009 amendments were made to the legislation governing the rules over free campaign advertising which states that those parties which do not receive 3% of the votes in parliamentary elections and 2% in presidential elections will not be granted free campaign advertising in subsequent elections (Kynev 2009).

One positive feature of the law on parties is the provision for the state funding of parties. However, it is only those parties that have seats in the State *Duma* which are eligible for such funds. Parties outside the *Duma* have to rely on membership fees and donations.

The dissolution of parties

In 1999, 149 registered parties and political associations were registered with the Ministry of Justice and thereby had the right to participate in elections. However, as a result of the amendments to party and electoral laws discussed above, scores of parties have been merged, turned into public associations, or dissolved. Over the period 2003–2009 the number of parties dropped from 44 to just seven. Party contestation in regional assembly elections fell from an average of 8.1 in March 2006 to 4.6 in March 2010. Moreover, as can be seen from Table 2 there has been a steady decline in the number of 'effective parties' in almost all regional assemblies. There were particularly steep declines in Amur *Oblast'* where the number of effective parties fell from 7.73 in 2005 to 1.24 in 2008; in the Republic of Khakasiya there was a drop from 5.5 in 2004 to 1.31 in 2009; in Vladimir *Oblast'*, from 6.48 in 2005 to 1.73 in 2009; and in Ryazan *Oblast'*, from 5.9 to 1.69 in 2010 (Turovsky 2010).

At present the vast majority of regional elections are contested by only the four parties which currently have seats in the State *Duma*: United Russia, the Communist Party of the Russian Federation, the Liberal Democratic Party of Russia and Just Russia (*Spravedlivaya Rossiya*). The three parties outside the *Duma*—Right Cause,

TABLE 2

NUMBER OF EFFECTIVE PARTIES IN RUSSIAN REGIONAL ASSEMBLIES 2003–2010

	2003	*2004*	*2005*	*2006*	*2007*	*2008*	*2009*	*2010*
Adygeya				2.97				
Altai Republic				4.25				2.14
Bashkortostan						1.01		
Buryatiya					1.2			
Dagestan					1.16			
Ingushetiya	2.82					1.07		
Kabardino-Balkariya	1.06						1.09	
Kalmykiya	1.7					1.48		
Karachaevo-Cherkessiya		1.31					1.1	
Kareliya				2.4				
Komi Republic					2.75			
Mari El		3.29					1.21	
Mordoviya	1.03				1.01			
Sakha (Yakutiya)						1.55		
North Ossetiya					1.2			
Tatarstan		1.04					1.04	
Tuva				2.04				
Udmurtiya					1.35			
Khakasiya		5.5					1.31	
Chehen Republic			1.21			1.01		
Chuvashiya				1.51				
Altai *Krai*		4.3				1.56		
Zabaykalski *Krai*		2.76				1.37		
Kamchatski *Krai*					1.19			
Krasnodar					1.15			
Krasnoyarsk					2.15			
Perm				2.97				
Primorski *Krai*				1.51				
Stavropol'					4.19			
Khabarovsk			2.06					1.83
Amur			7.73			1.24		
Arkhangel'sk							1.61	
Astrakhan				2.35				
Belgorod			1.42					
Bryansk		2.86					1.56	
Vladimir			6.48				1.73	
Volgograd	2.78						1.77	
Vologda	2.3				2.24			
Voronezh			3.93					1.24
Ivanovo			3.19			1.26		
Irkutsk		3.45				1.6		
Kaliningrad				2.7				
Kaluga		2.09						1.54
Kemerovo						1.01		
Kirov				4.05				
Kostroma			3.69					
Kurgan		4.77						2.4
Kursk				2.16				
Leningrad *Oblast'*					2.97			
Lipetsk				1.46				
Magadan			4.02					
Moscow *Oblast'*					1.6			
Murmansk					2.18			
Nizhni Novgorod				1.99				

(*continued*)

TABLE 2
(*Continued*)

	2003	*2004*	*2005*	*2006*	*2007*	*2008*	*2009*	*2010*
Novgorod				1.82				
Novosibirsk			3.22					
Omsk					1.43			
Orenburg				2.05				
Orel					2.51			
Penza					1.14			
Pskov					1.93			
Rostov						1.1		
Ryazan			5.9					1.69
Samara					3.18			
Saratov					1.25			
Sakhalin		6.72				1.5		
Sverdlovsk		1.99				1.31		2.53
Smolensk					1.63			
Tambov			2.2					
Tver'			2.88					
Tomsk					1.69			
Tula		6.02					1.43	
Tyumen					1.13			
Ul'yanovsk	4.2					1.16		
Chelyabinsk			1.33					
Yaroslavl'		4.7				1.51		
Moscow City			1.67				1.12	
St Petersburg					2.71			
Yevreyskaya Autonomous *Okrug*				1.4				
Nenets Autonomous *Okrug*			4.64				2.22	
Khanty-Mansi Autonomous *Okrug*				1.27				
Chukotski Autonomous *Okrug*			1.11					
Yamalo-Nenets Autonomous *Okrug*			1.12					1.16

Notes: the 'effective number of parties' is calculated according to the method devised by Molinar (1991) (Low=1; Medium=2; High=3–4; Very High=5+).
Source: Turovsky (2010).

Patriots of Russia and *Yabloko*—have been able to contest and win seats in only a tiny number of regions. Two of these parties are Kremlin inspired creations. Just Russia was forged out of the amalgam of the Party of Pensioners, the Russian Party of Life (*Rossiiskaya Partiya Zhizni*) and *Rodina*; Right Cause was manufactured by the Kremlin out of the ruins of the Union of Right Forces, The Democratic Party of Russia and Civil Power.

As Table 3 shows, United Russia (in April 2010) had the largest number of party members (1,931,667), followed closely by the Liberal Democratic Party of Russia with 1,885,573. The other parties have substantially lower numbers. Thus, for example, Just Russia has 402,017 members, the Communist Party of the Russian Federation has 152,844, Patriots of Russia 87,344, Right Cause 61,691 and *Yabloko* 55,930.

Turning to an examination of the levels of party membership in the regions, as can be seen in Table 4 all of the parties with the exception of United Russia have memberships which comprise less than 1% of their regional electorates. United Russia

TABLE 3
PARTY MEMBERSHIP AND NUMBER OF REGIONAL BRANCHES (APRIL 2010)

Party	*Number of members*	*Number of regional branches*
United Russia	1,931,667	83
Liberal Democratic Party of Russia	1,885,573	83
Just Russia	402,017	82
Communist Party of the Russian Federation	152,844	80
Patriots of Russia	87,344	80
Right Cause	61,691	74
Yabloko	55,930	76

Source: Ministry of Justice website, available at: http://minjust.lgg.ru/ru/activity/nko/partii/, accessed 10 June 2010.

fares a little better with most regions scoring memberships of between 1% and 2%. There are unusually (and suspiciously) high levels of United Russia party members in Kabardino-Balkariya (8.7%), Orel (6.4%), Dagestan (5.2%), Ingushetiya (4.6%), Tuva (5.0%), Khakasiya (4.9%), Sakha-Yakutiya (4.7%), Mordoviya (4.1%) and Chechnya (4.0%).

United Russia's monopoly of power

As Table 5 demonstrates, United Russia totally dominates Russia's regional assemblies with a total of 73.0% of the seats. Moreover, the 'party of power' commands a majority in 81 of the 83 regions. Only in St Petersburg where it has 46% of the seats, and Sverdlovsk *Oblast' Duma* where it holds 42%, does it have a plurality, rather than an outright majority. Moreover, in 62 regions United Russia has over two-thirds of assembly seats, and in seven regions over 90% of the deputies are members of the 'party of power': Kemerovo *Oblast'* (97.2%), Republic of Mordoviya (95.8%), Republic of Bashkortostan (95.0%), Moscow City (91.5%), Republic of Tatarstan (91.0%), Republic of Chechnya (90.2%) and Rostov *Oblast'* (90.0%). The Communist Party is a long way behind in second place with a total of 10.3% of the seats; Just Russia comes third with 7.3%, followed by the Liberal Democratic Party of Russia with 4.1%. The Patriots of Russia have only 22 seats and Right Cause a mere two seats. *Yabloko* has been completely eliminated in recent regional elections and currently holds no seats. In addition there are just 135 deputies (3.4%) who have no party allegiance.

United Russia's domination of regional assemblies is especially important now that the party that wins the most seats in a regional legislature has the right to nominate the candidate for the post of regional governor. It is perhaps no coincidence that this new ruling has coincided with United Russia's electoral success in the regions.

The nationalisation of parties under Putin and Medvedev

According to the conclusions of a major study devoted to the nationalisation of parties in Russia that was carried out by Turovsky, of the four parties which gained seats in

TABLE 4

PARTY MEMBERSHIP IN THE REGIONS IN JANUARY 2010 (AS A PERCENT OF MEMBERS OF THE REGIONAL ELECTORATE)

Regions	*Number of members of regional electorate*	*United Russia*	*KPRF*	*Just Russia*	*LDPR*[a]	*Yabloko*[a]	*Patriots of Russia*	*Right Cause*
		No. (%)	*No. (%)*	*No. (%)*	*No. (%)*	*No. (%)*	*No. (%)*	*No. (%)*
Adygeya	332,234	8,048 (2.4)	900 (0.27)	1,873 (0.56)	1,120 (0.33)	395 (0.11)	1,530 (0.46)	899 (0.27)
Altai	142,421	3,646 (2.6)	575 (0.40)	1,310 (0.91)	867 (0.60)	535 (0.37)	636 (0.44)	562 (0.39)
Bashkortostan	2,961,055	70,059 (2.4)	3,353 (0.11)	6,667 (0.22)	2,884 (0.09)	1,584 (0.05)	1,158 (0.03)	843 (0.02)
Buryatiya	701,413	14,055 (2.0)	1,819 (0.25)	12,927 (1.84)	1,103 (0.15)	501 (0.07)	1,587 (0.22)	705 (0.10)
Dagestan	1,447,708	75,469 (5.2)	57,49 (0.40)	6,872 (0.47)	1,364 (0.09)	259 (0.01)	6,870 (0.47)	3,688 (0.25)
Ingushetiya	170,149	7,852 (4.6)	301 (0.20)	2,635 (1.54)	1,534 (0.90)	1,402 (0.82)	813 (0.47)	–
Kabardino-Balkariya	518,451	45,398 (8.7)	1,635 (0.30)	14,409 (2.77)	1,021 (0.19)	–	1,062 (0.20)	700 (0.13)
Kalmykiya	212,808	5,781 (2.7)	746 (0.35)	2,303 (1.08)	1,074 (0.50)	515 (0.24)	307 (0.14)	546 (0.25)
Karachaevo-Cherkesskaya	313,156	10,487 (3.3)	821 (0.30)	4,580 (1.46)	2,733 (0.87)	961 (0.30)	950 (0.30)	805 (0.25)
Kareliya	557,662	4,509 (0.8)	770 (0.13)	782 (0.14)	1,200 (0.21)	2,774 (0.49)	840 (0.15)	578 (0.10)
Komi	743,064	8,499 (1.1)	639 (0.08)	1,608 (0.21)	1,852 (0.24)	526 (0.07)	320 (0.04)	360 (0.04)
Marii El	550,257	16,068 (2.9)	1,401 (0.25)	1,167 (0.21)	1,610 (0.29)	533 (0.09)	603 (0.10)	561 (0.10)
Mordoviya	665,204	27,775 (4.1)	1,257 (0.18)	2,590 (0.38)	1,728 (0.25)	517 (0.07)	1,874 (0.28)	598 (0.08)
Sakha-Yakutiya	591,726	27,895 (4.7)	1,873 (0.31)	3,428 (0.57)	764 (0.12)	354 (0.05)	774 (0.13)	585 (0.09)
North Ossetiya-Alaniya	490,240	1,345 (0.2)	2,567 (0.52)	2,664 (0.54)	1,200 (0.24)	334 (0.06)	1,983 (0.40)	827 (0.16)
Tatarstan	2,867,987	128,964 (4.5)	1,435 (0.05)	15,329 (0.53)	542 (0.01)	646 (0.02)	1,268 (0.04)	1,300 (0.04)
Tuva	170,402	8,533 (5.0)	903 (0.52)	1,341 (0.78)	773 (0.45)	255 (0.14)	1,120 (0.65)	–
Udmurtiya	1,222,792	27,227 (2.2)	1,315 (0.10)	1,956 (0.15)	1,980 (0.16)	326 (0.02)	358 (0.02)	556 (0.04)
Khakasiya	375,643	18,275 (4.9)	662 (0.17)	1,106 (0.29)	1,957 (0.52)	353 (0.09)	2,104 (0.56)	558 (0.14)
Chechnya	576,493	23,226 (4.0)	314 (0.05)	12,310 (2.13)	1,503 (0.26)	648 (0.11)	1,119 (0.19)	–
Chuvash	981,561	29,299 (3.0)	3,022 (0.30)	4,072 (0.41)	3,218 (0.32)	992 (0.10)	2,047 (0.20)	862 (0.08)
Altai *Krai*	1,973,572	28,276 (1.4)	3,115 (0.15)	9,651 (0.48)	5,300 (0.26)	988 (0.05)	914 (0.04)	755 (0.03)
Zabaikalskii	799,827	12,418 (1.5)	2,011 (0.25)	2,963 (0.37)	5,770 (0.72)	775 (0.09)	450 (0.05)	764 (0.09)
Kamchatskii	263,198	5,841 (2.2)	363 (0.13)	1,096 (0.41)	654 (0.24)	–	602 (0.22)	285 (0.10)
Krasnodar	3,819,774	95,652 (2.5)	5,481 (0.14)	8,525 (0.22)	20,902 (0.54)	664 (0.01)	962 (0.02)	906 (0.02)

(continued)

TABLE 4
(Continued)

Regions	*Number of members of regional electorate*	*United Russia* No. (%)	*KPRF* No. (%)	*Just Russia* No. (%)	*LDPR*[a] No. (%)	*Yabloko*[a] No. (%)	*Patriots of Russia* No. (%)	*Right Cause* No. (%)
Krasnoyarsk	2,147,244	39,280 (1.8)	4,922 (0.22)	4,463 (0.20)	4,602 (0.21)	1,169 (0.05)	1,230 (0.06)	1,220 (0.05)
Permskii	2,116,315	21,407 (1.0)	1,357 (0.06)	6,456 (0.30)	2,457 (0.11)	1,365 (0.06)	3,253 (0.15)	764 (0.05)
Primorskii	1,511,446	42,593 (2.8)	2,012 (0.13)	2915 (0.19)	2,055 (0.13)	647 (0.04)	351 (0.02)	1,387 (0.09)
Stavropol'	1,944,660	28,243 (1.4)	3,441 (0.17)	14,823 (0.76)	1,413 (0.07)	1,365 (0.07)	606 (0.03)	1,059 (0.05)
Khabarovsk	1,059,850	12,701 (1.2)	992 (0.10)	1,677 (0.15)	1,583 (0.14)	531 (0.05)	1,269 (0.12)	251 (0.02)
Amur *Oblast'*	650,850	8,102 (1.2)	1,293 (0.20)	2,073 (0.31)	927 (0.14)	300 (0.04)	502 (0.07)	548 (0.08)
Arkhangel'	1,000,099	7,175 (0.7)	1,227 (0.12)	4,400 (0.43)	1,441 (0.14)	504 (0.05)	1,604 (0.16)	802 (0.08)
Astrakhan	762,153	12,122 (1.6)	1,450 (0.20)	953 (0.12)	797 (0.10)	1,081 (0.14)	869 (0.11)	1,001 (0.13)
Belgorod	1,220,797	19,371 (1.6)	2,797 (0.23)	2,787 (0.22)	1,300 (0.10)	683 (0.05)	1,079 (0.08)	821 (0.06)
Bryansk	1,046,819	17,095 (1.6)	2,872 (0.27)	4,788 (0.45)	1,422 (0.13)	686 (0.06)	657 (0.06)	703 (0.06)
Vladimir	1,215,001	9,779 (0.8)	1,178 (0.96)	2,775 (0.22)	1,781 (0.14)	566 (0.04)	1,175 (0.09)	325 (0.02)
Volgograd	1,966,338	34,020 (1.7)	7,238 (0.36)	11,061 (0.56)	3,730 (0.18)	353 (0.01)	3,996 (0.20)	1,040 (0.05)
Vologda	987,549	7,908 (0.80)	898 (0.10)	2,533 (0.25)	1,700 (0.17)	552 (0.05)	590 (0.06)	508 (0.05)
Voronezh	1,921,386	30,494 (1.6)	3,157 (0.16)	5,250 (0.27)	3,790 (0.19)	526 (0.02)	2,069 (0.10)	2,309 (0.1)
Ivanovo	884,192	11,390 (1.3)	883 (0.10)	2,852 (0.32)	1,792 (0.20)	617 (0.06)	611 (0.06)	709 (0.8)
Irkutsk	1,876,130	29,990 (1.6)	3,054 (0.16)	5,735 (0.30)	3,857 (0.20)	511 (0.02)	1,413 (0.07)	649 (0.03)
Kaliningrad	744,244	11,559 (1.5)	833 (0.11)	2,630 (0.35)	669 (0.08)	931 (0.12)	669 (0.08)	718 (0.1)
Kaluga	812,386	18,556 (2.3)	1,220 (0.15)	3,863 (0.47)	1,241 (0.15)	1,906 (0.23)	1,323 (0.16)	554 (0.6)
Kemerovo	2,132,479	25,712 (1.2)	1,305 (0.06)	1,778 (0.08)	2,994 (0.14)	726 (0.03)	266 (0.01)	690 (0.03)
Kirov	1,137,144	16,789 (1.5)	1,158 (0.10)	2,314 (0.20)	2,841 (0.24)	477 (0.04)	2,369 (0.20)	734 (0.06)
Kostroma	571,872	11,229 (2.0)	768 (0.13)	1,838 (0.32)	1,458 (0.24)	306 (0.05)	538 (0.09)	814 (0.1)
Kurgan	773,110	13,623 (1.8)	927 (0.11)	2,221 (0.28)	1,598 (0.20)	580 (0.07)	936 (0.12)	937 (0.1)
Kursk	969,808	22,559 (2.3)	2,100 (0.21)	9,343 (0.96)	1,350 (0.13)	350 (0.03)	915 (0.09)	–
Leningrad	1,309,970	10,757 (0.82)	1,569 (0.11)	2,356 (0.17)	3,445 (0.26)	749 (0.05)	888 (0.06)	569 (0.04)
Lipetsk	950,001	13,232 (1.4)	1,747 (0.18)	3,152 (0.33)	1,085 (0.11)	283 (0.02)	560 (0.05)	847 (0.08)

(continued)

TABLE 4
(Continued)

Regions	*Number of members of regional electorate*	*United Russia* No. (%)	*KPRF* No. (%)	*Just Russia* No. (%)	*LDPR*[a] No. (%)	*Yabloko*[a] No. (%)	*Patriots of Russia* No. (%)	*Right Cause* No. (%)
Magadan	120,780	4,512	259	1,581	1,187	–	793	309
		(3.7)	(0.21)	(1.30)	(0.98)		(0.65)	(0.25)
Moscow *Oblast'*	5,538,805	76,924	7,561	16,000	4,630	1,409	1,060	1,554
		(1.4)	(0.13)	(0.28)	(0.08)	(0.02)	(0.01)	(0.02)
Murmansk	688,846	8,098	684	3,310	1,197	268	404	977
		(1.1)	(0.09)	(0.48)	(0.17)	(0.03)	(0.05)	(0.14)
Nizhegorod	2,737,471	33,158	2,353	4,867	3,575	570	1,159	585
		(1.2)	(0.08)	(0.17)	(0.13)	(0.02)	(0.04)	(0.02)
Novgorod	535,682	5,839	769	1,405	2,240	670	421	1,004
		(1.1)	(0.14)	(0.26)	(0.41)	(0.12)	(0.07)	(0.18)
Novosibirsk	2,099,694	30,353	2,685	4,261	2,669	628	890	805
		(1.4)	(0.12)	(0.20)	(0.12)	(0.02)	(0.04)	(0.03)
Omsk	1,504,204	19,650	2,418	2,867	1,400	566	350	762
		(1.3)	(0.16)	(0.19)	(0.09)	(0.03)	(0.02)	(0.05)
Orenburg	1,631,751	19,206	2,495	2,434	2,441	520	787	734
		(1.2)	(0.15)	(0.14)	(0.14)	(0.03)	(0.04)	(0.04)
Orel	661,107	42,350	2,227	4,388	1,246	801	968	564
		(6.40)	(0.33)	(0.66)	(0.18)	(0.12)	(0.08)	(0.03)
Penza	1,129,289	27,090	2,067	9,560	1,996	636	2,350	–
		(2.4)	(0.18)	(0.84)	(0.17)	(0.05)	(0.20)	
Pskov	587,613	10,678	990	11,361	2,035	266	516	–
		(1.80)	(0.16)	(1.93)	(0.34)	(0.04)	(0.08)	
Rostov	3,307,315	51,441	3,014	13,458	3,143	365	2,082	1,057
		(1.50)	(0.10)	(0.40)	(0.09)	(0.01)	(0.06)	(0.03)
Ryazan'	964,197	13,408	2,201	4,176	1,870	283	1,102	915
		(1.4)	(0.22)	(0.43)	(0.19)	(0.02)	(0.11)	(0.09)
Samara	2,513,381	33,941	1,985	9,823	3,571	723	1,237	1,014
		(1.3)	(0.07)	(0.39)	(0.14)	(0.02)	(0.04)	(0.04)
Saratov	2,002,031	41,209	2,020	14,479	4,519	787	689	1,031
		(2.05)	(0.10)	(0.72)	(0.22)	(0.03)	(0.03)	(0.05)
Sakhalin	396,422	5,062	686	1,117	1,354	506	279	696
		(1.3)	(0.17)	(0.28)	(0.34)	(0.12)	(0.07)	(0.17)
Sverdlovsk	3,474,777	55,357	1,822	2,593	3,563	2,276	1,152	1,047
		(1.6)	(0.05)	(0.07)	(0.10)	(0.06)	(0.03)	(0.03)
Smolensk	825,318	12,756	2,013	4,121	2,888	2,832	292	825
		(1.5)	(0.24)	(0.49)	(0.34)	(0.34)	(0.03)	(0.1)
Tambov	859,606	14,591	1,612	5,724	2,556	1,276	542	806
		(1.7)	(0.18)	(0.66)	(0.29)	(0.14)	(0.06)	(0.09)
Tver'	1,161,886	15,497	1,332	4,149	1,321	471	529	806
		(1.3)	(0.11)	(0.35)	(0.11)	(0.04)	(0.04)	(0.06)
Tomsk	757,692	9,847	897	2,813	1,602	567	621	827
		(1.3)	(0.11)	(0.37)	(0.21)	(0.07)	(0.08)	(0.1)
Tula	1,288,003	19,078	2,838	6,495	1,654	1,181	1,189	1,654
		(1.5)	(0.22)	(0.50)	(0.12)	(0.09)	(0.09)	(0.12)
Tyumen'	1,027,746	16,143	1,060	1,873	1,070	511	671	820
		(1.6)	(0.10)	(0.18)	(0.10)	(0.04)	(0.06)	(0.07)
Ul'yanovsk	1,079,683	22,526	1,152	8,605	2,277	507	832	683
		(2.0)	(0.10)	(0.79)	(0.21)	(0.04)	(0.07)	(0.06)
Chelyabinsk	2,729,605	38,117	1,746	17,551	3,365	589	651	565
		(1.4)	(0.06)	(0.64)	(0.12)	(0.02)	(0.02)	(0.02)

(continued)

TABLE 4
(*Continued*)

Regions	*Number of members of regional electorate*	*United Russia* No. (%)	*KPRF* No. (%)	*Just Russia* No. (%)	*LDPR*[a] No. (%)	*Yabloko*[a] No. (%)	*Patriots of Russia* No. (%)	*Right Cause* No. (%)
Yaroslavl'	1,069,387	15,285 (1.4)	819 (0.07)	1,231 (0.15)	2,347 (0.21)	488 (0.04)	525 (0.04)	825 (0.07)
Moscow city	7,040,798	118,959 (1.7)	6,656 (0.10)	3,556 (0.05)	2,790 (0.03)	1,025 (0.01)	368 (0.005)	531 (0.007)
St Petersburg	3,389,957	27,077 (0.8)	2,048 (0.06)	12,283 (0.36)	1,090 (0.03)	871 (0.02)	257 (0.007)	1,273 (0.03)
Evreiskaya Autonomous *Okrug*	138,232	2,912 (2.1)	471 (0.34)	837 (0.60)	367 (0.26)	–	290 (0.20)	452 (0.32)
Nenets	30,780	1,343 (4.36)	–	393 (1.27)	420 (1.3)	–	–	–
Khansy-Mansiiskii	1,060,795	14,290 (1.3)	437 (0.04)	1,550 (0.14)	1,665 (0.15)	256 (0.02)	–	295 (0.02)
Chukotka	36,908	1,146 (3.1)	–	304 (0.82)	300 (0.81)	–	–	–
Yamalo-Nenets	359,378	9,702 2.7	284 0.07	1,009 0.28	1,344 0.37	–	–	301

Notes: [a]data on party membership for the LDPR is for January 2009; data for *Yabloko* is for March 2010. *Source*: data on party membership calculated by the author from the Ministry of Justice website (http://minjust.lgg.ru/ru/activity/nko/partii/, accessed 20 June 2010). Data on the size of regional electorates is provided on the Central Electoral Commission website (http://www.cikf.ru/print.jsp, accessed 4 June 2010).

the State *Duma* in 2007, United Russia had the most geographically even electoral support with a variation coefficient of 0.17, followed by the Communist Party at 0.36, LDPR at 0.41, and Just Russia at 0.45.[9]

Turning to the territorial representation of parties in regional assembly elections, United Russia has seats in all 83 regional assemblies and the Communists have seats in 79 regional assemblies. Just Russia and the LDPR have seats in 64 and 55 regions, respectively. In sharp contrast the Patriots of Russia are represented in just seven regional assemblies, Right Cause in two regions and, as noted above, *Yabloko* is no longer represented in any of the regional assemblies (see Table 5).

United or disunited Russia?

Whilst United Russia dominates regional assemblies it is far from united. As Kynev concludes,

> the formal dominance of the party of power in the regions has hidden the fierce struggle for power which has taken place between interest groups (clienteles, cliques and clans). The real struggle for power now takes place behind closed doors within the ranks of United Russia whose public display of unity is an illusion. (2010, p. 149)

[9]The variation coefficient is a standard deviation multiplied by the mean. Low < 0.3, Medium = 0.3–0.5, High > 0.5.

TABLE 5
PARTY MEMBERSHIP OF REGIONAL ASSEMBLIES (APRIL 2010)

	United Russia	*KPRF*	*Just Russia*	*LDPR*	*Yabloko*	*Patriots of Russia*	*Right Cause*	*Parties which no longer exist*	*Non-party*
Number of regions where parties have seats	83	79	64	55	0	7	2	10	–
Number of seats	2,845	401	286	161	0	22	2	47	135
Percentage of seats	73.0	10.3	7.3	4.1	0	0.56	0.05	1.2	3.5

Source: calculated by the author from data provided on the Central Electoral Commission website (http:/ www.cikrf.ru, accessed 7 June 2010) and also from Kynev (2009).

Indeed, it would now appear that there may be as many different United Russias as there are regions.

It is also becoming more common for members of the same party who represent different regional elite groups to stand against each other in elections. For example, in October 2008, in the election for the Mayor of Nizhnii Tagil, five members of United Russia (including two deputy-mayors) stood against the official candidate of United Russia, Aleksei Chekanov, who came third in the election (Kynev 2010, p. 146). There are also countless examples of representatives of regional businesses hedging their bets and supporting more than one party and even putting forth candidates for regional assembly elections in more than one party list.

Changes to party and electoral legislation under Medvedev

Since Medvedev was elected president in 2008 there have been a number of positive changes to election rules and party legislation: first, according to legislation adopted in April 2009, the minimum number of members a party needs to be registered has been reduced. From 1 January 2010 to 1 January 2012, it has been lowered from 50,000 to 45,000 (with 450 members in over half the regions instead of 500, and not less than 200 in the remaining regions—down from 250). From 2012 it will be lowered further to 40,000 members with 400 in each region and 150 members in the remaining regions.[10]

Second, legislation adopted in early 2009 abolished the electoral deposit. Regional elections which were held in October 2009 and March 2010 were the first to be held under the new system whereby candidates and parties could only register by submitting signatures. Third, in February 2010 legislation was adopted which states

[10]Federal Law, 28 April 2009, No. 75, 'O vnesenii izmenenii v Federal'nyi zakon "O politicheskikh partiyakh" v svyazi s poetapnym snizheniem minimal'noi chislennosti chlenov politicheskikh partii', *Rossiskaya Gazeta*, 5 May 2009. See http://www.rg.ru/2009/05/05/partii-dok.html, accessed 7 June 2010.

that parties with seats in regional assemblies will also be able to participate in regional elections without having to collect signatures. Moreover, parties with seats in one third of regional assemblies will no longer need to collect signatures to stand for *Duma* elections or for the Russian Federation Presidency.[11] Fourth, those parties which receive 5–6% of the votes will gain one seat in regional assemblies and those parties which win between 6% and 7% of the votes will be guaranteed two seats.

Conclusion

A major problem as regards building democracy in Russia has been the weakness of parties and the party system. As has been demonstrated, Russian parties, with the exception of United Russia, currently suffer from very low levels of 'party nationalisation' and 'institutionalisation'. Many of the regional branches of parties have been captured by regional business groups and as Kynev stresses, it is now quite difficult to know to what extent the regional branches of parties can be considered as 'collective actors, rather than the artificial conglomerates of elite groups' (2010, p. 146).

In the absence of strong parties, clientelism, not party politics, dominates regional politics. Competition between regional elites takes place not only between parties but within parties, and the composition of regional legislatures largely reflects the makeup of the respective elites. Such developments have seriously compromised the ideological foundations and political identity of many of the regional branches of political parties and dealt a serious blow to the consolidation of a nationwide party system in Russia. They have also thwarted Russia's democratic transition. As Mainwaring and Scully (1995, p. 27) observe, democracy tends to thrive 'when party systems have been institutionalised'. Where parties are not institutionalised, 'democratic politics is more erratic, establishing legitimacy is more difficult, and governing is more complicated .... Powerful economic elites tend to have privileged access to policy makers... patrimonial practices often prevail, and legislatures tend to be weakly developed'.

University of Dundee

References

Dawisha, K. (1997) 'Democratization and Political Participation: Research Concepts and Methodologies', in Dawisha, K. & Parrot, B. (eds) (1997) *The Consolidation of Democracy in East-Central Europe* (Cambridge, Cambridge University Press), p. 55.

Enyedi, Z. (2006) 'Party Politics in Post-Communist Transition', in Katz, R. S. & Crotty, W. (eds) (2006).

Fleron, J., Ahl, R. & Lane, F. (1998) 'Where Now in the Study of Russian Political Parties?', in Lowenhardt, J. (ed.) (1998), p. 231.

Gel'man, V. (2006) 'From Feckless Pluralism to Dominant Power Politics: The Transformation of Russia's Party System', *Democratization*, 13, 4.

Gel'man, V. & Ross, C. (eds) (2010) *The Politics of Sub-National Authoritarianism in Russia* (Farnham, Ashgate).

[11]Federal Law, 9 February 2009, N3-F3, 'O vnesenii izmenenii v otdel'nye zakonodatel'nye akty Rossiiskoi Federatsii v svyazi s otmenoi ozbiratel'nogo zaloga pri provedenii vyborov', *Rossiiskaya Gazeta*, 11 February 2009.

Gel'man, V., Ryzhenkov, S. & Brie, M. (2003) *Making and Breaking Democratic Transitions: The Comparative Politics of Russia's Regions* (Lanham, MD, Rowman and Littlefield).

Gibson, E. (2004) 'Federalism and Democracy: Theoretical Connections and Cautionary Insights', in Gibson, E. (ed.) (2004) *Federalism and Democracy in Latin America* (Baltimore, MD & London, The Johns Hopkins University Press).

Golosov, G. V. (2004) *Political Parties in the Regions of Russia: Democracy Unclaimed* (Boulder, CO & London, Lynne Rienner).

Golosov, G. V. (2006) *Rossiiskaya Partiinaya Sistema i Regional'naya Politika 1993–2003* (St Petersburg, European University at St Petersburg).

Hale, H. E. (2006) *Why Not Parties in Russia? Democracy, Federalism, and the State* (Cambridge, Cambridge University Press).

Hopkin, J. & van Houten, P (2009) 'Decentralization and State-Wide Parties: Introduction', *Party Politics*, 15, 2.

Ivanchenko, A. V. & Lyubarev, A. E. (2006) *Rossiiskie Vybory ot Perestroiki do Suverennoi Democratii* (Moscow, Aspekt Press), p. 17.

Jones, M. P. & Mainwaring, S. (2003) 'The Nationalization of Parties and Party Systems. An Empirical Measure and Application to the Americas', *Party Politics*, 9, 2.

Kasuya, Y. & Moenius, J. (2008) 'The Nationalisation of Party Systems: Conceptual Issues and Alternative District Focused Measures', *Electoral Studies*, 27, 1.

Katz, R. S. & Crotty, W. (eds) (2006) *Handbook of Party Politics* (London, Thousand Oaks, CA & New Delhi, Sage Publications).

Kynev, A. (2008) 'Proportsionalizatsiya Regional'nykh Vyborov: Polozhenie Rgional'nykh Parlamentov v Rossii i Itogi Pervovo Tsikla Regional'noi Izbiratel'noi Reformy', *Sravnitel'noe Konstitutsionnoe Obozrenie*, 5, 66.

Kynev, A. (2009) *Vybory Parlamentov Rossiiskikh Regionov 2003–2009: Pervyi Tskikl Vnedreniya Proportsional'noi Izbiratel'noi Sistemy* (Moscow, Tsentre 'Panorama').

Kynev, A. (2010) 'Party Politics in the Russian Regions: Competition of Interest Groups Under the Guise of Parties', in Gel'man, V. & Ross, C. (eds) (2010).

Kynev, A. & Glubotskii, A. (2003) 'Politicheskie Partii v Zakonodatel'nykh Sobraniyakh Sub'ektov RF (situatsiya na vensu 2003 goda)', *Polis*, 6.

Lago, I. & Montero, J. R. (2010) 'The Nationalisation of Party Systems Revisited. A New Measure Based on Parties' Entry Decisions, Electoral Results and District Magnitude', Paper presented to the *Canadian Political Science Association*, Concordia University, Montreal, 1–3 June.

Lowenhardt, J. (ed.) (1998) *Party Politics in Post-Communist Russia* (London & Portland, OR, Frank Cass).

Mainwaring, S. (1998) 'Party Systems in the Third Wave', *Journal of Democracy*, 9, 3, July.

Mainwairing, S. & Scully, T. R. (eds) (1995) *Building Democratic Institutions: Party Systems in Latin America* (Stanford, CA, Stanford University Press).

Mainwaring, S. & Torcal, M. (2006) 'Party System Institutionalization and Party System Theory After the Third Wave of Democratization', in Katz, R. S. & Crotty, W. (eds) (2006).

McFaul, M. (2000) 'Party Formation and Non-Formation in Russia', Carnegie Endowment for International Peace, *Working Paper*, 12, May (Washington, DC, Carnegie Endowment for International Peace).

Molinar, J. (1991) 'Counting the Number of Parties: An Alternative Index', *American Political Science Review*, 85, 4.

Panov, P. (2009) 'Russian Political Parties and Regional Processes: The Problem of Effective Representation', in Ross, C. & Campbell, A. (eds) (2009) *Federalism and Local Politics in Russia* (London & New York, Routledge).

Pridham, G. & Lewis, P. (1996) 'Introduction: Stabilising Fragile Democracies and Party System Development', in Pridham, G. & Lewis, P. (eds) (1996) *Stabilising Fragile Democracies: Comparing New Party Systems in Southern and Eastern Europe* (London & New York, Routledge).

Ross, C. (2002) *Federalism and Democratisation in Russia* (Manchester, Manchester University Press).

Ross, C. (2009) *Local Politics and Democratisation in Russia* (London & New York, Routledge).

Ross, C. (2010) 'Sub-National Elections and the Development of Semi-Authoritarian Regimes', in Gel'man, V. & Ross, C. (eds) (2010).

Thorlakson, L. (2009) 'Patterns of Party Integration, Influence and Autonomy in Seven Federations', *Party Politics*, 15, 2.

Turovsky, R. (2010) 'Party Systems in Post-Communist States: New Trends and Bifurcations', paper presented to the *ICCEES Conference*, Stockholm, 26 July–1 August.

Webb, P. & Lewis, P. G. (1998) 'The Lessons of Comparative Politics: Russian Political Parties as Independent Variables?', in Lowenhardt, J. (ed.) (1998).

Local Regimes, Sub-national Governance and the 'Power Vertical' in Contemporary Russia

VLADIMIR GEL'MAN & SERGEI RYZHENKOV

THE EMERGENCE OF LOCAL REGIMES,[1] OR RELATIVELY stable patterns of sub-national governance, became an important logical consequence of the turbulent political and economic changes in Russia's regions and cities during the periods of the 1990s and the 2000s. We posit that these developments could be analysed within the theoretical framework of 'urban regimes', which have been conducted in studies of American and West European urban politics and governance over the two last decades (Mossberger & Stoker 2001; Ledyaev 2008). Despite the major differences which exist between local regimes in contemporary Russia and in the West, and their highly divergent political and institutional environments, the placement of Russian local regimes within a theoretical and comparative perspective opens new horizons for their analysis. It also provides us with a better understanding of their general trends as well as some of their peculiarities.

The 'local regime' is defined here as a complex of political institutions, actors, and the resources and strategies available to them, which determine the conduct of local politics, local policy and local governance. Local regimes could be attributed to various territorial units at any level if they exhibited some autonomy of local politics and governance *vis-à-vis* the higher levels of authority. They perform under the hierarchically structured influence of three major factors: (1) exogenous structural characteristics of local regimes (geographical locations, natural resources, socio-economic profiles, and more broadly, in a national and international developmental context); (2) political opportunities, which set up the political and institutional environment of local regimes and the incentives for their actors; and (3) patterns of governance at higher levels of authority implemented at the local level by conducting certain policies. Concurrently, outcomes of local regimes emerge as a result of the interactions of their actors within the framework of political institutions. These outcomes affect all three major inter-related local areas—local politics, local policies and local governance.

It is widely accepted that trajectories of local regimes in post-communist Russia over the period of the 1990s and the 2000s resembled pendulum-like swings

[1]In this essay, we refer to 'local' as a category which combines both regions and cities.

(Petrov 2004; Gel'man 2009). In the early 1990s the collapse of the Soviet Union, the breakdown of communist rule, and the launching of market reforms caused spontaneous decentralisation and democratisation at the local level. These trends occurred against the background of protracted economic transformation, the decline of coercive and distributive capacities of the Russian state and deep conflicts among local economic interest groups (Stoner-Weiss 2006; Zubarevich 2010). It is not surprising that emerging local regimes demonstrated a great diversity in terms of local politics (Gel'man *et al.* 2003). However, given the fiscal crisis during the 1990s in Russia and the *de facto* devolution of social obligations of the Russian state from the federal government to sub-national governments, in terms of local governance most of these local regimes were merely oriented toward the maintenance of the *status quo*, which was based upon redistributive social policies. These local regimes routinely divided scarce budgetary resources, their amounts heavily dependent upon transfers from higher levels of authority, and maintained the basic infrastructure and housing assets of cities and regions. The key actors of local regimes were involved in 'the privatization of gains' and 'the socialization of losses' (Gel'man *et al.* 2003, p. 56). These local regimes emerged in the majority of Russia's cities and regions and demonstrated the predominance of local-based distributional coalitions (Shirickov 2010), which involved major dependent social groups such as pensioners and public sector employees, local businesses closely linked with local authorities (Brie 2004), and also criminal 'violent entrepreneurs' (Volkov 2002).

In the 2000s, the dynamics of Russian local regimes qualitatively changed. The tremendous economic growth in Russia (until the 2008–2009 economic crisis) accompanied by the large-scale recentralisation of governance and the rise of authoritarian tendencies, led to a major shift of Russia's sub-national authoritarianism from a decentralised to a centralised party-based model (Gel'man 2010). For local regimes—first and foremost, in Russia's large cities—these changes led to the emergence of elements of regimes of growth and development. They were based upon booming construction, real estate, retail and related sectors of local economies. These processes also affected the nature of local governance, which was faced with similar challenges that previously determined the agenda of urban regimes in American and Western European cities. In particular, the increasing value of urban land and real estate as developmental resources, and the rise of the influence of local and nationwide business actors on local governance (Zubarevich 2010), contributed to more proactive local policies, especially in those policy areas such as urban planning and land use, which were prone to the escalation of conflicts among major actors. To some extent, these developments were akin to the emergence of 'growth coalitions' in a number of American cities (Ledyaev 2008). Meanwhile, Russian local regimes were rather distinct from their US counterparts in terms of configurations of actors, structural characteristics and political opportunities (Tev 2006). The institutions and actors of Russia's local regimes as well as the patterns of local governance were greatly influenced by the major political and institutional changes of the 2000s. These changes included the shift from local autonomy to the partial re-establishment of a hierarchical model of regional and urban governance (the 'power vertical') (Sharafutdinova 2010a); the major decay, if not the total elimination of electoral contestation in local as well as in national politics (Golosov 2008); and the abolition of popular elections of regional governors and, in many cases, of city mayors (Gel'man & Lankina 2008).

How do local regimes in Russia's regions and cities function under the conditions of the 'power vertical' and sub-national authoritarianism while experiencing uncertain economic prospects? What about factors which affect the features of local politics and local governance, and what about the incentives for actors of the local regimes within the framework of politics and governance in the country as a whole? This essay seeks to explore these issues based upon our previous studies (Gel'man 2009, 2010; Ryzhenkov 2010) and through the observations and interpretations of research by other scholars. In the first section, we present the general evolutionary logic of Russia's local regimes within the hierarchy of the 'power vertical', the related principal–agent problems, and attempts at their resolution. Then, we offer a preliminary analysis of incentives and control mechanisms, which are embedded in the 'power vertical', and an account of costs and challenges of this pattern of local governance in Russia. Possible perspectives of further evolution of Russia's local regimes in a theoretical and comparative context are discussed in the concluding part of the essay.

The 'power vertical' and local regimes: institutions and incentives

The building of the 'power vertical' in the context of Russia's politics of the 2000s was one of the cornerstones of the recentralisation of governance and institutionalisation of both nationwide and sub-national authoritarianisms (Gel'man 2009, 2010). In political terms, the mechanism of the 'power vertical' is based upon several formal and informal 'rules of the game' for local regimes and their actors: the hierarchical subordination of regional chief executives (governors) as well as city mayors to the Kremlin; the *de facto* prohibition of open political competition of local elites on electoral and legislative arenas, and the forced co-optation and integration of the majority of key actors of local regimes into the 'party of power', United Russia (*Edinaya Rossiya*) (Golosov 2008); and making actors of local regimes responsible for the provision of favourable results of national and regional elections, requested by the centre, and for the prevention of actual mass protests.

Political consequences of these changes for Russia's local regimes included not only the institutional decay of regional legislatures (Shirickov 2010) and branches of political parties (Kynev 2010), but also the continuous decline of local autonomy (Gel'man & Lankina 2008) and the shrinking space for public participation (Belokurova 2010). They also heavily affected patterns of local governance in Russia's regions and cities.

Emerging Russian local regimes in the 1990s were faced with numerous conflicts resulting from the open competition between local distributional coalitions for the limited pool of resources, such as budgetary funds, and the assets of privatising enterprises, and administrative rents. They were also faced with the transformation recession and the fiscal crisis of the Russian state (Shirickov 2010; Zubarevich 2010). Most of these conflicts were resolved as zero-sum games because of the influence of structural characteristics of local regimes, which determined the constellations of their actors. The federal centre indirectly (and often ineffectively) had an influence on these conflicts by the use of institutional engineering (Gel'man *et al.* 2003). But even in the 1990s, some successful local regimes were able not only to extract additional rents due to resource endowments (for example in Tatarstan) (Matsuzato 2001), or due to the special status of locality as in Moscow (Brie 2004), but also to pursue a policy of growth and development at the local level. In these local regimes, equivalents of 'growth coalitions' emerged (Tev 2006). The dominance of executive officials and their business cronies also allowed for other subordinated actors, who exchanged their access to local political and economic markets, to refuse to challenge the *status quo* (Zubarevich 2010). This informal deal, or 'imposed consensus' brought some benefits to both dominant and subordinated actors. The former spent fewer resources on co-optation rather than coercion, while the latter increased their wealth because of the growing amount of rents. In other words, newly emerging local regimes of growth and development turned into positive-sum games, if their 'growth coalitions' were led by local dominant actors.

The economic turnaround during the 2000s in Russia provided favourable conditions for the emergence of local regimes of growth and development in a number of large cities (Tev 2006). The 'opening' of local markets and the encroachment of Russian big business towards the provinces (Zubarevich 2010) greatly contributed to these changes. The inflow of capital as well as the increasing amount of rents fuelled the rise of new 'growth coalitions' in Russia's regions and cities. Due to the structural characteristics of local regimes and their political opportunities, the major turn in the developmental trend of Russia's local regimes did not always lead to changes in the constellations of local actors. In the 1990s, in the wake of the redistribution of property rights, regional and local officials served as 'veto players' in most of the local regimes (Pappe 2000). In the 2000s, in a number of cities, they preserved if not strengthened their dominance within the new local 'growth coalitions' in the manner of the 'predatory state' model of crony capitalism (Kang 2002, p. 15). At the same time, the equal partnership between local authorities and economic actors (the 'mutual hostages' model) and the dominance of big business in local regimes (the 'state capture' model) (Dininio & Orttung 2005) were typical only for a relatively small number of local regimes, such as, respectively, St Petersburg (in the former case) (Tev 2006) and mono-industrial company towns, such as Cherepovets (in the latter) (Bychkova & Gel'man 2010). It is no wonder that these 'growth coalitions', which included local authorities and their business cronies (with the *ad hoc* inclusion of some other actors), were by and large interested in diminishing the political competitiveness of local regimes. In fact, in the early 2000s the share of incumbent losses in elections of regional governors (Golosov 2008) and of city mayors was severely decreased. To put it bluntly, 'growth coalitions' avoided competition in local regimes due to their co-optation or (more rarely) by the use of coercion, while the growing local markets brought mutual benefits to all members of 'growth coalitions'. The building of a 'power vertical' not only strengthened the institutional foundations of these local regimes and contributed to their consolidation, but also offered new incentives for key local actors, first and foremost in the process of their interactions with the federal centre (Sharafutdinova 2010a). These incentives combined threats of selective top-down punishment of local actors (Petrov 2007) with the provision of various benefits to them by the federal centre (Ryzhenkov 2010).

As Barbara Geddes (1994) noted, in authoritarian regimes incentives for active involvement in reform policies are provided, not only because of the direct control by dictators over elites and the use of punishment for their poor performance, but also because of the abilities of political leaders to allocate resources and privileges among elites to achieve the regime's policy goals. The convergence between the policy goals of authoritarian rulers and their subordinated actors (including local ones) implies that the rulers have to provide loyal elites with power, status, wealth and career chances, as incentives for more efficient achievement of the regime's policy goals. These incentives include, *inter alia*,

> opportunities for upward mobility within the organisation; boundaries between the organisation and the rest of society that reduce opportunities for contact with groups that compete for the official's loyalty; intensive socialisation to organisation norms and values, which reduces the discrepancy between the informal subculture of members and the formal culture of organisation, and consequently reduces the incidence of members' taking advantage of their official positions to pursue personal gain. (Geddes 1994, pp. 193–94)

In the context of building the 'power vertical' in Russia similar incentives were provided to actors of the local regimes in Russia's regions and cities. Thus, an analysis of the patterns of governance of Russia's local regimes should focus on the context-bounded process of 'production' of these incentives.

In fact, for the maintenance of both loyalty and governability of local regimes within the framework of the 'power vertical', the federal centre needed to offer local actors juicy carrots rather than hard sticks. Even though during the stage of monopolisation of power and recentralisation of the state in the early 2000s, the centre relied upon top-down pressure on local actors, later on the 'power vertical' demonstrated more flexibility over maintaining local governance. This shift was caused by the rise of agency costs within the administrative hierarchy and the deepening of principal–agent problems (Gel'man 2009; Sharafutdinova 2010a). The strict adherence to top-down hierarchical relations against the interests of the lower echelons of the 'power vertical' would require from the centre tight control and the punishment of local actors for virtually all instances of wrongdoing, misbehaviour and poor performance. In theory, one can imagine that the centre would systematically use repressions toward lower-level officials of the 'power vertical'. However, despite the numerous cases of forced resignations of regional governors and, especially, city mayors (Turovsky 2010), the hierarchy of the 'power vertical' is far from an army-like chain of command, and it operates according to a different logic.

The popular argument that the 'power vertical' serves merely as a tool of subordination of the local regimes to the federal centre (Petrov 2007) is only partially true. We argue that the understanding of the logic of the 'power vertical' should take into account its multiple 'zigzags', 'turning points' and 'U-turns', and it is worth analysing not only by a normative critique but also through the lens of a positive political economy. Utilising the works of Barbara Geddes, we agree that 'the central problem for authoritarian regimes is the creation of an appropriate set of incentives to shape behaviour of their own officials' (Geddes 1994, p. 193). From this point of view, the 'power vertical' should be considered not only as a tool of maintaining loyalty and governability of low-level officials by the threat of imposition of top-down sanctions, but also as a stimulus for local regime actors through the use of selective informal incentives. Local actors served the centre's interests mostly because their inclusion into the 'power vertical' rewarded them with extra benefits in the form of exclusive gains that were unavailable to those actors who were not included in the 'power vertical'. The major condition for local beneficiaries is that their opportunistic behaviour should not prevent the centre from achieving its strategic policy goals. Thus, the dual system of local governance which serves the interests of both local actors and the centre has emerged within the framework of the 'power vertical'.

In the most general sense, the centre's goals included the preservation of a stable economic and social order, in which the ruling group was unchallenged, it supported the relative well-being of the population-at-large, and maintained its patronage over disadvantaged social groups. For example, Denis Tev, in his study of the emerging 'growth coalition' in St Petersburg, noted that 'under conditions of political centralisation in Russia, especially after the shift from popular elections of regional executives ... to presidential appointments, the agenda of local elites was defined by the strategic goals of the federal centre, and that economic growth plays a primary role among these goals' (Tev 2006, p. 104). His analysis convincingly demonstrates that an active policy of urban development brought major benefits to the city leadership and their allies—not only because they implemented the strategic goals of the 'power vertical' but also because these goals coincided with the self-interests of local actors. Thus, the local regime achieved those goals which were set up by the centre and its rulers also were able to pursue their own selfish interests.

In the early 2000s, during the first stage of the 'federal reform' (Reddaway & Orttung 2003–2004), these goals were pursued by the policy of centralisation of resources and the demise of the autonomy of sub-national governments and institutions. However, in fact the centre granted autonomy to specific actors included in the hierarchy of the 'power vertical'. The centre built the 'power vertical' using the informal institutionalisation of political rents, which were divided between actors of the local regimes and the centre itself.

In the 1990s however, this type of principal–agent relationship between the centre and local regimes was unfeasible due to the economic recession and the lack of political resources. Even if the centre was able to defeat the local regimes politically, it could not offer their actors sufficient rewards for their loyalty. This is why local actors in the 1990s often ignored the centre's requests, and arbitrarily appropriated and used major resources. But during the 2000s when the formal and informal autonomy of the local regimes was diminished, if not eliminated, the centre was able to reward loyal and capable local agents systematically and to successfully motivate them to serve its interests.

If the centre's requests were satisfied and the local regimes of growth and development performed successfully it resulted in stability and legitimacy for both the local regimes and the regime in the country as a whole. Subordinated local actors could pursue a broad range of their self-interests, especially given the poor protection of property rights in Russian regions and cities, which forced local businesses to seek close informal connections with local authorities (Yakovlev 2006). Economic growth and rising consumer demand increased the profitability of local businesses, but these profits were used not only for the expansion of business as such but also for the protection of private property through investments in the public ventures of regional and local authorities (including major developmental projects) as well as in their own private enterprises. For instance, in Perm the city mayor, and then the regional governor, Yuri Trutnev, owned a major retail business; Trutnev's successor Oleg Chirkunov was also a large business owner; and the new city mayor Igor' Shubin also became a key player in the construction industry, the most dynamic sector of the local economy (Borisova 2010). In pursuit of self-interest, regional and city authorities actively used their dominance in local regimes for the attraction of investments. They offered businesses favourable terms to participate in local public projects. For example, the former governor of the Ryazan *Oblast'* Georgii Shpak aggressively pursued the goal of attracting Moscow-based investors into the region and the city of Ryazan (Avdonin 2006). In Perm, Chirkunov actively lobbied construction and development companies which were based outside the region. Moreover, one should not consider these private interests of public officials just as a systematic distortion of local governance. Indeed, these practices of governance (both in the local regimes and in the country as a whole) served as the major foundation of the strong Russian state. It maintained and developed the state capacity of the economic and social orders at the local and nationwide levels (Ryzhenkov 2010). In this capacity the Russian state served both the collective interests of the insiders of the 'power vertical' as a group (or, rather, an estate), and the private interests of owners of private resources, which played a major role in local economic development.

In its quest to maintain the loyalty of local actors the centre was forced to use both carrots and sticks. The multiple tools of control included not only appointments, dismissals and replacements of regional and local officials, but also the exclusion of some participants from participation in elections and 'contract-ordered' criminal investigations against disloyal politicians, officials and businessmen. Given the fact that almost all actors of the local regimes pursued their private interests in local governance, these instruments not only maintained their loyalty to the 'power vertical', but were also used by the centre as an additional mechanism of control. Almost every local actor could easily be accused of criminal acts, and the threat of criminal prosecution was an even more efficient tool for maintaining control than its actual use. As a consequence, local actors were genuinely interested in the successful implementation of policies which served both the centre's goals and their own self-interests. One should note that top-down punishments of local actors took place under two circumstances: either because their rent-seeking activities contradicted the centre's interests or (more rarely) because their poor performance undermined the legitimacy and stability of the local regimes and to some extent that of the centre.

In Russia's case—both at the level of the local regimes and at the national level—the dual model of local governance is typical for authoritarian 'Gony capitalism' but demonstrates certain special features. Adam Przeworski pointed out three interrelated principles of interactions between the 'power apparatus' (political leaders) and subordinated actors under authoritarian regimes (Przeworski 1991, p. 48): the existence of some room for manoeuvre for agents but undisputable punishment for actions which violate the principal's interests; the status of the principal as a virtually unlimited supreme ruler, who is able to impose arbitrary evaluations and decisions; and the specific divisions within the 'power apparatus' into competing cliques. The strong impact of the first and the last conditions on the 'power vertical' in Russia is undeniable.

From this perspective, local governance in Russia fits the following criteria:

> ... instrumental action under authoritarianism is limited to cases in which those actors who enjoy room for manoeuvre know that the power apparatus is indifferent to some outcomes.... Acting instrumentally makes sense for them only if they know that the power apparatus will not punish them for their actions and that it can tolerate the outcome they want. (Przeworski 1991, p. 48)

To put it bluntly, the centre requested two things from the lower echelons of the 'power vertical'. First, it called for the maintenance of mass patronage, which required the use of business resources for the purposes of social development. If local actors were able to achieve public policy goals, the centre was tolerant not only with regard to their pursuit of private interests but also in the choice of methods which they used to achieve their goals. The genuinely patrimonial type of governance currently in operation in the Chechen Republic is probably the most notorious example, but it is certainly not unique in this respect. Secondly, the centre required the local regimes to produce electoral results to the liking of the Kremlin as well as the prevention of mass protest activism. Since the planned voting results are sent by the Kremlin to the local regimes well in advance of the polls, the capacity of local actors to bring home the votes in the required percentages is the key criterion which is used to measure their political efficiency. This fact contributed to the spread in scale and scope of electoral fraud. A number of observers argued that by 2007–2008 Russia's local regimes had turned from unfree elections (with systematic exclusion of disloyal or independent parties or candidates) to fake elections, where local electoral commissions officially submitted requests for the achievement of specific electoral results regardless of the actual voting behaviour of their citizens (Mebane & Kalinin 2009). Even though regional and local actors pursue their own goals in the wake of election campaigns, the risks of punishment from the centre for 'inappropriate' results provides them with additional incentives for fraud, incentives which are similar to those which were found in the Soviet planned economy (Harrison 2009).

Authoritarian divisions within the 'power vertical' meant neither the separation of powers nor the existence of open intra-elite conflict between organised political factions. Rather, these divisions implied behind-the-scenes competition between various cliques for influence on key decision-makers and for informal positions in key arenas of governance. Russia's local regimes all demonstrated similar trends, including relationships of their actors with the centre. The competition among cliques within the 'power vertical' (both on the same level of government and between these levels) for extraction of rents became an inherent feature of Russia's local regimes; a side effect of the informal distribution of rights between local agents by the centre as a principal. Yet, these divisions undermined the centre's capacity to control local agents. The centre was forced to limit the struggles between local cliques in order to diminish its agency costs. There is no doubt that this hidden and informal competition of local actors worsened the quality of local governance. Thus, the centre required that United Russia (UR), besides performing its core functions, should establish and maintain a kind of corporate solidarity within the 'power vertical'.[2] Yet, it is far from achieving the 'socialisation' outlined by Geddes: United Russia is unable to reduce 'the incidence of members taking advantage of their official positions to pursue personal gain' (Geddes 1994, p. 194), even though this task is at least openly stated as a part of UR's agenda. In a more general sense, the divisions within the 'power vertical' are unavoidable side effects of the lack of competitive elections, which could allow actors with divergent interests to define *pro tempore* winners on the electoral arena (Przeworski 1991, p. 13).

The second feature of the authoritarian division within the 'power apparatus' is that the local regimes are also affected by sectoral 'power verticals', which link local actors to certain patrons at the level of the federal authorities or even of the top leadership. This mechanism played a powerful role in the informal system of local governance because it could not be bypassed in the process of appointments or dismissals in the lower echelons of the 'power vertical' and it is important for the survival of local regime actors in their behind-the-scenes struggles against powerful competitors. The centre made the key decisions on appointments, dismissals and replacements at the very top level (Titkov 2007) under the influence of a number of factors. They included, *inter alia*, the maintenance of the balance between sectoral 'power verticals' and cliques and the use of a 'divide and conquer' strategy as a tool for prevention of open intra-elite conflicts. This approach was vividly illustrated in the wake of the removal of some long-standing regional leaders (such as the President of Bashkortostan, Murtaza Rakhimov and the Mayor of Moscow, Yuri Luzhkov), who not only lost their powerful positions by being replaced by Kremlin loyalists but also lost their control over local assets, which were claimed by several major nationwide financial and industrial groups (Sharafutdinova 2010b; Zubarevich 2010).

To summarise, the evolution of Russia's local regimes during the process of the centralisation of the state and their functioning in the political context of authoritarianism coexisted with the hierarchical dual model of local governance within the framework of the 'power vertical'. Moreover, the centre provided various contradictory incentives for local actors against the background of the possible prevalence of both distributional coalitions and 'growth coalitions' in local regimes of Russia's regions and cities. The major features of the evolutionary trajectory of Russia's local regimes are outlined in Table 1.

Local regimes and the 'power vertical': costs and challenges

The formation of Russia's local regimes in the 1990s and the 2000s faced multiple conflicts amongst their actors, and the building of a 'power vertical' by no means resolved them successfully. Rather, these conflicts became routinised, and their political content was replaced by an administrative form of 'bargaining' over the redistribution of growing rents (Shirickov 2010, pp. 178–79). But this mechanism of

[2]Actually, the Communist Party of the Soviet Union performed similar functions of local governance in the Soviet times (Rutland 1993); but while the Communist Party was the major actor, which exercised control over the state apparatus and could impose sanctions for violations of formal and informal 'rules of the game', today the role of the 'party of power' is quite limited. In fact, most local branches of United Russia are just one of the competing cliques of the local regimes.

TABLE 1

MAJOR FEATURES OF EVOLUTIONARY TRAJECTORIES OF LOCAL REGIMES IN RUSSIA'S REGIONS AND CITIES

Period	*Nationwide economic context*	*Nationwide political context*	*Political opportunities*	*Centre's policies towards local regimes*	*Patterns of development of local regimes*	*Major actors of local regimes*
1970s–1980s	Economic stagnation	Communist regime	Narrow, closed opportunity structure	Centralised hierarchy, the rise of principal–agent problems	Maintenance of the *status quo*, centralised party-based sub-national authoritarianism	Local officials and sectoral branch agencies (localism and departmentalism)
1991–1998	Transformation recession	Inconsistent and partial democratisation	Widening, unclear 'rules of the game', power grab by local elites	Major decentralisation	Maintenance of the *status quo*, in some regions and cities—the emergence of growth machines, political diversity of local regimes, trend toward decentralised sub-national authoritarianism	Various segments of local elites and their subordinates, the predominance of distributional coalitions, in some regions and cities—the emergence of growth coalitions
2000–2008	Rapid economic growth	The rise of authoritarianism	Shrinking, building of 'power vertical'	Recentralisation, the rise of principal–agent problems	The rise of growth machines in most big cities, trend toward centralised party-based sub-national authoritarianism	Various segments of local elites and their subordinates, large nationwide companies, the rise of growth coalitions in many regions and cities
2010–?	Unclear economic prospects	Consolidation of authoritarianism	Narrow, closed opportunity structure	Strengthening of the 'power vertical', the aggravation of principal–agent problems	Parallel trends of growth and maintenance of the *status quo*, centralised party-based sub-national authoritarianism	Large nationwide companies, various segments of local elites and their subordinates, coexistence of growth and distributional coalitions

local governance proved itself vulnerable *vis-à-vis* exogenous challenges, as the experience of the 2008–2009 economic crisis illustrates. In fact, for local regimes this crisis played the role of a 'natural experiment', which shed some light on the issue of adaptability of the 'zigzags' and 'U-turns' of the 'power vertical' to the changing external conditions without major revision of its foundation.

The impact of actors on the performance of local regimes was limited in comparison with their structural characteristics and political opportunities. Similar to the spread of local regime 'growth coalitions' which were driven by economic growth and the increase of rents, the crisis of 2008–2009 contributed to the revival of distributional coalitions (Zubarevich 2010)—not only in crisis-ridden mono-industrial company towns but also in some previously successful local regimes of growth and development (such as Kaliningrad, where major local protest actions were visible in early 2010). The structural characteristics of local regimes, on the one hand, and the systematic diminution of their political opportunities, on the other, led to a shrinking of their resource base and a revival of local regimes of the maintenance of the *status quo*. This is not to say that the evolution of Russia's local regimes has fundamentally shifted. Rather, these two types—local regimes of growth and development and local regimes of the maintenance of the *status quo*—are coexisting with each other. But this coexistence is far from peaceful and it has been accompanied by a new wave of conflicts amongst local actors. Moreover, the preservation of the current 'rules of the game' and the transfer to local regimes of the problem of crisis-driven costs—both political (the threat of intra-elite conflicts and mass protests) and economic (the deficit of local budgets and further rise of tariffs, especially housing costs)—became the major priority of the centre's policy towards local regimes. This policy contributed to the aggravation of the key problems inherent in the dual model of local governance in Russia.

First, the maintenance of the electoral dominance of UR with the use of fake elections is faced with new problems because the toughening of the centre's control over local actors did not compensate for the decline of positive incentives to their loyalty. Thus, despite the *de facto* prohibition of inter-party competition—both in the local regimes and in the country as a whole—the mayoral elections in 2009–2010 (for example in Smolensk, Murmansk, and Nizhny Tagil) demonstrated the rise of intra-party competition within UR in which its candidates competed with each other for shrinking sources of rents. Some attempts by the centre to prevent this competition and to impose sanctions on violators of party discipline had limited success, and sometimes even led to electoral victories for either independent or opposition-backed candidates (for example, in Irkutsk). The same trends were typical of a number of elections of municipal councils (Kynev 2010). The centre, from its position, was unable or unwilling to offer local actors viable positive alternatives, while the proposed measures for widening the political opportunities of the local regimes, such as the increase in the number of deputies of regional legislatures and the delivery of seats in regional legislatures to 'small' parties, were certainly insufficient.

Second, the fierce struggle for the redistribution of rents poses a major blow to city mayors and the heads of district administrations, which were the 'weakest link' of the 'power vertical' nearly by default. Even before the beginning of the economic crisis in 2008 top-down pressures on them—ranging from forced resignations to 'contract-ordered' criminal investigations—were nearly ubiquitous (Monitoring 2008). The deepening of contradictions between local actors led not only to an increase in this pressure, but also to further institutional changes. In the wake of local government reforms in 2004–2005 about one third of Russia's cities eliminated popular elections of their mayors merely due to the influence of local political factors (Gel'man & Lankina 2008). In 2009–2010 new attempts to replace elected mayors by hired city managers became more active and widespread. They affected even those regions and cities where the competition between governors and city mayors previously constituted the heart of local politics—such as in Yekaterinburg and Nizhnii Novgorod. These institutional changes led to a further decline of local political and economic autonomy and contributed to the institutional decay of local regimes. However, the replacement of city mayors, as well as the more proactive replacement of regional governors pursued by Dmitry Medvedev in comparison with his predecessor (Titkov 2007; Turovsky 2010), could not resolve the rising principal–agent problems within the framework of the 'power vertical'.

Finally, in 2010 the Kremlin proposed a draft of a new law, which would impose the mandatory use of proportional or mixed electoral systems to all large municipalities (of over 30,000 voters). This reform was oriented not to strengthen UR's position at the local level (technically, this goal could be easily achieved due to the further spread of electoral fraud) but, rather, to exclude intra-party competition within UR (due to an open power struggle of several representatives of UR in the same electoral districts) and to replace it by cartel-like deals inside the 'party of power'. However, the 'privatisation' of local branches of political parties by key economic actors became a side effect of artificial party penetration of municipal councils (Kynev 2010). The village of Khomutinino (Chelyabinsk *Oblast'*) serves as the most outrageous case in this respect. In the wake of municipal council elections in 2009, local branches of four parliamentary parties were established there, and 300 out of the 1,200 local residents joined the ranks of UR, which was led by the director of the sanatorium, the largest local employer. The list of Just Russia (*Spravedlivaya Rossiya*) was led by the chief of the sanatorium's security, and the list of Communists was headed by the deputy director of the same sanatorium, so the municipal government became essentially captured by sanatorium employees. In sum, the corrosion of the 'power vertical' from within became the side effect of the preservation of the monolithic unity of the 'power vertical' at any cost, which also contributed to the aggravation of principal–agent problems.

Contrary to the expectations of a number of observers, the crisis of 2008–2009 and its aftermath has not caused (at least, as yet) a major rise of non-conventional mass participation in Russia's local regimes. Even in the 1990s, the protest activism at the local level was primarily a function of struggles among elites (Robertson 2007). The period of the 2000s brought few new colours to this picture. Even though the wave of protest actions from Vladivostok to Kaliningrad and from Arkhangelsk to Irkutsk was rather large, it barely affected local regimes and changed neither the configurations of local actors and institutions nor the mechanisms of local governance. The potential of protest mobilisation was limited to local 'rebellions', while the organisational weakness of protest social movements, constrained by political opportunity structures at the level of the local regimes and in the country as a whole, did not allow scattered local protest initiatives to resolve collective action problems and to prevent their coordination. Meanwhile, most of these local protests could be labelled as NIMBY ('Not In My Back Yard'), which were oriented toward partial solutions of local issues on a case-by-case basis (Belokurova 2010), rather than toward reforms of the local regimes as such. Therefore the rise of these protest movements did not pose major challenges for the local regimes. As a rule, they were either co-opted by the ruling groups, who partially satisfied the requests of the protest groups (as in Pikalevo) or were coerced due to the pressure of authorities on local activists (as in Kaliningrad). Thus, trends of local protests could not develop beyond some uncontrolled 'rebellions'. It is not surprising therefore, that new local actors, who would be able to systematically challenge established local regimes, did not emerge in Russia's regions and cities. One might expect that the preservation of the current political opportunity structures at the level of local regimes and in the country as a whole would prevent changes of patterns of mass participation in Russia's regions and cities. Furthermore it is no wonder that the growing potential of the formation of possible alternatives to the existing local regimes remains poorly mobilised.

One might draw certain parallels between principal–agent problems in the Soviet system of territorial governance in the 1970s–1980s with those within the contemporary 'power vertical' in Russia. The aspiration of the centre to impose social costs on local actors against the background of decline of positive incentives to their loyalty, the selective transfer of resources and powers to several leaders of local regimes, the taboo on open political contestation, and the rise of costs of centralised control to a prohibitively high level, are typical of the contemporary 'power vertical' as they were for the period of the 1970s and 1980s (Rutland 1993). Yet, it proved to be impossible to improve the Soviet system of territorial governance; indeed, it was eliminated at the end. In light of this experience, attempts at a partial revival of late-Soviet practices of local politics and local governances in Russia's local regimes in the 2010s look at least dubious.

Nevertheless (at least up until the time of writing), the 'power vertical' was able to diminish recent challenges (and possible future challenges) to the local regimes. It also postponed their risks but contributed to the decline in quality of local governance and deepening principal–agent problems. However, in the short term, the challenges and contradictions of local regimes are likely to increase due to the influence of several factors: the declining amount of rents at the local level and an even more intensive struggle for its redistribution; the rising tensions between distributional coalitions and 'growth coalitions' within the local regimes; and the rising demand of the urban middle class for improving the quality of local governance and, consequently, the possible formation of an equivalent to a progressive movement in Russia's cities, which could also affect local regimes.

These challenges are driven by the general logic of modernisation processes in Russia's regions and cities and the structural characteristics of Russia's local regimes. Although the existing political opportunities of the 'power vertical' are oriented toward the prevention of this kind of development of the local regimes, the aggravation of these conflicts and contradictions in Russia's local regimes is merely just a matter of time.

Conclusion: the 'power vertical' and the prospects of local regimes

Recent studies of urban regimes in Western Europe and North America tend to be actor-centred and merely focused on the composition and interests of local coalitions and their developmental strategies (Mossberger & Stoker 2001). Alternatively, some comparative studies of local regimes in Africa (Boone 2003) and Latin America (Gibson 2005) have convincingly demonstrated that the nature of their evolutionary trajectories is path-dependent and often self-enforcing even regardless of the changing nationwide political and economic contexts. The framework of analysis of Russia's local regimes outlined above combines both perspectives, the predominance of structural conditions and the key role of political opportunities. The embeddedness of the institutions of local regimes is entrenched due to the complex legacies of the Soviet period (Gel'man *et al.* 2003) and due to the political consequences of reforms from the 1990s and 2000s (Golosov 2008). While the power mechanisms of most of Russia's local regimes are rather self-enforcing, attempts at the consolidation and co-optation of local regimes into the 'power vertical' have contributed to the preservation of sub-national authoritarianism (Gel'man 2010).

However, it is not so clear as to what extent the 'power vertical' and the centre's policies towards local regimes are really changing patterns of local governance or are just maintaining the *status quo*. This issue is worth further research, oriented to an in-depth analysis of the role of federal and local actors, and, more generally, to the role of agency in local governance, which is heavily determined by structural characteristics of Russia's local regimes (Zubarevich 2010)—similar to those of Third World countries. Apparently, the federal centre is oriented to the improvement in quality of local governance and an increase in the performance of the local regimes. It is important for the centre, not only in instrumental political terms, even though the popular perceptions of the efficiency of local regimes will enhance their legitimacy (as well as the legitimacy of Russia's nationwide regime) but it is also important due to the centre's strategic policy goal of economic modernisation of Russia and its regions and cities. Yet, Russia's rulers, who are keeping major leverages of control over the state machinery, would like to achieve both the strengthening and the sustaining of it. Will the centre be able to curb the opportunistic behaviour of actors of the local regimes within the framework of the 'power vertical' and the emerging dual system of local governance?

Besides top-down pressure on local actors, the centre's strategic policy towards the local regimes involves a number of other important components. First, it implies legalisation of ownership of private assets, which were seized by local elites as part of their administrative rents, and *de facto* recognition of the private businesses of local politicians and officials (even though they often officially belong to dummy intermediaries). Second, formal legalisation of dual governance practices has led to a rise in the incomes and bonuses of local officials, who are able to use public resources for their private consumption. But the centre's policy towards local regimes has also led to the aggravation of long-term problems of local governance. The official legalisation of the incomes of local officials and the *de facto* recognition of the servants of the 'power vertical' as a kind of estate has led to a rise in social inequality and an increase in costs of social control at the local level. Also, the very fact that local officials and politicians owned their private businesses contributed to the poor protection of property rights and distorted local markets, which negatively affected the outcomes of local regimes in the arena of local governance.

Finally, the rule *by* law, which became the major tool of dominance in local regimes and substitutes for the rule *of* law, has also led to further institutional decay and a lock-in of bad governance equilibrium both at the level of local regimes and in the country as a whole. Furthermore, the decline of resource rents and unclear prospects for economic growth have posed a difficult dilemma for the federal centre. Further centralisation of economic resources would diminish the share of rents of local actors. Thus, the centre should either toughen its control over local regimes or provide them with new sources of rents in order to maintain the loyalty of local actors. In this respect, the policy of modernisation will forcefully drive subordinated actors to cooperate with the centre in order to establish new (or to revive previous) growth coalitions and to pursue local developmental policy in order to continue rent extraction on a new basis. This evolution of local regimes in Russia's regions and cities will bring benefits to both the federal centre (which is interested in further economic growth) and to local actors (who are interested in the preservation, if not in an increase in their rents). The point is that now local actors have to invest more efforts into local development in order to achieve their opportunistic goals. But despite the convergence of public interests and self-interests of local actors in the developmental evolution of the local regimes, the 'power vertical' provided more incentives for short-term rent-seeking rather than for growth-oriented policies of the local regimes (which, from their perspective, in the short term could bring more rents to local actors). Also, the centre's interest in the preservation of power mechanisms of the local regimes has led to the reproduction rather than the circulation of local elites and contributed to the survival of incumbents regardless of their performance: even though the centre would like to improve the quality of local governance, the 'power vertical' inhibits these changes.

As yet, it is unlikely that the federal centre will provide strong incentives for the transformation of the local regimes, which will lead to long-term cohabitation of sub-national authoritarianism with sustainable growth and development in Russia's regions and cities. Meanwhile, the further trajectories of the local regimes in Russia, to a great degree, will depend upon the resolution of one major issue—whether the cohabitation of sub-national authoritarianism in local politics and the attempts of modernisation of local governance will bring sustainable growth and development to Russia's regions and cities in the long haul.

European University at St Petersburg
Russian State University for Humanities

References

Avdonin V. (2006) 'Ryazanskaya oblast' v 2006 godu', in *Regional'nyi monitoring*, Carnegie Moscow Centre, available at: http://monitoring.carnegie.ru/2006/12/ryazan/avdonin-vladimir-ryazanskaya-oblast-v-2006-m-godu/, accessed 28 April 2010.

Belokurova, E. (2010) 'NGO and Politics in Russian Regions', in Gel'man, V. & Ross, C. (eds) (2010), pp. 107–22.

Boone, C. (2003) *Political Topographies of the African State: Territorial Authority and Institutional Choice* (Cambridge, Cambridge University Press).

Borisova, N. (2010) 'Perm: lokal'nyi rezhim v krupnom rossiiskom gorode', *Neprikosnovennyi zapas*, 2, pp. 92–102.

Brie, M. (2004) 'The Moscow Political Regime: The Emergence of a New Urban Political Machine', in Evans, A. & Gel'man, V. (eds) (2004) *The Politics of Local Government in Russia* (Lanham, MD, Rowman and Littlefield), pp. 203–34.

Bychkova, O. & Gel'man, V. (2010) 'Ekonomicheskie aktory i lokal'nye rezhimy v krupnykh gorodakh Rossii', *Neprikosnovennyi zapas*, 2, pp. 73–82.

Dininio, P. & Orttung, R. (2005) 'Explaining Patterns of Corruption in the Russian Regions', *World Politics*, 57, 4, pp. 500–29.

Geddes, B. (1994) *Politician's Dilemma: Building State Capacity in Latin America* (Berkeley & Los Angeles, University of California Press).

Gel'man, V. (2009) 'Leviathan's Return? The Policy of Recentralization in Contemporary Russia', in Ross, C. & Campbell, A. (eds) (2009) *Federalism and Local Politics in Russia* (London, Routledge), pp. 1–24.

Gel'man, V. (2010) 'The Dynamics of Sub-National Authoritarianism: Russia in Comparative Perspective', in Gel'man, V. & Ross, C. (eds) *Federalism and Local Politics in Russia* (2010), pp. 1–18.

Gel'man, V. & Lankina T. (2008) 'Authoritarian versus Democratic Diffusions: Explaining Institutional Choices in Russia's Local Government', *Post-Soviet Affairs*, 24, 1, pp. 40–62.

Gel'man, V. & Ross, C. (eds) (2010) *The Politics of Sub-National Authoritarianism in Russia* (Farnham, Ashgate).

Gel'man, V., Ryzhenkov, S. & Brie, M. (2003) *Making and Breaking Democratic Transitions: The Comparative Politics of Russia's Regions* (Lanham, MD, Rowman and Littlefield).

Gibson, E. (2005) 'Boundary Control: Subnational Authoritarianism in Democratic Countries', *World Politics*, 58, 1, pp. 101–32.

Golosov, G. (2008) 'Elektoral'nyi avtoritarizm v Rossii', *Pro et Contra*, 12, 1, pp. 22–35.

Harrison, M. (2009) 'Forging Success: Soviet Managers and Accounting Fraud, 1943 to 1962', *Warwick Economic Research Papers*, University of Warwick, Number 909, available at: http://www2.warwick.ac.uk/fac/soc/economics/research/papers_2009/twerp_909.pdf, accessed 23 May 2010.

Kang, D. (2002) *Crony Capitalism: Corruption and Development in South Korea and the Philippines* (Cambridge, Cambridge University Press).

Kynev, A. (2010) 'Party Politics in the Russian Regions: Competition of Interest Groups under the Guise of Parties', in Gel'man, V. & Ross, C. (eds) (2010), pp. 135–50.

Ledyaev, V. (2008) 'Gorodskie politicheskie rezhimy: teoriya i opyt empiricheskogo issledovaniya', *Politicheskaya nauka*, 3, pp. 32–60.

Matsuzato, K. (2001) 'From Ethno-Bonapartism to Centralized Caciquismo: Characteristics and Origins of the Tatarstan Political Regime, 1990–2000', *Journal of Communist Studies and Transition Politics*, 17, 4, pp. 43–77.

Mebane, W. & Kalinin, K. (2009) 'Comparative Election Fraud Detection', Paper presented at the *Annual Meeting of the American Political Science Association*, Toronto, 3–6 September, available at: http://papers.ssrn.com/sol3/papers.cfm?abstract_id=1450078, accessed 10 January 2011.

Monitoring (2008) *Monitoring faktov davleniya na glav munitsipal'nykh obrazovanii*, Public Chamber of the Russian Federation, Commission on Local Government and Housing Policy, Mimeo, 27 August, available at: http://www.oprf.ru/files/Otstavqui.doc, accessed 28 April 2010.

Mossberger, K. & Stoker, G. (2001) 'The Evolution of Urban Regime Theory: The Challenge of Conceptualization', *Urban Affairs Review*, 36, 6, pp. 810–35.

Pappe, Y. (2000) 'Treugol'nik sobstvennikov v regional'noi promyshlennosti', in Klimanov, V. & Zubarevich, N. (eds) (2000) *Politika i ekonomika v regional'nom izmerenii* (Moscow & St Petersburg, Letnii Sad), pp. 109–20.

Petrov, N. (2004) 'Federalism', in McFaul, M., Petrov, N. & Ryabov, A. (eds) (2004) *Between Dictatorship and Democracy: Russian Post-Communist Political Reform* (Washington, DC, Carnegie Endowment for International Peace), pp. 213–38.

Petrov, N. (2007) 'Corporatism vs. Regionalism', *Pro et Contra*, 11, 4–5, pp. 75–89.

Przeworski, A. (1991) *Democracy and the Market: Political and Economic Reforms in Eastern Europe and Latin America* (Cambridge, Cambridge University Press).

Reddaway, P. & Orttung, R. (eds) (2003–2004) *The Dynamics of Russian Politics: Putin's Reform of Federal–Regional Relations, vol. 1–2* (Lanham, MD, Rowman and Littlefield).

Robertson, G. (2007) 'Strikes and Labor Organizations in Hybrid Regimes', *American Political Science Review*, 101, 4, pp. 781–98.

Rutland, P. (1993) *The Politics of Economic Stagnation in the Soviet Union: The Role of Local Party Organs in Economic Management* (Cambridge, Cambridge University Press).

Ryzhenkov, S. (2010) 'Lokal'nye rezhimy i vertikal' vlasti', *Neprikosnovennyi zapas*, 2, pp. 63–72.

Sharafutdinova, G. (2010a) 'Subnational Governance in Russia: How Putin Changed the Contract with His Agents and the Problems it Created for Medvedev', *Publius*, 40, 4, pp. 672–96.

Sharafutdinova, G. (2010b) 'Redistributing Sovereignty and Property under Putin: A View from Resource-Rich Republics of the Russian Federation', in Gel'man, V. & Ross, C. (eds) (2010), pp. 191–210.

Shirickov, A. (2010) *Anatomiya bezdeistviya: politicheskie instituty i byudzhetnye konflikty v regionakh Rossii* (St Petersburg, European University at St Petersburg Press).

Stoner-Weiss, K. (2006) *Resisting the State: Reform and Retrenchment in Post-Soviet Russia* (Cambridge, Cambridge University Press).

Tev, D. (2006) 'Politekonomicheskii podkhod v analize mestnoi vlasti. K voprosu o koalitsii, pravyashchei v Sankt-Peterburge', *Politex*, 2, 2, pp. 99–121.

Titkov, A. (2007) 'Krizis naznachenii', *Pro et Contra*, 11, 4–5, pp. 90–103.

Turovsky, R. (2010) 'How Russian Governors are Appointed: Inertia and Radicalism in Central Policy', *Russian Politics and Law*, 48, 1, pp. 58–79.

Volkov, V. (2002) *Violent Entrepreneurship: The Role of Force in the Making of Russian Capitalism* (Ithaca, NY, Cornell University Press).

Yakovlev, A. (2006) 'The Evolution of Business–State Interactions in Russia: From State Capture to Business Capture?', *Europe-Asia Studies*, 58, 7, pp. 1033–56.

Zubarevich, N. (2010) 'State–Business Relations in Russia's Regions', in Gel'man, V. & Ross, C. (eds) (2010), pp. 211–26.

The Clash of Regionalisms and Caucasian Conflicts

RICHARD SAKWA

THE RECOGNITION OF THE INDEPENDENCE OF Abkhaziya and South Ossetiya on 26 August 2008, following the five-day Russo-Georgian War (8–12 August), at a stroke created a new dynamic in Russia's ethnic and federal relations and in the politics of the Caucasus as a whole. Nation and state building aspirations were heightened across the region. For the first time the independent political status of sub-national entities was recognised in post-Soviet Eurasia, and this could come to threaten Russia itself. The initial disintegration of Yugoslavia had occurred along the lines of the constituent republics, but the recognition by the United States and some of its allies of Kosovo's unilateral declaration of independence in February 2008 broke the unspoken taboo against the recognition of sub-republican units that had governed processes of state formation in the post-communist world (Pavković & Radan 2007, Chapter 5). The war demonstrated that the process of the disintegration of the USSR was far from over, but had only been 'frozen' for some two decades. Russia was now forced to deal with Caucasian conflicts in a more fluid and broader international context, while intensifying concerns about Russia's own territorial integrity. Although the threat of outright separatism has waned, the adhesive bonds of the Caucasus with Russia have also weakened (Malashenko 2009). The interconnectedness of the various conflicts has now become evident (Cheterian 2008).

Competing regionalisms

Four types of regionalism are in operation in the Caucasus (see Table 1). The first encompasses the sub-national units, focusing on intra-state and ethnic issues. Each of the micro-regionalisms in the area has a distinct dynamic with its metropole, including some that have shifted their allegiance to an external capital (Abkhaziya, Nagorno-Karabakh and South Ossetiya). The second is the Caucasus considered as a single meso-regional unit, although divided into southern and northern sub-regions. Here the fundamental dynamic is between states or proto-states. Third is the macro-region encompassing the Caucasus, the Transcaspian states in Central Asia, Turkey and Iran where the fundamental dynamic is the relationship between putative and actual regional hegemons with their potential suzerains. Finally, there is a mega-region which

TABLE 1
OVERLAPPING REGIONALISMS

Type of region	*Relevant examples*	*Encompassing*
Micro-region	Chechnya, Dagestan, Abkhaziya, South Ossetiya, Nagorno-Karabakh, Samtskhe-Javakhetiya	Various sub-national regions of the south Caucasian unitary states; intra-state and ethnic issues
Meso-region	The Caucasus	North Caucasus, South Caucasus; covering inter-state relations; comparable to the Balkan meso-region
Macro-region	Caspian, Black Sea and post-Soviet Eurasia and Near East	The Caucasus, Transcaspian states, Near East (Turkey, Iran); issues regarding regional hegemons and interested parties
Mega-region	Western Europe, Post-Soviet Eurasia and Greater Middle East	The CIS, Caspian, Black Sea littoral states, Near and Middle East, European Union; relations between great powers

brings in the various external great powers, comprising the Commonwealth of Independent States (CIS), the Caspian and Black Sea littoral states along with the European Union (EU) and the United States.

Kimitaka Matsuzato (2005, p. 10) asks whether 'meso-areas are analytic (constructive) or, on the contrary, ontological (really existing)', a question that applies to regions at all levels. This issue is especially pertinent to meso-regions such as the Caucasus, with its conventional sub-division along the line of the Caucasian mountain ridge. The Georgian war demonstrated that this division is misleading, and that the analytic division of the area into the North and South Caucasus (Transcaucasia) does not capture the ontological truth that in fact we are dealing with a single unit. This is not simply a matter of semantics but affects the way that the region's problems are conceptualised. Micro-regional dynamics of relations with a preferred or actual host state are located in a broader geopolitical context and shared history that cuts across contingent state borders.

If in the 1990s the centre of conflict in Europe was found in the Balkan meso-region, in the 2000s the source of division and tension moved to the Caucasus. The geographical shift also represents a change in the sequencing of the conflicts. The Balkan wars of the 1990s emerged out of the decay of a supranational state—Yugoslavia—and the creation of successor nation-states. The borders of nations and states did not coincide, and thus wars were provoked. The conflicts in the Caucasus today share this characteristic but with a distinctive twist: the new states were born relatively easily, and were recognised as such by the international community, but it is their consolidation that has generated numerous conflicts. A number of separate states are looking for ways to affirm their political identity, and this comes into conflict with the struggles of other nations to create their own political communities. A further difference is that in the Balkans, although the competing interests of the great powers were not absent, the battles on the whole remained meso-regional in focus, whereas the conflicts in the Caucasus today are intensely bound up with the assertion of the power of a regional hegemon at the meso-regional level and great power rivalries at the mega-regional level. Indeed, the contemporary Caucasus is reminiscent of the Balkans in the nineteenth and early twentieth centuries, where spheres of interest overlapped. It is here that our four-fold categorisation of *matreshka*-style regionalism has heuristic value.

The Caucasus is part of several superimposed regions, each with its own intra-regional dynamics and extra-regional concerns, and in which contesting political projects collide. In terms of our multi-dimensional model, the collisions are often tangential and indirect, operating on different planes, accompanied by the temporal dimension. The great projects of our time interact in incommensurable spheres. Hence the American Secretary of State, Condoleezza Rice (2008), at the time of the Russo-Georgian War noted that Russia behaved in a nineteenth century manner in a twenty-first century context.[1] This was disingenuous, to say the least, since it would be naïve to assume that the United States had no 'nineteenth century' geopolitical interests in the region. The erosion of the bloc politics of the Cold War era has once again rendered the Caucasus the cockpit for the clash of incommensurable political projects of our time.

Political events in the Caucasus thus have an inherently multi-faceted character. The logic of developments in Georgia, in Abkhaziya, South Ossetiya, Nagorno-Karabakh and any number of other trouble spots have a meso-regional dynamic, but each of these conflicts has several other dimensions, each with its own characteristics. The question then becomes the relationship between these various levels. It is always easy to blame the global powers for local problems, and there has been no lack of this in discussion of the events of August 2008. Some of the practices of the Cold War have returned, when the superpowers did not enter into direct conflict but fought numerous proxy wars in Asia and Africa. The smaller states became victims of the larger conflict, and a similar process is at work today. As far as Russia is concerned, Georgia under President Mikheil Saakashvili became an American client-state in which its own national interests were subordinated to the superpower's mega-regional ambition, and thus failed to engage with solutions to its micro-problems of national integration at the level of the meso-region balance of power. Georgia, however, hoped to mobilise the resources available from the mega-region, above all the United States, to solve its problems; but by seeking to bypass the macro-regional level, it soon found itself isolated. This is a graphic illustration of how competing representations of the most relevant regional context for a particular issue creates parallel universes with a refracted interaction between them.

This is reflected in Russia's attempt to assert the hegemony of the macro-regional level on the various micro-regional conflicts in the North Caucasus. Although cases have been taken to the European Court of Human Rights (ECtHR) in Strasbourg, which by June 2009 had delivered 102 judgments on Chechen matters, and the Council of Europe at various points was involved in the Chechen conflict, on the whole Russia successfully localised the conflict. Equally, the influx of foreign *jihad*ists has been reduced to a trickle, although it appears there is a significant financial involvement of external agencies. Although external actors inspire some of the movements in the region, these ideas have gained traction because of the intransigent nature of endogenous problems.

[1]For the context to this, see Tsygankov (2009a, 2009b).

Over time the impact of a particular regional level waxes and wanes. The Russo–Georgian War was in effect about the reassertion of the centrality of the macro-regional level, and this has been Russia's policy throughout the CIS. However, this has not prevented the rise of mega-regional power. At the heart of the growing impact of the mega-regional factor is the enhanced role of the EU in the Caucasus. The development of the Eastern Partnership (EaP) from 2009 built on the European Neighbourhood Policy (ENP), which was launched in 2003 to develop a programme that sought to make the region safe for Europe by advancing a transformative agenda that would bring local norms into conformity with alternative macro-regional standards. The end of the eastward expansion of the EU has been compensated for by an active regionalisation policy, operating within the framework of the 'new regionalism' of international relations theory (Ágh 2010, p. 1239). These 'external regions' have been subjected to what in Euro-parlance is known as 'external governance', the attempt to achieve a soft transformation of the areas concerned without actually engaging in the accession process. However, instead of the EU developing as a genuine intermediary that could extend its peace-building dynamic to the Caucasus, it was in danger of becoming just another source of contestation and conflict.

In the Balkans the EU has been a genuine force for reconciliation and development, whereas in the Caucasus, because of the contesting regionalisms, it runs the risk of becoming an instrument of division. The EU acted as an honest broker in the 2008 conflict largely because of the adroitness of the French presidency, but it has too many contradictory aspirations to allow it to act unequivocally in conformity with its expressed normative values (Zielonka 2007). The general rule appears to be that projects like that of the EU succeed when contesting regionalisms are reduced to one overwhelmingly powerful hegemonic actor, with competing representations of regionalism either negated or marginalised. The enlargement to Central Europe in the 2000s was a relatively simple matter of extending the EU to a region where the historical challengers had withdrawn. Within the CIS macro-region this does not hold, and here the EU is just one of several competing regional visions. The EU's ambition to become a self-contained hegemonic macro-region has now been placed on indefinite hold and the EU will now have to learn to share the continent with alternative meso-regions.

The macro-regional level has been increasingly activated as a result of the Russo–Georgian War, and the shift to this plane already represented a victory for Russia, but it also empowered other actors at this level. Turkey's plans for a South Caucasus Regional Stability Platform in the wake of the 2008 war built on earlier initiatives to provide an inclusive security regime for the region. Russia and Turkey represent alternative meso-regional hegemonic powers. They are both partners and rivals, especially in the energy sphere and in the struggle for influence in the region. Just as in Russia's relations with China, the relationship with Turkey can be described as an 'axis of convenience' (Lo 2008). Turkey no longer shares a border with Russia so there is no direct confrontation over territory, but the two countries still look with concern at each other. Both are aware of the new opportunities, accompanied by the burden of the historical legacy, and aspire to become macro-regional hegemons. Their relationship with the mega-regional powers and institutions is unstable and potentially disruptive and both encounter resistance by meso-regional actors. They share borders with a region that is increasingly unstable and which is becoming the object of geopolitical contestation (Warhola & Mitchell 2006). Turkey had also become disenchanted with America's so-called 'war on terror', but Russia's war against Chechen separatism and other manifestations had provoked a rapid deterioration of relations in the early 2000s (Warhola & Mitchell 2006, pp. 135–38). This provides a salutary warning of the rapidly changing dynamics of relations between the two and in the region in general.

A new 'axis of opportunity' is taking shape across the macro-region. As the two major 'outsider' powers in Europe, there is an ineluctable geopolitical commonality between Russia and Turkey that has the potential to become the basis for a long-term rapprochement. However, both Russia and Turkey are aware that an 'alliance of the outsiders' would be catastrophic for both, reinforcing their marginal status and condemning them to a fruitless international politics of opposition. The two countries are certainly not planning to create an 'axis of the excluded', and there is no attempt to create a systemic balancing organisation, but the 'odd coupling' of Turkey and Russia in international politics is based on substantive issues: 'Turkish anger at US policy in Iraq ... dovetails with longer-term Russian disgruntlement over America's encroachment on Moscow's sphere of influence' (Hill & Taspiner 2006, p. 81). With the disappearance of the Soviet Union, Turkey and the US no longer have a common enemy; and on a number of issues, including transport corridors, Russia and Turkey have growing common interests (Hill & Taspiner 2006, p. 83). More broadly, 'Russia and Turkey are undergoing parallel revivals of their imperial state traditions', with Russian Orthodoxy and Sunni Islam assuming increasing significance in the respective countries. Both are set to become regional powers, and closer alliance between the two acts as a 'hedge', 'if not outright alternative, to trans-Atlantic and European ties' (Hill & Taspiner 2006, p. 85).

After the Russo–Georgian War Russian commentators suggested that Turkey would be turning to Moscow as part of a fundamental geopolitical reorientation (Torbakov 2008, p. 25). Russo–Turkish rapprochement has particular appeal for the Russian military. The parallels between the Turkish intervention in Northern Cyprus in 1974 and the Russian intervention in the South Caucasus in 2008, followed in due course by the recognition of the respective entities, has forced a rethinking of strategic alliances. The existence of a group of Russophiles with anti-Western views in the Turkish military, mockingly dubbed by some the 'Young Russians', creates the framework for an 'alliance of the excluded' between the two countries. Their bottom line appears to be that 'America has betrayed Turkey; the country will never fit into the EU; and to avoid isolation, Turkey should become a member of a Eurasian alliance that will be built around a resurgent Russia' (Torbakov 2005, p. 27). The unthinkable is now being thought, reflecting the unblocking of the geopolitical logjam following the long end of the Cold War. However, there is a no less powerful lobby in Turkey arguing that the country has to reinforce its alliance with the West to keep 'Russia's strategic ambitions in check' (Torbakov 2005, p. 31). By the same token, Russian strategists are wary of Turkey's ambitions in the South Caucasus and as a 'neo-Ottoman' regional power in the Middle East.

The Georgia crisis of 2008 took place at a time when both Russia and Turkey began to demonstrate greater independence in foreign policy, even a degree of unilateralism.

Russia no longer believed in the possibility of deep partnership with the West and sought to re-establish itself as a great power in Eurasia, while Turkey placed less emphasis on NATO and strove to become a regional power. Russia has tried to maintain a multi-dimensional partnership with Turkey while advancing geopolitical pluralism in post-Soviet Eurasia and its traditional links with allies and friends in the Caucasus. Turkish policy makers, despite the 'zero-problem' strategy, are well aware that the geopolitical game in post-Soviet Eurasia will now take much harsher forms. Concessions to Armenia risk alienating Azerbaijan and *vice versa*. The difference now is that the regional powers have more of a free hand. The US, and the West in general, has been to a degree discredited by the failure of its adventurism in Georgia; propping up an authoritarian and dangerous client regime under the guise of advancing democracy, something that had been quite common during the Cold War. The view that joining NATO was the democratic thing to do, as in Ukraine, suffered a severe blow. The US tried to achieve a fundamental geopolitical reorientation of the South Caucasus and the whole region, and its failure undermined its credibility as a provider and guarantor of security.

Russia now faces a range of similar issues in its relations with post-war South Ossetiya and Abkhaziya. Indeed, we can talk of the 'Cyprusification' of Russia's relations with the Caucasus, and more broadly the issue potentially hinders Russian integration with Western bodies, just as the Cyprus question impedes Turkey's accession to the EU. With the EU insisting on the territorial integrity of Georgia in circumstances where it is almost inconceivable to envisage South Ossetiya and Abkhaziya returning to Georgian sovereignty (at least to a Georgia as presently constituted), the problem looks all set to become as endemic as the Cyprus question.

The recognition of multi-level regionalism offers a new way of thinking about regional conflict, and could thus offer a way of transcending the entrenched divisions at the micro-regional level and the multiplying evidence of zero-sum politics at the mega-regional level. Instead of regional actors acting against each other to intensify local or global problems, certain basic truths have emerged. One of these is that micro-regional problems need meso-regional and macro-regional solutions. It is pointless to expect that NATO enlargement to the area will resolve any regional problem—it would instead only exacerbate and entrench them. Equally, the growth in the influence of the EU in the area could be highly positive, but only if it is decoupled from global geopolitical agendas and instead focuses on what the EU was originally established to achieve—to rid Europe of the scourge of war. The interminable struggle over pipeline routes acts as an ersatz war, notably between Russia and the EU over contesting plans for Nabucco and South Stream routes to bring gas from the Caspian macro-region to the European mega-region. There is no agreement on the legitimate interests of Russia and Turkey in the region and what political form they could take. This allowed other mega-regional actors to make a bid for meso-regional hegemony.

The reunification of the Caucasus

The nature of the 'region' in question and character of the conflicts that have plagued the area since the demise of the Soviet Union, and the relationship between the two, remain contested (King 2008; de Waal 2010). In addition to defining a geographical region bounded by two seas (the Caspian and Black) and strung along both sides of the mountain range of that name, the Caucasus is a geopolitical term coined in the eighteenth century, but which in the Soviet and post-Soviet eras was divided into sharply defined sub-regions (Akkieva 2008). The viability of existing political boundaries is now coming increasingly into question, with peoples divided by what many consider to be artificial borders (for example, the Lezgins, the Ossets and the Circassiyan peoples).

The wars in Chechnya, the persistent low-level insurgency in Northeastern Caucasus (primarily Dagestan, Chechnya and Ingushetiya), and the Russo–Georgian War of August 2008 have had a profound impact on the region and on the way that we think about it. The conventional north–south division between the North Caucasus and what in Soviet parlance was Transcaucasia is complemented by an east–west axis, reflecting two traditional differing patterns of resistance to Russian power. The Northeast Caucasus (Dagestan, Chechnya and Ingushetiya) has always had difficulty relating to the specific concerns of the northwestern part (Kabardino-Balkariya, Karachaevo-Cherkessiya and Adygeya), while Ossetiya as an Orthodox enclave in the middle has had concerns of its own. The security of the whole region, however, pivots on Chechnya; while in the south, Georgia has been crucial—and so it remains to this day.

The new dynamic was recognised by the creation on 19 January 2010 of a new North Caucasus Federal District that hived off six republics and one region from the Southern Federal District: Dagestan, Chechnya, Ingushetiya, North Ossetiya, Kabardino-Balkariya, Karachaevo-Cherkessiya, and Stavropol region. President Dmitry Medvedev appointed Alexander Khloponin, the former governor of Krasnoyarsk *Krai*, to head the new body, whose capital was in Pyatigorsk in Stavropol region, and urged him to apply 'primarily economic methods', rather than coercive strategies (Medvedev 2010). The new district split the North Caucasus on an east–west axis, and in part was prompted by an attempt to insulate the western part from the insurgency in the east, especially with the Winter Olympics of 2014 in mind, to be held in Sochi in Krasnodar *Krai*. The putative creation of a giant South Russian region was considered a way of managing micro-regional conflicts.

Since the wars of the early nineteenth century the Caucasian mountain ridge has been taken as the dividing line between the North and the South Caucasus, but there has never been such a firm division in practice. The wars in Chechnya and the North Caucasus as a whole were in part a strategic response to the incorporation of Georgia in 1801, and later the whole southern region, into the Russian empire. The defence of the Georgian Military Highway over the mountains to the south was one of Russia's strategic preoccupations for over a century. The opening of the 3.6 km-long Roki tunnel linking North and South Ossetiya in 1985 brought together not just the two parts of a single ethnic and religious group but symbolically forged a permanent all-weather link between the two regions. The geographical barrier was not transcended, however, and this was reflected in the existence of a separate Soviet Transcaucasian group of forces based in Tbilisi, subordinate to the Caucasian Military District. In the post-communist era as well, although the framework for relations with the North Caucasus is Russian regional policy while foreign policy covers transactions with the South Caucasus, this distinction is increasingly blurred. In his landmark study of geopolitics in the region, Gadzhiev (2001, p. 292) insists that 'both blocs must be considered as part of a seamless unit'.

The creation of a Caucasian Mountain Republic in the early communist years was intended to provide unity across the smaller ethnic groups, although the independence of the Transcaucasian republics revealed the fragility of that construct. No sooner did the Soviet Union disintegrate than the interaction of the two parts of the region was restored. In September 1991 South Ossetiyan leaders pleaded with President Boris Yel'tsin to incorporate the region into the Russian Federation.[2] The presence of Chechen forces in South Ossetiya in the August 2008 war was reminiscent of the role played by Shamil Basaev in the Abkhaz wars in the early 1990s on behalf of the dream of a recreated Caucasian Mountain Republic, taking the form at that time of Musa Shanibov's Confederation of the Mountain Peoples of the Caucasus (*Konfederatsiya gorskikh narodov Kavkaza*, CMPC). The fighters in Georgia then returned to continue the struggle in Chechnya, an experience that Moscow was keen to avoid repeating. The use of the Pankisi Gorge in Georgia by Chechen insurgents for recuperation and regrouping (until 2004 when Saakashvili came to an agreement with Moscow to put an end to the practice) demonstrated the strategic link between the two parts of the region.

The 2008 war brought into focus two aspects of politics in the region. First, the Caucasus represents a single security system, and the interactions between permeable borders gained greater salience (Buzan *et al.* 1997). Chechnya has now clearly become part of a larger security community on a north–south and east–west axis. Russian forces once again look set to be permanently stationed in 'Transcaucasia' (the return of the term is itself significant), changing the geopolitical balance of the region and reversing the long retreat begun in 1991. Until 2008 the status of Russia's last base in the region, Gudauta in Abkhaziya, was tenuous and the subject of intense diplomatic efforts by Georgia and its allies, but the base is now secure and has been joined by others, notably a Russian naval presence in Ochamchira. This is a shallow-water port and is unable to take any but the smaller vessels from the Russian Black Sea fleet based in Sevastopol. In April 2009 Russia took over effective control of Abkhaziya's and South Ossetiya's borders, ensuring their development as independent states. On 17 February 2010 the Abkhaz leader, Sergei Bagapsh, signed a deal with Moscow to create a 'unified military base' in Abkhaziya for 49 years, with the option of prolongation. The date was carefully chosen, since on 17 February 1810 Abkhaziya had become a Russian protectorate, with Russia conclusively replacing the Ottoman Empire as the dominant force in the Caucasus (Lavrov 2009a; Tseluiko 2009).[3] Russia, moreover, has been able relatively to insulate the whole region from outside interference (with the partial exception of Turkey). Iran, for example, has been careful not to become engaged, allowing Russia a *droit de regard* over the whole area. The 2008 war signalled to the Western powers that it was entering a highly charged region, and although they have certainly not withdrawn, the United States, NATO and the EU have since then acted with greater circumspection.[4] The area, however, remains

[2]Author's interviews with anonymous individuals in the Russian White House, 9 September 1991.

[3]For an overview, see Barabanov *et al.* (2009).

[4]This is not to suggest that the US, for example, has accepted geopolitical defeat in the region. President Barack Obama took a firm stand on the Georgian question at the 6–7 July 2009 Moscow summit, followed by a visit to Georgia by Vice President Joseph Biden on 22 July.

the most volatile in the whole of post-Soviet Eurasia and the likely flashpoint for future conflict.

Second, the region has emerged as a single political region, however fragmented. Developments south of the Caucasian ridge influence political evolution to the north. Russian recognition of the independence of Abkhaziya and South Ossetiya encouraged separatist sentiments north of the mountains, notably among various Circassiyan communities, while stimulating talk of a 'greater Ossetiya' (Malashenko 2008, p. 7). As a result of the war, South Ossetiya emerged as a new dependent Russian quasi-region, while Abkhaziya is more independent and viable. It would be misleading to call it a client state, however much its fundamental security and economic well-being are dependent on Russia.[5]

This may well have implications for the development of Russian regionalism as a whole. The existence of independent but subaltern regions provides an alternative model for the Russian state's interactions with its own sub-national units. Discussion of the various conflicts in the Caucasus is usually posed in terms of threats to the integrity of the Russian state, and while this is understandable in the light of the disintegration of the Soviet Union and Chechnya's struggles for independence, the latter were the exception. Malashenko (2008, p. 7) argues that the North Caucasian peoples support the maintenance of Russian statehood, and in that framework are active players in the endless bargaining for privileges and concessions. He concludes that 'the North Caucasus today as never before is part of the Caucasus'. The reunification of the region is one of the major political consequences of the Five-Day War.

The Chechen conflict and multi-level regionalism

In the meantime, we are faced with endemic entrenched conflicts in sub-national regions. One of the most intractable centres on Chechnya, which from the first had a pronounced meso-regional facet. The incursion in summer 1999 into Dagestan by the 'Islamic Army of the Caucasus'[6] was perceived by exponents of the broader war as part of the historical tradition of resistance to Russian occupation by Islamicised national fighters.[7] According to Basaev, a grand council of field commanders, the so-called state committee of defence of the Chechen Republic of Ichkeriya[8] met on 22 July 2002 and approved the extension of the war to the rest of the North Caucasus (Kavkazcenter 2006). Basaev was appointed the commander of military operations on three fronts (eastern, western and northern), while Abdul-Khalim Sadulaev, the head of the *jamaat* in Argun and an advisor on religious affairs to the president of

[5]For a prescient call to consider recognition of the three south Caucasian proto-republics, see Kolstø and Blakkisrud (2008).

[6]The *jihad*ist insurgency planned to link up with the Sharia enclave of the Kadar Zone, the Wahhabi communities in the villages of Karamakhi and Chabanmakhi.

[7]This was the view, for example, of Yasin Rasulov, an ideologue from Dagestan State University, killed in Makhachkala on 10 April 2006 during an operation by special forces (Roshchin 2009).

[8]The Chechen Republic of Ichkeriya was the name for the historical part of Chechnya conquered by the tsarist army in 1852. It was adopted by Chechen nationalists from the 1990s to symbolise resistance to Russia.

ChRI (*Chechenskaya Respublika Ichkeriya*), was selected as vice president (Roshchin 2009).

From nationalism to jihad

There is no evidence that Aslan Maskhadov (the President of Chechnya elected in 1997, following the Khasavyurt peace agreement with Russia) repudiated this strategy, although in tactical terms he demonstrated a degree of flexibility. For example, on 14 January 2005 he tried to impose a unilateral ceasefire to give peace negotiations a chance, but this was probably far too little far too late (Ware 2005), and certainly could not reverse the dynamic of multi-level conflict. Mistrust was sharply exacerbated by the Beslan events of 1–3 September 2004, in which 1,100 pupils, teachers and parents in School No.1 in the North Ossetiyan town were taken hostage by militants, resulting in the death of 396 people, mostly hostages (Phillips 2007). In an interview a few months later Maskhadov seemed oblivious to the regional context of the struggle. He declared 'I'm deeply convinced that [President Vladimir] Putin is far from reality about what is really going on in Chechnya today', and argued that the security forces were feeding him false information. He suggested that everything could be resolved if he and Putin were to meet face-to-face (echoing Jokhar Dudaev's plea to this effect on the eve of the first Chechen war in 1994): 'If we are able to open the eyes of our opponents, the Russian leaders, peace can be established'.[9] This was not to be, and Maskhadov was assassinated by Russian forces on 8 March 2005. His death further weakened the classic nationalist wing of the insurgency, and the importance grew of other forces that Maskhadov had long failed to contain, let alone confront.

The multi-faceted nature of what is conventionally called 'the insurgency' should be stressed. Already by 1995 nationalist aspirations were tempered by a local reading of *jihad*ist ideologies, which by and large subsumed Chechen concerns into a much broader regional struggle for affirmation and recognition (Falkowski 2007).[10] Even the designation of the conflict from autumn 1999 as the 'second Chechen war' is misleading, since from the beginning this was a struggle that encompassed not just neighbouring Dagestan (the original *casus belli* for the military intervention) but the broader North Caucasian region, which itself was just one front for movements in the larger Near East macro-region, stretching from Afghanistan to Yemen.[11]

A common criticism of much of the existing literature is that it tends to view the conflicts in the North Caucasus through the lens of 'Russian studies', and thus allegedly smuggles in numerous unaddressed assumptions while limiting analysis to only one regional context. The regional analysis attempted here is intended to be at least a small step in correcting this methodological bias, although it is attended by the no less serious danger of importing a geopolitical perspective that may once again occlude the numerous streams and concerns that feed the unrest in the Caucasus.[12] There is certainly scope for further detailed ethnographical and comparative work on

[9] *RFE/RL Russian Political Weekly*, 6, 6, 10 March 2006.

[10] For overviews of Islam in Russia, see Hahn (2007) and Yemelianova (2002).

[11] For overviews, see Derluguian (2005), Radnitz (2006), Sagramoso (2007) and Wilhellmsen (2005).

[12] For a discussion of the military aspects of the conflict, see Kramer (2005).

politics in the region, for which a 'Russian studies' perspective is entirely appropriate. A recent comparative analysis of state building in Chechnya and Ingushetiya, for example, reveals the marginality of the *teip* (clan) social formation (Sokirianskaia 2010). A self-consciously constructivist approach is offered by Moore (2006) as a way out of the impasse, but this post-structural approach runs the risk of dissolving all structures into the mediated play of elusive agents.

With Maskhadov's death, leadership of the organised insurgency passed to Sadulaev. Whereas in his last months Maskhadov had sought to find a route towards negotiations, Sadulaev, the self-declared President of the ChRI, had no interest in peace talks other than those that would lead to the recognition of Chechen independence. He broadened the war to encompass the whole of the North Caucasus, and in May 2005 the 'North Caucasian front' was established to coordinate insurgent actions. On 2 May 2005 he divided the western 'front' into seven sectors (Ingushetiya, North Ossetiya, Kabardino-Balkariya, Stavropol *Krai*, Karachaevo-Cherkessiya, Adygeya and Krasnodar) and named commanders of those sectors. He also appointed new commanders of the eastern 'front' as a whole and of four of its sectors (Gudermes, Argun, Kurchaloi and Grozny).[13] Basaev, the architect of the Beslan assault, was now brought in as first deputy prime minister. Their aim was to establish an Islamic state in Chechnya and to achieve the 'decolonisation' of the whole North Caucasian region through a 'national liberation struggle', although 'nationalism' was less the governing ideology than a *jihad*ist inflexion of political Islam.

The nationalistic state building rationale of the original Chechen revolt gave way to *jihad*. In November 2005 Sadulaev declared that there would be no peace negotiations with the Russians until 'the Caucasus is freed from the boot of the Russian occupiers'.[14] Thus Maskhadov's death provoked the further radicalisation of the militants and the extension of the insurgency, although it is not entirely clear whether Sadulaev supported the official creation of a theocratic mega-state. The original goal of building an independent Chechen state was now subsumed into a broader civilisational war against the corrupt West, with the Russian state, in their view, only its most boorish manifestation. This was the view of the chief ideologist of North Caucasian *jihad*, Movladi Udugov, propounded through his Kavkaz-Centre website.[15] The attack by over 200 militants on Nalchik, the capital of Kabardino-Balkariya, on 13–14 October 2005 was a clear sign of the widening of '*jihad*', as was the onset of a creeping civil war in Dagestan and Ingushetiya. The insurgency was attracting not just disaffected youth but members of the republican intelligentsia, indicating that the resistance was not only broadening but also deepening (Vatchagaev 2009). In their study, Moore and Tumelty (2008) assess the role of foreign fighters, and thus provide a broader canvas for the North Caucasian conflicts, and by the same token eschew the notion of 'insurgency' in favour of an analysis that connects local and global social networks that motivate the volunteers.

[13]'Zayavlenie Prezidenta ChRI', 15 May 2005, available at: http://chechenpress.org/events/2005/05/15/06.shtml, accessed 10 January 2011.

[14]*RFE/RL Russian Political Weekly*, 6, 6, 10 March 2006.

[15]Available at:www.kavkazcenter.com/eng, last accessed 8 October 2008.

By mid-2006 the nationalist insurgency had significantly waned, with most field commanders dead and the young recruits gravitating to the banner of radical Muslim fundamentalism (known in the North Caucasus as Wahhabism). This move only deepened the gulf between the separatists and the 'Chechenised' elite, which defended traditional Sufi practices against the onslaught of the Wahhabis. Sufi practices, it should be noted, also underwent a radicalisation towards greater fundamentalism. The authorities scored a number of successes against the militants. Sadulaev was killed on 17 June 2006, and on the night of 9–10 July 2006, on the eve of the G8 summit in St Petersburg, terrorist number one, Basaev, was killed.[16] Leadership of the insurgency passed to the veteran field commander, Dokku Umarov, who proved to be an effective guerrilla leader, opening up two new fronts, 'Urals' and 'Volga Region', confirming Putin's fears about the spread of the insurgency to the Russian heartland (Putin 2000, p. 140). Umarov's policies reinforced the shift in insurgent thinking away from national liberation and the secular rhetoric of freedom towards *jihad* and the universalism that is characteristic of political Islam.

Umarov declared the establishment of a Caucasus emirate, accompanied by the declaration of war across the region.[17] For this group the idea of the creation of an Ichkeriyan nation-state gave way to visions of Islamic universalism, allied with *al-Qaeda* (Hahn 2010). Chechen separatism and a centuries-long struggle for freedom from Russia were renounced in favour of global *jihad* against the proclaimed enemies of Islam (Hughes 2007b).[18] The national liberation trend in the insurgency, identified after the death of Maskhadov with Akhmed Zakaev in exile in London, remains the only group advancing the traditional agenda of national separatism and sovereign-state building. Although few in number, the creation of radical and well organised military *jamaats* made up of radical Muslims represented a major escalation of the war.

In October 2007 Umarov resigned as head of ChRI and declared himself the 'emir' of the militants in the Caucasus and the leader of *jihad*, while asserting that he was the only legitimate authority in the region.[19] This represented an internal coup within the insurgency, with power now seized by radical Islamists inspired above all by Movladi Udugov and his half-brother Issa Umarov despite grave misgivings even within the Salafist (Wahhabi) camp, let alone mainstream nationalists of the Zakaev type (dubbed 'Eurochechens' by the Salafists), who argued that the establishment of the emirate was an FSB stratagem (Vatchagaev 2008a). The declaration of an Islamic emirate covering the whole of the North Caucasus in effect meant the abolition of the Chechen Republic of Ichkeriya, the cause at the heart of the insurgency since 1991, and thus Zakaev's belief that Umarov's move was a Kremlin plot makes sense. Indeed, it was construed by supporters of the Zakaev line as an act of high treason (Amundsen

[16]According to an alternative version, Basaev died in an explosion of faulty munitions as he prepared another terrorist attack.

[17]'Ofitsial'nyi reliz zayavleniya Amira Dokki Umarova o provozglashenii Kavkazskogo Emirata', *Kavkaz tsentr*, 21 November 2007, available at: www.kavkazcenter.com/russ/content/2007/11/21/54480.shtml, accessed 10 January 2011.

[18]This is one of the works that is often considered representative of the misleading 'Russian studies' approach to the Caucasian conflicts.

[19]See http://www.kavkaz-uzel.ru/newstext/news/id/1200657.html, accessed 8 June 2008.

2008). For the new generation of separatists Ichkeriya meant little, reflecting the rise of non-Chechen leaders in the Caucasian insurgency, and equally, the triumph of the radical Islamist movement over the nationalists. While Western commentators such as Tony Wood (2007) make sophisticated arguments in favour of Chechen independence, exponents of classical notions of national self-determination were now outflanked from both the 'left' (radical Islamists with a broader regional, if not universal, agenda) and from the 'right' (constrained separatism within the Russian state framework of the Kadyrov type).

Chechnya is no longer the centre of radical insurgency in the North Caucasus, and to that degree the insurgency in the republic has been defeated. Political Islam has come to the region, although refracted through the prism of post-Soviet realities (Mandaville 2007). The 'Caucasus Emirate' encompassed the republics of Dagestan, Chechnya, Ingushetiya, North Ossetiya-Alaniya, Kabardino-Balkariya and Karachaevo-Cherkessiya, and Stavropol and Krasnodar *krai*s. These regions were renamed '*vilayets*' (provinces), in deference to neo-Ottoman aspirations, with Chechnya, for example, renamed the *vilayat* of Nokhchicho, Ingushetiya the *vilayat* of Khyalgaicho, Ossetiya the *vilayet* of Iriston, and in a rather audacious step, Stavropol *Krai* became the *vilayet* of the Nogai Steppe. The Ottoman reference was intended to repudiate Tsarist, Soviet and Russian state-building efforts, and indeed the modern Turkish nation-building endeavour, in favour of a broader 'neo-mediaeval' community of overlapping state and religious authorities. The emirate was intended to provide a supra-ethnic form of allegiance that would unify the disparate ethnic struggles. Of course, this was little more than an aspiration advanced by radical Muslim groups focused, for example, on the Kavkaz Center website.[20] The idea was to rally all the militant *jamaats* into a single struggle, which would become the armed wing of the Caucasus emirate. In practice, however, the insurgency remains fragmented and divided along ethnic and regional lines.

Chechenisation and regional policy

From July 2000 the Russian government balanced its strategy of a military resolution of Chechen separatism by supporting a policy of Chechenisation promoted by Akhmat Kadyrov, a former resistance fighter and grand mufti of Chechnya who had been alienated by the rise of *jihad*ist ideologies. With his assassination in May 2004 power in due course was transferred to his son, Ramzan. Under the leadership of Kadyrov junior from March 2007 Chechnya emerged as an enclave in which the elements of the dual state prevalent elsewhere (between the constitutional state and a dominant power system in the form of an administrative regime) were attenuated to the point that it would be barely credible to describe the regime in operation there as 'hybrid' (Sakwa 2010a, 2010b). 'Chechenisation' allowed a negative transcendence of duality that intensified the prerogative powers of personalised leadership at the expense of the normative values and institutions of the constitutional state.

It is unclear whether the Kadyrov strategy has been able to resolve the Chechen war or whether it has done little more than change it into a 'frozen' conflict. In the

[20]Available at: http://www.kavkazcenter.com, accessed 8 October 2008.

long-term, the evaluation of 'Kadyrovism' focuses on the nature of the processes at work across the broader Caucasian region. Are they no more than 'legacy' conflicts, emerging out of the way that the Soviet Union collapsed? Or are they the outcome of a far deeper process, perhaps akin to decolonisation elsewhere? If the latter, then the Kadyrov option is at best a temporary solution which does not resolve the fundamental underlying pressures. Equally, Georgia's attempts to restore its 'territorial integrity' in this context may be considered as doomed as Serbia's ambition of restoring sovereignty over Kosovo. A common view suggests that from Shamil to Maskhadov and on to Sadulaev the Chechens have been engaged in a liberation struggle, including during the Soviet period (Gammer 2006). Thus the debate continues whether Russia is facing a guerrilla war, a liberation struggle, an Islamic *jihad*, or some combination of the three.

While Chechenisation was the broad strategy, support for Kadyrov is only one possible variant of its implementation. Kadyrov's poor relations with Russia's *siloviki* (security officials) is well known (Malashenko 2007b, p. 4). At various points the Kremlin was able to mobilise pro-Moscow but anti-Kadyrov groups (for example, the Yamadaev brothers) as a way of limiting a one-dimensional Chechenisation process. From our regional perspective, the fundamental question is the degree to which Chechenisation, and its Kadyrovite variant, was emulated elsewhere. Elements of Chechenisation are present throughout the North Caucasus, with federal resources propping up leaders and buying the support of regional elites accompanied by an increasing militarisation of the area to combat, in typically heavy-handed ways, the rise of political Islam. This is balanced, however, in a manner typical of the dual state, by contrary trends. The appointment of the former Constitutional Court judge Boris Ebzeev as governor of Karachai-Cherkessiya in July 2008 is a case in point.

Dmitry Kozak, the presidential envoy to the Southern Federal District between September 2004 and September 2007, criticised excessive centralisation, arguing that Moscow should only retain those powers that were necessary to maintain central control (Petrov 2007, p. 11). A report by Kozak in summer 2005 examined the situation in the region as a whole. The material leaked to the press spoke of corruption, clan-based political and criminal structures, a rampant shadow economy, and the widespread alienation of the population from ruling elites, threatening social stability and economic development. His statements suggested a shift from securitisation to socialisation as the dominant discourse in describing the endemic insurgency. Kozak noted the growing dualism in the region between constitutional principles and political practices, a feature that was institutionalised in the form of 'Chechenisation'. He foresaw 'the radicalisation and rise of extremism, and a widening gap between the prescriptions of the constitutional principles and democratic procedures and the processes that take place in reality' (Khinstein 2005). Elements of the socialisation strategy, accompanied by leadership renewal, were later implemented (Slider 2008).

Attempts to emulate the Kadyrov strategy elsewhere proved decisive failures. Heavy-handed repression in the region, the foisting of unrepresentative leaders on peoples who have traditionally worked on the basis of consensus (as in the removal of the popular leader of Ingushetiya, Ruslan Aushev, and the imposition in May 2002 of the security official Murat Zyazikov), impeded a solution that could be considered just by the majority of those involved (Sakwa 2005). The logic of regional consensus-building came into contradiction with Russia's state-building efforts. The death of Magomed Yevloev, the owner of the independent Ingushetia.ru website, on 31 August 2008, was particularly shocking. He had been a leading critic of the Kremlin-imposed administration in Ingushetiya, warning that the insurgency in the republic would only worsen unless the leadership changed. He was on the same plane from Moscow as the republic's head, Zyazikov, but on disembarking was detained by MVD personnel and he died soon after from a single bullet-wound to the head delivered in the police car taking him in for questioning.[21] In the ensuing unrest, in which calls for Zyazikov's resignation intensified, he dismissed them as the work of a handful of 'adventurers', and warned that 'The Americans are just waiting to destabilise [the situation] ... Maybe they would like to achieve what was done in South Ossetia'.[22]

The Medvedev administration moved cautiously but gradually turnover in regional leaderships gained momentum. Kozak's appointment in October 2008 as a deputy prime minister with responsibility for preparations for the 2014 Winter Olympics meant that the regional development ministry lost a powerful champion (Petrov 2008). The 'resignation' of the President of Ingushetiya, Zyazikov, on 30 October 2008, removed one of Russia's least successful regional leaders. Since coming to office in April 2002 he had presided over the republic's slide into an endemic low-level insurgency, in part inspired by the conflict with North Ossetiya over the Prigorodnyi district (Tlisova 2007), that threatened to turn into a civil war after the murder of Yevloev. The new governor, the career military officer who had commanded Russian troops in Kosovo in 1999, Yunus-Bek Yevkurov, was strongly critical of the region's law-enforcement agencies. The overall ambition appeared to be to implant a new generation of 'Medvedevite' governors with a profile similar to Medvedev's. As one report put it, Medvedev planned a mass rotation of regional heads to implant businessmen under 55 years of age who could break up clan loyalties.[23] If the Putin system of the 'power vertical' relied on buying the loyalty of regional strongmen, Medvedev began to modify this by appointing leaders with greater local legitimacy and flexibility. The inflexible vertical of power was not being dismantled, since Medvedev shared with Putin the fear that there could be a return to the 'pathological federalism' of the 1990s where the powers of the centre were hollowed out, but it was being modified. In broad terms Medvedev sought to restore balance in the dual state by strengthening the constitutional pillar. A step in this direction was the creation of the North Caucasus Federal District, accompanied by a shift to socio-economic amelioration.

Federal forces continued to be withdrawn from Chechnya, falling from 80,000 in early 2005 to about 37,000 a year later. More regiments with Chechen soldiers were formed, with the Vostok (East) and Zapad (West) battalions (formally subordinate to the Russian defence ministry) joined by the new Sever (North) and Yug (South)

[21]'New Details Emerge of Ingush Website Owner's Murder', *RFE/RL, Russia Report*, 16 February 2009.

[22]'Zyazikov Accuses US of Destabilizing Ingushetia', *North Caucasus Weekly*, 9, 34, 11 September 2008.

[23]*Vedomosti*, 24 July 2008; Slider (2010).

regiments in 2006 subordinate to the interior ministry (*Ministerstvo vnutrennykh del*, MVD). MVD forces, now largely Chechenised, began taking on more military responsibilities, despite the authorities fearing insurgent infiltration of the police forces. With the formal end of the 'counter-terrorist operation' announced on 16 April 2009 and the restoration of Chechnya to Russia's (fragmented) legal space, the Chechen government could act as a legitimate authority. This was symbolised by the opening of Grozny airport to international flights in December 2009. While military forces were being reduced in Chechnya, they were greatly increased in the North Caucasus as a whole, reflecting a shift in Moscow's own regional thinking from the sub-national to the meso-regional. The broadening of strategic vision was reflected in a new boldness in operations. The major military exercise Kavkaz-2008, for example, allowed Russia to deploy its forces in readiness to engage with challenges in the South Caucasus.

In his meeting with the Valdai International Discussion Club on 10 September 2008, Kadyrov accused the United States of fomenting unrest in the Caucasus, insisting that Russia's defeat of Georgian forces was the appropriate response, and he backed Russia's recognition of the two regions.[24] He admitted that Chechen units and paramilitaries had fought alongside the Russian forces in Georgia: 'We Chechens are obliged to be in the front line with Russia because we are warriors, and we know what war is'.[25] Once again in June 2009 Kadyrov insisted that 'it is precisely from the side of America that work is being carried out aimed at the disintegration of the sovereign Russian state. It is not terrorists, not Islamists'.[26] Kadyrov asserted that the West was behind the insurgency in the North Caucasus, hoping to 'sever the Caucasus from Russia'.[27] Kadyrovism thus has a foreign policy component, advancing a resolutely anti-Western line and acting as an instrument of Russian policy in relations with the South Caucasus. Kadyrov, however, remained a maverick actor, and under his leadership traditional ambitions to create a 'greater Chechnya', incorporating not only Ingushetiya, which shares a Vainakh culture, but also Dagestan that would give the republic access to the sea, was given expression (Dannreuther & March 2008, p. 106).

Meso-regional implications and the limits of separatism

With effective victory in the Chechen conflict Russia restored its regional predominance. Predictions that Russia would disengage from the Caucasus proved false, and the roll-over effect from one plane of regionalism to another was clear. As Dannreuther and March (2008, p. 102) put it, 'Putin's policy of "Chechenisation" undoubtedly played a significant role in improving Russia's fortunes in the Caucasus'. This was reinforced by victory over Georgia in 2008, which reasserted elements of a wider geopolitical hegemony throughout the whole Caucasian region. Clearly this is

[24] *Moscow Times*, 12 September 2008.

[25] 'Kadyrov Accuses US of Fomenting Unrest in the Caucasus', *North Caucasus Weekly*, 9, 34, 11 September 2008.

[26] 'Kadyrov Claims Umarov Gravely Wounded, Accuses US of Subversion', *Jamestown Foundation's Eurasia Daily Monitor*, 6, 112, 11 June 2009.

[27] 'Kavkaz—strategicheskii rubezh Rossii: Beseduyut Prezident Chechenskoi Respubliki Ramzan Kadyrov i glavnyi redaktor gazety "Zavtra" Aleksandr Prokhanov', *Zavtra*, 39, 23 September 2009.

extremely fragile at all levels. The Collective Security Treaty Organisation (CSTO) and the Shanghai Cooperation Organization (SCO) did not endorse Russia's recognition of the independence of the South Ossetiya and Abkhaziya; and equally, regional hegemony in the North Caucasus was challenged by persistent low-level insurgency. Its hold on the southern part relied on an unstable enclave policy and precarious balancing between Armenia and Azerbaijan. There are also broad regional processes in train, notably the accelerating retreat of ethnic Russians from the North Caucasian republics. Between the census dates of 1979 and 1989 the number of ethnic Russians fell by only 53,000 (4%) (Dzutsev 2009d); but in the next census period between 1989 and 2002 the number fell from 1.36 million to 950,000, a drop of 30% (Malashenko 2007a). Some 250,000 ethnic Russians left Chechnya between 1989 and 2002, some of whom Kadyrov hoped would now return to help restore the republic's oil industry.

Despite the long-standing calls of ethno-nationalists in Russia to cut the tie with the North Caucasus (the exemplary case is Alexander Solzhenitsyn), while neo-imperialists of the Vladimir Zhirinovsky type barely comment on the region as they focus on the greater game in the Near East macro-region, democratic statists in Moscow asserted that Russia would never agree to the Caucasus becoming independent. In a rare visit to Chechnya in October 2010 the first deputy head of the presidential administration, Vladislav Surkov (whose father was Chechen), asserted that 'The Caucasus is the foundation on which the whole of Russia stands'.[28] The dialectic between regional and global concerns underpins Russia's attempts to reinsert itself into the international system as a major player. Kotkin (2009, p. 137) notes that Russia 'remains a regional power that acts as a global superpower', while Tsygankov (2010, p. 43) is rather more specific about the relationship: '[Russia] seeks to remain regional by acting globally, thus distinguishing itself from established global powers in the West and rising global powers such as Brazil, China and India'. Equally, the loss of regional hegemony would undermine Russia's aspirations to return as a great power. Defeat in Chechnya or Dagestan would undermine regional and global aspirations for at least a generation.

Resolute action in August 2008 signalled that Russia was back as the regional hegemon, and provided a warning to the rest of the Caucasus. If Russia had failed to respond to the Georgian attack on the evening of 7 August, its position would have been weakened throughout the region. As Nalbandov argues, 'letting the Abkhaz and South Ossetiyans be defeated by Georgia would place Russia in a very uneasy, in the best case, position in relation to the nations of the Northern Caucasus whose kin the Georgian minorities were'. Russia represented an 'external homeland', to use Rogers Brubakers term, for the South Ossetians; and for Abkhaziya it acted as a 'surrogate lobby state' (Nalbandov 2009, p. 30). In the short term at least, Russia's exercise of military power tempered separatist ambitions by regional leaders, while the status of the Russian state was raised. Separatism in the 1990s had in part been encouraged by the view that Russia was a bankrupt enterprise, and while Putin had at least restored the perception that Russia was a going concern, it would fall to Medvedev to make membership an attractive proposition. There were three prongs to this strategy:

[28]'Top Kremlin Ideologue Visits Chechnya as Violence Mounts', *AFP*, 25 October 2010; *Johnson's Russia List*, 200, 2010, item 17.

leadership renewal, shifting from a securitisation to a socialisation discourse, and strengthening the constitutional state over the excesses of the administrative regime.

The Russo–Georgian War was a two-edged sword, with Russian republics possibly encouraged to emulate the independence of Abkhaziya and South Ossetiya. Both are dependent on Russia for economic survival, and indeed there is a pattern of rivalry between the two. Social hardship in South Ossetiya, moreover, led to the depopulation of the enclave (Milikishvili 2009). Recognising the independence of the region now inevitably led to the construction of a type of colonial administration and a regime dependent on Moscow. The danger was that this would become a more general pattern in the region. Paradoxically, independence only reinforced patterns of dependence. The continuing unstable security situation in the North Caucasus saw the radicalisation of separatist aspirations (Hagendoorn *et al.* 2008). From 2008, moreover, the economic crisis reduced the resources available and thus forced Moscow to insist that its southern regions try to find ways to pay their own way. Competition for shrinking resources exacerbated ethnic inter-clan conflict, notably in Dagestan and Karachaevo-Cherkessiya.

The response among the other peoples of the North Caucasus to the Russo–Georgian War divided broadly along ethnic lines. The Vainakh peoples (Chechens and Ingush) made up the first group who broadly sympathised with Georgia, even though some Chechen forces fought with the Russians, reflecting a gulf between elites and popular sentiments. The second group comprised those who unequivocally supported the Russian action, made up of the Adyghe-Cherkess peoples who are ethnically related to the Abkhaz and of course the North Ossetiyans, who naturally sympathised, and indeed supported, their ethnic kin in South Ossetiya. The third group is made up of the various peoples of Dagestan, who in general have enough problems of their own and thus took no defined line in the Russo–Georgian War. A fourth group is made up of the Karachais and Balkars, who have traditionally been close to the Svans from the Georgian highlands but who may share an ancient past with the Ossets. Ossets belong to the Iranian linguistic group, whereas the Karachais and Balkars are Turkic-speakers, thus raising questions about a common ancestry (Vatchagaev 2008b).

Regional responses to the Georgia conflict were mediated by history and ethnicity. Other traditions also came into play, notably Tbilisi's traditional role as the centre of the Caucasian region. Tbilisi had long been the capital of the Caucasian *guberniya*, and the cultural heart of the region, but with the fall of the Soviet Union the centre shifted to Rostov-on-Don, where it remains to this day, although now sharing authority with Pyatigorsk. On coming to power, Saakashvili had collaborated with Russian forces in preventing the use of Georgia (above all the Pankisi gorge) as a reserve base for the Chechen insurgency. Despite this, Vainakh sympathies for Georgia remained. Even during the war it appears that Chechens in the Vostok battalion saved Georgian civilians from revenge attacks by Ossets. The battalion was commanded by Kadyrov's enemy Sulim Yamadaev, whose enhanced political status won as a result of the war only enraged Kadyrov. The latter launched criminal charges against Yamadaev, but to save face and in recognition of his services Yamadaev was honourably discharged with the rank of lieutenant colonel of the Russian armed forces. He was subsequently assassinated in Dubai on 28 March 2009. Even radicals like Umarov adopted a wait-and-see position, although warning the Caucasian peoples not to succumb to 'Russian intrigues' (Vatchagaev 2008b).

One of the main peoples to be inspired by the recognition of the new states in Georgia is the Circassiyans (the Adyghe), who have long entertained aspirations to unite their disparate membership into a single republic. The Adyghe are the indigenous inhabitants of Northwest Caucasus who resisted the Russian advance from 1763 to 1864. At the conclusion of the Russian–Caucasian War from 1817 to 1864 the great majority were deported to the Ottoman Empire, accompanied by dreadful suffering and loss of life. According to Circassiyan sources,[29] some 1.5 million were massacred or deported. Cossacks were moved in to settle the evacuated area and continued to act as a type of garrison estate in the North Caucasus. With the annexation of Georgia, Russia's strategic concern was to ensure the security of the northern end of the Georgian Military Highway in Ossetiya, a region that cooperated with the Russians (Miller 2007). Defeat in the Crimean War (1853–1856) intensified Russia's sense of strategic vulnerability (Richmond 2008). As Stephen Shenfield (2008) stresses, the past is very much a living presence in the politics of the region. Although plans to merge Adygeiya with Krasnodar *Krai* were probably sensible in purely administrative terms, such a forced unification would represent a repudiation of Russia's untidy yet functioning principle of federal representation of ethnic identities. Various alternative plans have been mooted, notably the creation of a 'greater Circassiya' bringing together all of Russia's republics with a Circassiyan identity (notably Adygeiya and Kabardiya), as well as (more provocatively) Abkhaziya on the other side of the mountains.

There is an extensive Circassiyan diaspora scattered across the Near and Middle East, concentrated in particular in Turkey and Jordan, and as part of the Russian programme for the return of 'compatriots' plans were launched for their gradual resettlement to the Caucasus, although this contained many contradictions (Tlisova 2010). It was not a move welcomed, for example, by the Terek Cossacks, who instead had long called for the abolition of the ethnic North Caucasian republics, which they regarded as economically unviable and corrupt (Dzutsev 2009c).

Within Georgia, there has been pressure for greater autonomy in Samtskhe-Javakhetiya, a region populated largely by ethnic Armenians. In the wake of the Russo–Georgian War the authorities reacted with typically heavy-handed brutality, arresting a number of activists who appeared to be innocent of breaking any specific laws. At the same time, the president of the National Assembly of Azerbaijanis of Georgia, Dashgyn Gulmannadov, released a declaration calling for Georgia to be transformed into a confederation of Georgians, Abhaziyans and Ossetiyans, while Azerbaijani was to become one of the country's state languages.[30] The declaration was considered part of Russia's efforts to undermine the integrity of Georgia, although it had been a long-standing element in Russia's thinking about resolving the problem of

[29]See, for example, Antero Leizinger, 'The Circassian Genocide', *Circassian World: Independent web source*, available at: http://www.circassianworld.com/new/war-and-genocide/1121-circassian-genocide-leitzinger.html, accessed 10 January 2011.

[30]'Nastalo vremya dobivat'sya svoikh natsional'nykh tselei: Prezident Natsional'noi assamblei azerbaidzhantsev Gruzii', 30 January 2009, available at: http://www.regnum.ru/news/1118358.html, accessed 10 January 2011.

the breakaway republics while retaining Georgian territorial integrity. As so often in Caucasian politics, the real target may have been the attempt to stimulate separatist aspirations among Azerbaijan's own ethnic minorities, in particular the Talysh, Avars and Lezgins. Equally, there is a suspicion in Armenia that there is an Azerbaijani hand in the unrest in Javakhetiya, while Moscow is accused of seeking the further dismemberment of Georgia by encouraging Armenian separatism. Complicating the issue is the gradual return of Meskhetian Turks to their historic homeland in Samtskhe-Javakhetiya, a process opposed by the Armenians and one that has stalled since the Georgian war.

The absence of a founding moment in Georgia in which all of its territories acceded to the post-Soviet republic provoked the various secessions. Questions over the degree to which South Ossetiya is a nation state in any generally accepted definition of the term prompted a powerful movement to merge with its northern twin. President Eduard Kokoity made clear his desire to join the Russian Federation, stressing that a united Ossetiya had joined Russia in 1774, although this is not a position endorsed by the Russian leadership.[31] A natural process of unification with North Ossetiya is taking place on the ground, with innumerable personal and other links. The border between the two regions is becoming increasingly porous.

When it comes to the recognition of secessionist territories, there is a question of why Kosovo (and indeed Montenegro), followed by Abkhaziya and South Ossetiya, could gain a degree of international recognition for their independence, and other regions, notably Chechnya in our case, were condemned to remain within the larger unit of which they formed part. Why indeed South Ossetiya and not Chechnya was a question that was a particularly relevant for the Russian authorities. In an interview with the BBC Russian service on 23 April 2009, the Russian foreign minister, Sergei Lavrov (2009b), was asked the question directly: 'Does the recognition by Russia of Abkhaziya and South Ossetiya mean that Russia's national republics have an analogous right to independence from Russia if they want it?' Lavrov referred to international law in response, noting that Article 51 of the United Nations recognises the right of a state to self-defence if attacked, and thus Russia had a right to respond to Georgia's attack on Russian peacekeepers and civilians in South Ossetiya. He also noted that the two territories quite legitimately applied the stipulations of the USSR law of 3 April 1990 on self-determination and thus had the right to secede from Georgia, which itself had seceded from the USSR using the provisions of the same law. South Ossetiya and Abkhaziya had followed all due procedures, including holding referendums, adopted constitutions, elected parliaments and government, and since 1991 had gained *de facto* a certain separate legal personality. Lavrov went on to argue that 'unlike the Western sponsors of independent Kosovo, we recognized South Ossetiya and Abkhaziya not for geopolitical purposes, but in the interests of security and the very survival of the Abkhaz and South Ossetiyan peoples and of regional stability as a whole'.

[31]On 11 September 2008 he told the members of the Valdai Club that he sought the republic's entry into the RF, but within a couple of hours he was forced to retract his statement (Samarina 2008, pp. 1, 4).

Despite the formal end of the conflict in Chechnya, it became clear that security in the region was indivisible. This was reflected in attempts by the interior ministries in Chechnya and Ingushetiya to coordinate their actions, although Dagestan demonstratively distanced itself from the initiative.[32] As Kadyrov put it in a press conference on 17 May 2009 in Ingushetiya: 'We have agreed that we will fight against the militants together, regardless of which territory they are in. ... I have waited long for this day' (Dzutsev 2009b). In his mind this reinforced long-held Chechen aspirations for the reunification of the two republics, something that is strongly resisted by Ingush elites. While events in the Caucasus have been kept relatively isolated in military terms, their political impact on shaping the Russian state has paradoxically increased.

Conclusion

For as long as Russia has been an independent state in the post-Soviet era, it has been engaged in wars, counter-insurgency operations and socio-religious conflicts in the Caucasus (Hahn 2008). Russia's military engagement has been a mix of conventional warfare and 'state terrorism', if terrorism is defined as the targeting of non-combatants. This was seen at its most vivid in Chechnya, where the insurgency, at least initially, was in part a classic national liberation movement with terrorist features (Hughes 2007a). The character of the conflict repeatedly changed, and became increasingly a type of civil war within Chechnya and the region as a whole between separatist militants and those willing to seek accommodation with Moscow, accompanied by a change in ideological emphasis in the former from a national liberation to an Islamist supra-national rhetoric (Falkowski 2007). The declaration of the Caucasus emirate in November 2007 subordinated Chechen national goals to the broader struggle for an expansive anti-modern and anti-statist form of universal Islam.

The changing pattern of conflicts in the Caucasus affected the character of state building in Moscow, although their constitutive impact took some unexpected forms. Undoubtedly venal concerns were involved, notably a share of the funds devoted to the restoration of the Chechen Republic, but more importantly, the methods employed in the struggle against the insurgency across the region fostered a broader process of the meta-corruption of the political system in its entirety. Bribery and corruption is one thing, but the persistent use of extra-judicial mechanisms to achieve short-term victories in the long-run undermined the coherence of the state in whose name these methods were used. Equally, 'Chechenisation' represented an extreme form of the segmented regionalism that had characterised Russia's federal system in the 1990s. The existence of this enclave of extra-constitutionalism threatened to undermine the legitimacy of the Russian state in its entirety.

The 'normalisation' of Chechnya was accompanied by a degree of Chechenisation of Russia, a distinctive type of 'blowback' whose full repercussions are yet to be felt. The establishment of what is in effect an enclave of the arbitrary state (despite its contradictions with the central version of this state) was at best a partial solution if Russia was serious about its commitments to democracy and the

[32] 'What is Ramzan Kadyrov's New Game Plan?', *RFE/RL, Russia Report*, 21 May 2009.

treaties to which it signed up as part of its commitments on joining the Council of Europe and other bodies. It is for this reason that Medvedev sought to 'regionalise', and thus to dilute and partially reverse, Kadyrovism as a form of outsourced rule (Sakwa 2010a). Equally, territories which labour under the title of 'frozen conflict' are typically denigrated as 'criminal enclaves' by the titular nation, and the term describes less the actual level of banditry as the fact that their disputed status makes legal cross border activities almost impossible, and thus enterprises are forced to circumvent by fair means or foul what in most cases are economic embargos. Chechnya, however, is in a different category, since its legal status is not contested in international law, but its ambivalent political status is entrenched by a set of informal political practices, which in turn reinforces informal practices in the Russian government as a whole.

The Russo-Georgian War created a new geopolitical environment in the Caucasus. Hitherto obscured regional dimensions came into greater prominence, while others lost some of their salience. The Moscow Declaration of November 2008 by the Russian, Armenian and Azerbaijani presidents added a new urgency to resolving the Nagorno-Karabakh question, while Armenian–Turkish rapprochement gained added pace. There would be no immediate breakthroughs on these or other conflicts, but it was clear that a new fluidity was introduced into regional problems. In this essay I have argued that a multi-level approach to regionalism fosters differentiated approaches to some of the most difficult issues in the region. As De Waal (2010, p. 226) puts it, 'More division and conflict can be avoided if the different parts of the South Caucasus start to think less like individual actors and more like members of a region'. When analysis operates on only one plane, a partial view is provided (Asmus 2010). This applies as much to analysis of a particular conflict, as we saw in our examination of Chechnya, as it does to regional studies as a whole.

The existence of sub-national struggles can be understood not only in the context of meso-regions, in our case the Caucasus, but also in the framework of macro-regions and mega-regions. The attempt to establish a national political community intersects with other regionalisms. The question whether the whole former Soviet area constitutes a single definable proto-political community is countered by the advance into the region of a new form of political community in the form of the EU, and both are countered by the vision of a security community advanced by the United States. The creation of two largely unrecognised statelets in the South Caucasus and an intensifying insurgency further north means that all the states in the region have become 'trapped' in a sovereignty–recognition impasse that can only be transcended when the various regional layers come into alignment. The recognition of competing regionalisms is only the first, but necessary, step to overcome the clash of regionalisms.

The University of Kent

References

Ágh, A. (2010) 'Regionalisation as a Driving Force of EU Widening: Recovering from the EU "Carrot Crisis" in the "East"', *Europe-Asia Studies*, 62, 8, October, pp. 1239–66.

Akkieva, S. (2008) 'The Caucasus: One or Many? A View from the Region', *Nationalities Papers*, 36, 2, May, pp. 253–73.

Amundsen, I. (2008) 'Clarity in the Chechen Resistance', *Chechnya Weekly*, 9, 3, 24 January.
Asmus, R. (2010) *A Little War that Shook the World: Georgia, Russia and the Future of the West* (Basingstoke, Palgrave Macmillan).
Barabanov, M., Lavrov, A. & Tseluiko, V. (eds) (2009) *Tanki avgusta: Sbornik statei* (Moscow, Tsentr Strategii i Tekhnologii), available at: http://www.cast.ru/comments/?id=351, accessed 9 October 2010.
Buzan, B., Waever, W. & de Wilde, J. (1997) *Security: A New Framework for Analysis* (Boulder, CO, Lynne Rienner Publishers).
Cheterian, V. (2008) *War and Peace in the Caucasus: Ethnic Politics and the New Geopolitics* (New York, Columbia University Press).
Dannreuther, R. & March, L. (2008) 'Chechnya: Has Moscow Won?', *Survival*, 50, 4, pp. 97–112.
De Waal, T. (2010) *The Caucasus: An Introduction* (Oxford, Oxford University Press).
Derluguian, G. M. (2005) *Bourdieu's Secret Admirer in the Caucasus: A World-System Biography* (Chicago, IL, University of Chicago Press).
Dzutsev, V. (2009a) 'Moscow and Grozny Maintain the Illusion that the War has Ended', *Jamestown Foundation's North Caucasus Weekly*, 10, 18, 8 May.
Dzutsev, V. (2009b) 'Moscow Sees Chechnya's Kadyrov as a Silver Bullet for the North Caucasus', *North Caucasus Weekly*, 10, 20, 22 May.
Dzutsev, V. (2009c) 'North Caucasus Cossacks are also Victims of Moscow's Policies in the Region', *Jamestown Foundation's Eurasia Daily Monitor*, 6, 134, 14 July.
Dzutsev, V. (2009d) 'North Caucasus' Ethnic Russian Population Shrinks as Indigenous Populations Grow', *Jamestown Foundation's Eurasia Daily Monitor*, 6, 210, 13 November.
Falkowski, M. (2007) 'Chechnya: Between a Caucasian Jihad and "Hidden" Separatism', *OSW Policy Brief*, January (Warsaw, Centre for Eastern Studies).
Gadzhiev, K. S. (2001) *Geopolitika kavkaza* (Moscow, Mezhdunarodnye otnosheniya).
Gammer, M. (2006) *The Lone Wolf and the Bear: Three Centuries of Chechen Defiance of Russian Rule* (Pittsburgh, University of Pittsburgh Press).
Hagendoorn, L., Poppe, E. & Minescu, A. (2008) 'Support for Separatism in Ethnic Republics of the Russian Federation', *Europe-Asia Studies*, 60, 3, pp. 353–73.
Hahn, G. M. (2007) *Russia's Islamic Challenge* (New Haven, CT, Yale University Press).
Hahn, G. M. (2008) 'The *Jihadi* Insurgency and the Russian Counterinsurgency in the North Caucasus', *Post-Soviet Affairs*, 24, 1, pp. 1–39.
Hahn, G. M. (2010) 'Caucasus Emirate (CE) Mujahedin', Monterey Terrorism and Research Program (MonTREP), Monterey Institute for International Studies, *Islam, Islamism and Politics in Eurasia Report*, 9, 24 February.
Hill, F. & Taspiner, O. (2006) 'Turkey and Russia: Axis of the Excluded?', *Survival*, 48, 1, pp. 81–92.
Hughes, J. (2007a) 'The Chechnya Conflict: Freedom Fighters or Terrorists?', *Demokratizatsiya*, 15, 3, pp. 293–311.
Hughes, J. (2007b) *Chechnya: From Nationalism to Jihad* (Philadelphia, PA, University of Pennsylvania Press).
Kavkazcenter (2006) 'Basaev Threatens to Cross the Volga', *Chechnya Weekly*, VII, 2, 12 January, available at: http://www.kavkazcenter.com/russ/archive.php, accessed 8 October 2008.
Khinstein, A. (2005) 'Prodaem Kavkaz', *Moskovskii komsomolets*, 16 June.
King, C. (2008) *The Ghost of Freedom: A History of the Caucasus* (Oxford, Oxford University Press).
Kolstø, P. & Blakkisrud, H. (2008), 'Living with Non-Recognition: State- and Nation-building in South Caucasian Quasi-states', *Europe-Asia Studies*, 60, 3, pp. 483–509.
Kotkin, S. (2009) 'The Unbalanced Triangle: What Chinese–Russian Relations Mean for the United States', *Foreign Affairs*, 88, 5, pp. 130–38.
Kramer, M. (2005) 'Guerrilla Warfare, Counterinsurgency and Terrorism in the North Caucasus: The Military Dimension of the Russian–Chechen Conflict', *Europe-Asia Studies*, 57, 2, March, pp. 209–90.
Lavrov, A. (2009a) 'Poslevoennoe obustroistvo vooruzhennykh sil Rossii v novopriznannykh respublikakh Abkhaziya i Yuzhnaya Osetiya', in Barabanov, M. *et al.* (eds) (2009), pp. 127–40.
Lavrov, S. (2009b) 'Interview of the Russian Minister of Foreign Affairs with the BBC Russian Service', 23 April, available at: www.mid.ru.
Lo, B. (2008) *Axis of Convenience: Moscow, Beijing and the New Geopolitics* (London, Blackwell for RIIA & Washington, DC, Brookings Institution Press).
Malashenko, A. (2007a) 'Khotyat li russkie v Chechniyu', *Nezavisimaya gazeta: NG Regiony*, 23 July.
Malashenko, A. (2007b) 'The Two Faces of Chechnya', Carnegie Moscow Center, *Briefing*, 9, 3, July.

Malashenko, A. (2008) 'Privychnoe sostoranie nestabil'nosti: o vozmozhnykh posledstviyakh nedavnei kavkazskoi voiny', *Nezavisimaya gazeta*, 8 October, p. 7.
Malashenko, A. (2009) 'Losing the Caucasus', Carnegie Moscow Center, *Briefing*, 11, 3, August.
Mandaville, P. (2007) *Global Political Islam* (London, Routledge).
Matsuzato, K. (2005) 'Preface', in Matsuzato, K. (ed.) (2005) *Emerging Meso-Areas in the Former Socialist Countries: Histories Revived or Improvised* (Sapporo, Slavic Research Center, Hokkaido University).
Medvedev, D. (2010) 'V Rossii obrazovan novyi federal'nyi okrug—Severo-Kavkazskii', available at: http://www.kremlin.ru/transcripts/6664, accessed 10 January 2010.
Milikishvili, A. (2009) 'Moscow and Tskhinvali Finally Agree Russian Federal Aid Deal for South Ossetia', *Jamestown Foundation's Eurasia Daily Monitor*, 6, 65, 6 April.
Miller, A. I. (ed.) (2007) *Severnyi Kavkaz v sostave Rossiiskoi Imperii* (Moscow, Novoe Literaturnoe Obozrenie).
Moore, C. (2006) 'Reading the Hermeneutics of Violence: The Literary Turn and Chechnya', *Global Society*, 20, 2, April, pp. 179–98.
Moore, C. & Tumelty, P. (2008) 'Foreign Fighters and the Case of Chechnya: A Critical Assessment', *Studies in Conflict and Terrorism*, 31, 5, pp. 412–33.
Nalbandov, R. (2009) 'Battle of Two Logics: Appropriateness and Consequentiality in Russian Interventions in Georgia', *Caucasian Review of International Affairs*, 3, 1, Winter, pp. 20–35.
Pavković, A. & Radan, P. (2007) *Creating New States: Theory and Practice of Secession* (Aldershot, Ashgate).
Petrov, N. (2007) 'Kozak's Regional Recipe', *Moscow Times*, 6 November.
Petrov, N. (2008) 'Moscow Losing Clout in the Regions', *Moscow Times*, 28 October.
Phillips, T. (2007) *Beslan: The Tragedy of School No. 1* (London, Granta Books).
Putin, V. (2000) *First Person: An Astonishingly Frank Self-Portrait by Russia's President Vladimir Putin* [with Nataliya Gevorkyan, Natalya Timakova & Andrei Kolesnikov, translated by Catherine A. Fitzpatrick] (London, Hutchinson).
Radnitz, S. (2006) 'Look Who's Talking! Islamic Discourse in the Chechen Wars', *Nationalities Papers*, 34, 2, May, pp. 237–56.
Rice, C. (2008) 'Rice Speech at German Marshall Fund on US–Russia Relations: US, Europe Must Not Allow Russia's Aggression, Says Secretary Rice', 18 September, Washington, DC, US Department of State, available at: http://www.america.gov/st/texttrans-english/2008/September/20080918155132eaifas0.4152033.html, accessed 29 November 2010.
Richmond, W. (2008) *The Northwest Caucasus: Past, Present, Future* (London, Routledge).
Roshchin, M. (2009) 'Caucasus Emirate: Virtual Myth or Reality?', *North Caucasus Weekly*, 10, 10, 13 March.
Russell, J. (2002) 'Mujahedeen, Mafia, Madmen: Russian Perceptions of Chechens During the Wars in Chechnya, 1994–96 and 1999–2001', *Journal of Communist Studies and Transition Politics*, 18, 1, March, pp. 73–96.
Russell, J. (2005) 'Terrorists, Bandits, Spooks and Thieves: Russian Demonisation of the Chechens Before and Since 9/11', *Third World Quarterly*, 26, 1, pp. 101–16.
Sagramoso, D. (2007) 'Violence and Conflict in the Russian North Caucasus', *International Affairs*, 83, 4, pp. 681–705.
Sakwa, R. (ed.) (2005) *Chechnya: From Past to Future* (London, Anthem Press & Sterling, VA, Stylus Publishers).
Sakwa, R. (2010a) 'The Dual State in Russia', *Post-Soviet Affairs*, 26, 3, July–September, pp. 185–206.
Sakwa, R. (2010b) 'The Revenge of the Caucasus: Chechenization and the Dual State in Russia', *Nationalities Papers*, 38, 5, September, pp. 601–22.
Samarina, A. (2008) 'Eduard Kokoity progovorilsya', *Nezavisimaya gazeta*, 12–13 September, pp. 1–4.
Shenfield, S. (2008) 'The Circassians', Special Issue of *JRL Research and Analytical Supplement* No. 42, May, *Johnson's Russia List*, 93.
Slider, D. (2008) 'Putin's "Southern Strategy": Dmitriy Kozak and the Dilemmas of Recentralization', *Post-Soviet Affairs*, 24, 2, April–June, pp. 177–97.
Slider, D. (2010) 'Medvedev and the Governors', *Russian Analytical Digest*, 86, 16 November, pp. 2–4.
Smirnov, A. (2006) 'Russian Generals Warn of New Rebel Offensive in the North Caucasus', *Jamestown Foundation's Eurasia Daily Monitor*, 3, 8, 12 January.
Sokirianskaia, E. (2010) 'State-Building and Political Integration in Ingushetia and Chechnya (1991–2009)', *Russian Analytical Digest*, 86, 16 November, pp. 4–7.
Tlisova, F. (2007) 'Understanding the Roots of the Conflict in Ingushetia', *Chechnya Weekly*, 8, 38, 4 October.

Tlisova, F. (2010) 'Moscow Uses Commission on "Historical Falsification" to Deny Circassian Rights', Jamestown Foundation's *Eurasia Daily Monitor*, 7, 14, 21 January.
Torbakov, I. (2008) *The Georgia Crisis and Russia–Turkey Relations* (Washington, DC, The Jamestown Foundation).
Tseluiko, V. (2009) 'Nastoryashchee i budushchee gruzino-rossiiskogo konflikta: Voennyi aspekt', in Barabanov, M. *et al.* (eds) (2009), pp. 85–108.
Tsygankov, A. P. (2009a) 'Blaming Moscow: The Power of the Anti-Russia Lobby', *Global Dialogue*, 11, Winter/Spring, Special Issue 'After Georgia', available at: http://www.worlddialogue.org/content.php?id=448, accessed 10 January 2010.
Tsygankov, A. P. (2009b) *Russophobia: Anti-Russian Lobby and American Foreign Policy* (Basingstoke, Palgrave Macmillan).
Tsygankov, A. P. (2010) 'Russia's Power and Alliances in the 21st Century', *Politics*, 30, S1, pp. 43–51.
Vatchagaev, M. (2008a) 'Zakaev's Attempts to Persuade Dokka [Doku] Umarov are in Vain', *North Caucasus Weekly*, 9, 24, 19 June.
Vatchagaev, M. (2008b) 'The Chechen Reaction to the Georgian Crisis', *North Caucasus Weekly*, 9, 34, 11 September.
Vatchagaev, M. (2009) 'No Let Up in Insurgent Attacks in the North Caucasus', *Jamestown Foundation's Eurasia Daily Monitor*, 6, 113, 12 June.
Ware, R. B. (2005) 'A Multitude of Evils: Mythology and Political Failure in Chechnya', in Sakwa, R. (ed.) (2005), pp. 79–116.
Warhola, J. W. &. Mitchell, W. A. (2006) 'The Warming of Turkish–Russian Relations: Motives and Implications', *Demokratizatsiya*, 14, 1, pp. 127–43.
Wilhellmsen, J. (2005) 'Between a Rock and a Hard Place: The Islamisation of the Chechen Separatist Movement', *Europe-Asia Studies*, 57, 1, January, pp. 35–59.
Wood, T. (2007) *Chechnya: The Case for Independence* (London, Verso).
Yemelianova, G. (2002) *Russia and Islam: A Historical Survey* (Basingstoke, Palgrave).
Zielonka, J. (2007) *Europe as Empire: The Nature of the Enlarged European Union* (Oxford, Oxford University Press).

Has the Russian Federation Been Chechenised?

ROBERT WARE

In every victory, there is a defeat; in every defeat, a victory. (Russian Proverb)

DID CHECHNYA CHECHENISE VLADIMIR PUTIN before Putin Chechenised Chechnya? To what extent was Vladimir Putin's approach to the administration of Russia, and particularly of the North Caucasus, influenced by crises that he faced during his first formative months of power in 1999? Did the Kremlin's Chechenisation programme become a template not only for the stabilisation of Chechnya, but for the long-term administration of its North Caucasian neighbours, and finally for the reconstitution of the Russian Federation? How have instabilities in the North Caucasus been affected by the evolution of Russian federalism, and how have they affected that evolution?

This article considers the extent to which instabilities in the North Caucasus and the evolution of the Russian Federation have shaped each other reciprocally since 1999. It suggests that Russia's federal recentralisation has inadvertently contributed to regional problems of political corruption, political alienation, and Islamist extremism, while these regional problems have contributed to authoritarian, bureaucratic, and centralising trends in the Russian Federation. It proposes that Russians have fallen into a vicious cycle of horizontal resistance and vertical reaction that may be as self-perpetuating as it is self-defeating.

Whereas many studies have examined the effects that the Russian Federation has had upon events in this region, there has been much less attention to ways in which the causal relationship has also been reversed.[1] Is there something faintly, if inadvertently, patronising in the tendency to ignore the other side of the causal relationship? Has there been a tendency to view the peoples of the North Caucasus in primarily passive roles, receiving policy directives and reacting to changes imposed upon them from Moscow, rather than as reciprocally causing important changes in the Russian Federation itself? In fact, events in the North Caucasus have caused exactly that at a series of crucial junctures. First, Putin became Russia's Prime Minister in August

The author is grateful to Cameron Ross and Sarah Lennon.

[1]An exception is Peter Reddaway *et al.* (2004, pp. 1–45).

1999, just one week after Chechnya-based militants invaded Dagestan, and his administrative style was cast in the opening months of the ensuing war. Second, shortly after his presidential inauguration in May 2000, Putin announced the reorganisation of the Russian Federation on the model of Russia's seven military districts. Third, on 13 September 2004—barely one week after the Beslan hostage crisis, and in explicit response to 'terrorist' threats—Putin announced the centralised appointment of Russia's regional governors, and an overhaul of the Russian electoral system that promised additional strength for the party of power. Fourth, in January 2010, President Dmitry Medvedev announced the formation of the North Caucasus Federal District with a focus upon the endemic problems of the region.

Putin's Caucasian ascent

Throughout his terms as Russia's President, Boris Yel'tsin veered erratically through a series of prime ministerial appointments, finally selecting Sergei Stepashin in May 1999. And when militants from Chechnya invaded Dagestan on 2 August that year, the chaotic federal response was uncomfortably emblematic of Yel'tsin's bumbling administration. Chechnya had achieved *de facto* independence from Moscow in 1996, and particularly with the spread of Islamist militancy through the region there was concern, both in Moscow and in the West, that other North Caucasian republics would follow, perhaps jeopardising the cohesion of the Russian Federation as a whole (Evangelista 2002).

Thus the stakes could not have been higher for the Russian Federation, when—just one week after the invasion of Dagestan began—Yel'tsin appointed the obscure director of the Federal Security Service (FSB), Vladimir Putin, as prime minister. At the time, Putin seemed an unlikely prime minister; yet his self-assured approach to the military operation in Dagestan won immediate public approval, as did his belligerent reaction to apartment bombings in Moscow and Volgodansk that September (Ware 2005a, 2005b; Ware & Kisriev 2009).

Whatever the tendency in Putin's earlier career toward values of national security, military strength, and centralised control, these were brought to the fore as critical imperatives during Russia's defence of Dagestan in August and September of 1999, and in its subsequent invasion of Chechnya. By the time that Boris Yel'tsin resigned from the Russian presidency, such priorities were clearly ascendant over policies of decentralisation and local democratic control that characterised the Yel'tsin years. Indeed, since Yel'tsin's waffling on these points had much to do with the start of the first Chechen conflict, the vicious cycle of Russian federal evolution and North Caucasian conflict can be extended back at least as far as 1991.

From his first weeks in power, both Putin's administration and popular perceptions thereof were indelibly stamped by imperatives in the northeast Caucasus. His leadership style and administrative priorities were arguably cast during the military and political trauma of those initial months. It is symbolic of his dramatic ascent that at the stroke of the New Year 2000, the very moment of Yel'tsin's surprise resignation, Putin was not seated at the feet of his disgraced superior, but at the table of his new-found allies in Dagestan. 'I love the people of Dagestan', he toasted.[2]

Russian recentralisation

If the signature of Yel'tsin's administration had been radical decentralisation, Putin dedicated his presidency to precisely the opposite course and, in May 2000, he initiated his programme for the recentralisation of Russia. Given the early success of his militaristic approach to Dagestan and Chechnya, it came as little surprise that his bureaucratic model was Russian military organisation. Just as the latter was organised through its central command of seven districts, so was the new federal state. The North Caucasus fell into the nascent Southern Federal District, which was headed by General Victor Kazantsev from its inception on 18 May 2000 to 9 March 2004. Kazantsev led the federal military response to the invasions of Dagestan in 1999, and was a participant in both Chechen wars.

Initially this federal district was called 'Northern Caucasian', but the name was changed at Kazantsev's request. The name was altered ostensibly to reflect the fact that in addition to traditionally North Caucasian Republics (Dagestan, Chechnya, Ingushetiya, North Ossetiya, Kabardino-Balkariya, Karacheyvo-Cherkessiya and Adygeya), other southern Russian areas, such as Krasnadarskii and Stavropolskii *Krai*, the Rostovskaya *Oblast'* and two other territories, were also included. However, the revised title also indicated an altered geopolitical orientation wherein Moscow served as the point of reference. Thus a district may have been north of the main range of the Caucasus Mountains, but more importantly it was also south of Moscow.

The process of federal recentralisation had a distinctive effect on each of the members of the Southern District, as indeed it did on all 89 subjects of the Russian Federation. Yet the diverging paths that it took in Russia's three southern-most republics—Dagestan, Chechnya and Ingushetiya—proved to be of particular significance.

Russian recentralisation in Dagestan

During the final years of the USSR and the first years of Yel'tsin's presidency, power in Dagestan had devolved from Soviet verticality[3] toward the ancient, and horizontally pluralistic, traditions of Dagestan's 34 ethno-linguistic groups. An intense but largely peaceful power struggle among a multiplicity of Soviet elite members, ethnic leaders, village elders, mountain clans, and emerging entrepreneurs, culminated on 26 July 1994 in the adoption of an innovative democratic constitution (Ware & Kisriev 2001a). In accord with its pluralistic traditions, Dagestan had the only collegial executive in the Russian Federation, and the only executive that was not chosen directly by popular vote. In a series of three referenda, Dagestanis rejected a

[2]As of July 2009, Putin's toast was displayed on a billboard near government buildings on the main square of the Dagestani city of Makhachkala.

[3]Despite egalitarian aspirations of Marxist ideology, the Soviet government was organised in terms of a centralised, vertically hierarchical bureaucracy. This organisation contrasted with the egalitarian and pluralistic traditions of highland societies. Putin's recentralised bureaucracy is often described as 'the power vertical'.

popularly elected president for fear that the direct election of an individual leader would result in disproportionate power for a single ethnic group (Ware & Kisriev 2001a).

Dagestan's State Council (*Gossovet*) consisted of one representative from each of its 14 principal ethnic groups. Yet while tenure of the Chair of the State Council was intended to rotate, it was monopolised by the representative from the Dargin ethnic group, Magomedali Magomedov. Dagestan also developed an ethnic electoral system that provided legislative representation nearly precisely proportionate to the population of most ethnic groups (Ware & Kisriev 2001a). Thus as a natural result of local demographics and ancient traditions, Dagestan's constitution varied substantially from its federal counterpart.

In April 2000, almost immediately following Putin's election as president, federal officials requested that the attorney general of Dagestan, Imam Yaraliev, identify all articles of the Dagestani Constitution that did not match the Constitution of the Russian Federation. Yaraliev identified 45 points of variance. When Moscow rejected a series of compromises, Dagestan's legislature made the requisite constitutional amendments. The following month Russia's Constitutional Court began a review of Dagestan's ethnic electoral system, thereby initiating a series of modifications that brought Dagestani elections into conformity with federal requirements over the next five years. Under federal pressure, Dagestan formally adopted a presidential system in 2003, nine years to the day after it had ratified its collegial executive (Ware & Kisriev 2001a, 2009).

Most Dagestanis viewed these changes with ambivalence. Throughout its nine years of operation, Dagestan's innovative democratic system had accomplished two primary objectives. It achieved ethnic proportionality, and it maintained political stability—even in those years when all surrounding territories were mired in protracted ethnic conflicts. Yet, Dagestan's economy remained stagnant, and available resources were increasingly monopolised by a shrinking circle of elites. Corruption was ubiquitous, economic disparities rankled traditionally egalitarian sensibilities and Islamist extremism smouldered. Since the pluralism of Dagestan's political system mitigated against a bold and comprehensive approach to these problems, many Dagestanis hoped that the federal imposition of a centralised administration would alleviate some of these problems.

Centralisation and Chechenisation

Federal forces crossed into Chechnya on 1 October 1999 and claimed control of its capital, Grozny, on 6 February 2000. Over the next decade fighting gradually diminished, but never completely ceased. On 12 June 2000, President Putin selected the Chechen mufti, Akhmed Kadyrov, to head the new loyalist Chechen administration. Putin's plan was to turn the Chechen conflict over to the Kadyrov regime, which would be integrated as a local extension of federally centralised bureaucratic structures. The plan was feasible because Chechens like Kadyrov had been alienated by Islamists, who had contributed to the fragmentation of Chechen society during its period of *de facto* independence from August 1996 to October 1999 (Ware 2005b). Kadyrov himself had fought against Russia in the first Chechen War, but was now prepared to align with old adversaries against his new Islamist enemies. Until his assassination in May 2004, Akhmed Kadyrov was a ruthless tactician, offering amnesties to Chechen militants at the same time that he made their operations more perilous. As more rebels switched sides, Kadyrov welcomed them into his administration, consolidated his power, and grew increasingly independent from Moscow.

At the time that the programme of Chechenisation was initiated in 2000, Chechnya was Russia's least integrated region in the sense that it was the only Russian Republic in which a war of separatism was being waged. The argument of this essay is that this programme of Chechenisation, which initially was designed for this dramatically exceptional republic, eventually became the template for the restructuring of the entire Russian Federation. These fundamental premises concerned the Kremlin's appointment of a local governor who was thereafter allowed to operate with substantial autonomy in exchange for guarantees of local stability and federal fealty. Thus the policy of Chechenisation was given an ironic twist in September 2004, when Putin announced that all local governors would be appointed by the Kremlin on terms that were to be broadly similar to those of Kadyrov. Yet this was not to be the only irony of Chechenisation.

The term 'Chechenisation' initially described a set of Kremlin policies that gave the Chechen administration of Akhmed Kadyrov responsibility for the conflict in Chechnya, aiming to relieve Russian troops of some combat duties by effectively predetermining a Chechen civil war. Putin's Chechenisation policy was consistent with Russian recentralisation in that both sought to stabilise the Republic under local leadership operating within the federal bureaucratic framework.

Yet the Chechenisation of the conflict also bore alternative connotations for those with opposing aspirations. For the Islamist ideologues of what later became the self-styled Caucasus Emirate, 'Chechenisation' suggested the export of Islamic *sharia* law throughout the North Caucasus, much as a *sharia* was established in Chechnya in February 1999. Chechenisation from this perspective presupposed the intensification of conflict between Russian and Islamist forces along with its expansion to other parts of the region. These aspirations were realised, for example, by attacks in Mozdok, North Ossetiya, on 5 June and 1 August 2003; in Nazran, Ingushetiya, on 21 June 2004; in Beslan, North Ossetiya on 1 September 2004; and in Nalchik, Kabardino-Balkariya on 13 October 2005.[4] In those years, journalists and policy makers commonly described these conflicts as 'spilling across Chechnya's borders to neighbouring republics'.[5] 'Chechenisation' in this sense suggested expanded violence, growing instability, and greater regional control for the Islamists.

[4]Although the aspiration endures and although his tactics have outlived him, all of these attacks were to one degree or another the work of Chechen leader, Shamil Basaev. Basaev never overcame the spectacular success of his raid on the town of Budenovsk on 15 June 1995. He spent the remaining 11 years of his life vainly trying to repeat it—even in his ill-fated invasions of Dagestan in 1999. During those years, much of the misery of this region, and much of the failure of the Chechen cause, may be attributed to Basaev's personal vanity. Salman Raduev's attack on Kizlyar, Dagestan in January 1996 was another catastrophic attempt to copy Budenovsk.

[5]See for example, 'Spreading Despair', *Human Rights Watch*, 21 September 2003; '75 Die as Chechen Rebels Stage Raid Across Border', *New York Times*, 23 June 2004; 'Conflict in Chechnya', British House of Commons Report, 7 February 2000.

Ironically, Chechenisation occurred in both of these senses at once: the conflict in Chechnya became a civil war that gradually sidelined Russian forces in Chechnya, even as it 'spilled into neighbouring republics'. Of course, the ostensibly 'overflowing' insurgency actually had much to do with endemic problems in surrounding territories. These problems included local variations on the themes of political corruption, economic disparity, organised crime and police brutality that provoked distinctive forms of militancy and protest. Over the years, these local distinctions added further nuances as the implications of Chechenisation rippled further outward from Chechnya, across the North Caucasus, and then across the breadth of Russia.

Second appointment in Chechnya

After Akhmed Kadyrov's assassination, for which Shamil Basaev claimed responsibility, real power soon passed to Kadyrov's son, Ramzan, who ruthlessly prosecuted his father's policies. Ramzan Kadyrov's personal militia overshadowed those of rival loyalist warlords, including Movladi Baysarov, Said-Magomed Kakiev and the Yamadaev brothers. By the beginning of 2008, Ramzan had eliminated his rivals, and had taken control of all other Defence and Interior Ministry Forces operating in Chechnya, with the sole exception of the Yamadaevs and their Vostok Battalion.

Moscow gradually ceded combat, administrative, and reconstructive responsibilities to former separatists in the Kadyrov administration, allocating vast sums of money to its Chechen proxies. Between 2002 and 2006, Moscow sent subsidies totalling R30.6 billion ($1.25 billion). In July 2007, Ramzan Kadyrov asked Putin for R168.8 billion ($6.6 billion) until the end of 2010 (Goble 2007). Moscow was ineffective in tracking this money, though federal audits uncovered evidence of widespread corruption. Nevertheless Kadyrov could present Chechenisation as a successful policy. Chechnya was being stabilised and reconstructed as a federal subject. In addition to rapid residential and commercial development in the republic's urban areas, Grozny had a refurbished university, a new hospital, and a new airport with daily flights to Moscow. The capital's central square was dominated by a new mosque, accommodating 10,000 worshippers. As the economy gradually recovered, future stability seemed assured.

How did Chechenisation culminate in centralised control and local autonomy?

In April 2008, tensions flared between Kadyrov and his last remaining rival, Sulim Yamadaev. Yamadaev commanded the Vostok Battalion of Chechen fighters, who operated under the auspices of Russian Military Intelligence (*Glavnoe Razvedyvatel'noe Upravlenie*, GRU). Approximately 375 Vostok troops had been responsible for combating rebels in eastern Chechnya, while Kadyrov personally controlled over 10,000 fighters.

In the city of Gudermes, on 14 April, a convoy of Vostok vehicles did not yield to Kadyrov's motorcade, causing a crash and a fatal skirmish. On 17 April, Chechnya's parliament urged Russian Defence Minister Anatoly Serdyukov to dissolve Vostok or replace Yamadaev. On 19 April, there was a meeting of Defence Ministry officials to consider the future of the Vostok Battalion. The meeting was attended by General Aleksandr Baranov, Commander of the North Caucasus Military District, and

General-Colonel Sergei Makarov, the Chief of the Staff of the District (Smirnov 2008). The military leadership decided to postpone a decision until after Dmitry Medvedev's presidential inauguration at the beginning of May. Immediately after the meeting, GRU Special Forces were dispatched to defend the main Vostok base against any hostile actions by Kadyrov's men. The move was widely seen as victory for Yamadaev, who called Kadyrov 'a coward' on a popular Russian radio programme that same day (Smirnov 2008), but Chechenisation had further surprises in store.

If Vladimir Putin's ascendance to the Russian presidency was the beginning of the end for Chechen independence, there is a sense in which Dmitry Medvedev's succession marked the quiet beginning of its reprise. In the week following his inauguration in May 2008, President Medvedev overruled powerful forces within the Russian Defence Ministry to consolidate Kadyrov's control. On 12 May, Kadyrov announced the suspension of Sulim Yamadaev as commander of the Vostok Battalion, and thereby eliminated the last Russian federal security agency that operated in the republic without Kadyrov's approval. On 5 April 2009, the Dubai police accused Adam Delimkhanov of ordering Yamadaev's assassination. Delimkhanov, who is Kadyrov's cousin and close friend, was a member of the Russian State *Duma* for the United Russia (*Edinaya Rossiya*) party. Delimkhanov denied the accusation.

As it turned out, the elimination of the Yamadaev brothers was the culmination of Putin's Chechenisation strategy, and signalled Medvedev's intent to sustain the policies of his predecessor in the North Caucasus. Ironically, Putin brought the North Caucasian republics under Moscow's bureaucratic power by ceding nearly complete local control and large economic subsidies to local elites in exchange for their loyalty to the Kremlin. Medvedev consolidated these policies in Chechnya by sidelining Defence Ministry officials in favour of Kadyrov. Having overcome the last federal agency in Chechnya, Ramzan Kadyrov and his Chechen administration operated in conditions that approached autonomy. After fighting for 15 years to prevent Chechen independence, Moscow subsidised its Chechenised approximation.

Chechenisation effectively meant that Putin and the Kadyrovs had followed one another in the centralisation of authority over their respective spheres of power. Putin was able to work with the Kadyrovs because all three were prepared to compromise other objectives in order to advance centralised authority against those centrifugal forces they encountered in their respective political arenas. By cooperating in their reversal of centrifugal tendencies initiated in the Gorbachev and Yel'tsin eras, Putin and the Kadyrovs achieved a compromise that recentralised the authority of the Russian Federation while allowing extensive autonomy to the bureaucratically-centralised Chechen administration.

In notes of further irony, it must not be forgotten that while this federal compromise was achieved often by brutal means, the precedent was set by Boris Yel'tsin's belated efforts to uphold vertical control in his attack on the Russian legislature in 1993 and his invasion of Chechnya in 1994. It should also be recalled that during its period of *de facto* independence from 1996 to 1999, Chechnya was fractured by intense competition among a raucous multitude of warlords and Islamists (foreign and domestic) culminating in conditions of social fragmentation that were even more dire than those of the Russian Federation itself.

The end of Russia's counter-terrorism operation in Chechnya

Russia's counter-terrorism operation in Chechnya began in 1999 under then Prime Minister Putin. Involving over 80,000 troops, the counter-terrorism operation restricted individual rights, allowed sometimes brutal searches of persons and entire villages, regulated movement and controlled the republic's infrastructure. As Ramzan Kadyrov consolidated power, the counter-terrorism operation was reduced to the operation of airports and customs, as well as a system of checkpoints manned by approximately 20,000 Russian troops. At a meeting in Moscow on 20 March 2009, Kadyrov asked Putin to terminate the counter-terrorism operation.[6] Kadyrov argued that the counter-terrorism operation was no longer useful since Chechnya had been stabilised, the counter-terrorism operation interfered with the development of the Chechen economy and the counter-terrorism operation inhibited private investment in local enterprises.

On 27 March President Dmitry Medvedev asked the FSB's National Anti-terrorist Committee (*Nazional'nyi Anti-Terroristicheskii Komitet*, NAK) to terminate the counter-terrorism operation. On the same day, FSB head Aleksandr Bortnikov said that lifting the counter-terrorism operation would assist the normalisation of the situation in Chechnya, while attracting investors and increasing external trade. On 30 March, a spokesman for the Interior Ministry observed that security issues were no greater in Chechnya than in the neighbouring republics of Dagestan and Ingushetiya, where there was no counter-terrorism operation. On 27 April, the counter-terrorism operation was formally concluded (Goble 2009), and after nine years, the Chechenisation of Chechnya was completed.

The Chechenisation of the North Caucasus

During the intervening years, the bureaucratic model that the Kremlin first introduced with its policy of Chechenisation was elaborated and extended to the administration, first of other North Caucasian republics, and then to all subjects of the Russian Federation. Throughout its proliferation, the distinctive hallmark of the model remained its focus on centralised bureaucratic control, combined with massive subsidies and substantial local autonomy, in exchange for stability and federal fealty.

Appointment in Ingushetiya

As he had first appointed Akhmed Kadyrov to rule Chechnya in 2000, Putin sought to extend central control by installing the president of the neighbouring Republic of Ingushetiya. In 2001, the Kremlin oversaw the removal of Ingushetiya's popularly elected and highly effective president, Ruslan Aushev. Though he had served as a general in Afghanistan, Aushev deplored the brutal military operations that Moscow was mounting in Chechnya. In Aushev's place, Moscow installed a bureaucrat, an obscure and pliable FSB colonel named Murat Zyazikov.

[6]Malashenko (2010); 'Russia Ends Chechnya Operation', *BBC News*, 16 April 2009, available at: http://news.bbc.co.uk/2/hi/europe/8001495.stm, accessed 12 January 2011.

Lacking a local political base, Zyazikov's authority depended more than Kadyrov's upon the unbridled force of federal security organisations. By 2003 young men were disappearing at an alarming rate in sometimes blatant abductions by law enforcement personnel. Along with endemic poverty and rampant government corruption, these disappearances fuelled a violent resistance with Islamist aspirations. On the night of 21 June 2004, Chechen and Ingush fighters launched well-coordinated attacks against law enforcement officials across Ingushetiya. Thereafter these attacks had become near-daily occurrences.

Appointment in Beslan

In August 2004, Shamil Basaev took credit for orchestrating explosions in the Moscow metro and on two of Russia's passenger aircraft. Then on 1 September, a group of mostly Chechen and Ingush militants operating under Basaev's direction commandeered School No. 1 in Beslan, North Ossetiya. They held over 1,100 hostages under harsh conditions in the school gymnasium. Following events that remain controversial, at least 334 hostages died, including 186 children. The episode shocked the world, convulsed Russia, and altered the course of Islamist militancy in the North Caucasus. Though his invasions of Dagestan had not substantially discredited Basaev outside of Russia, the events in Beslan were condemned across the Muslim world, and he was blamed even by some of his militant Chechen supporters.

Citing this security crisis, President Putin called for a strongly centralised federal bureaucracy. In his speech on 13 September 2004, he announced plans to augment federal control by giving the Russian President power to nominate regional governors with the 'endorsement' of regional legislatures, much as appointments previously made in Chechnya and Ingushetiya. In a sense, Russia's remaining 87 regions were now being 'Chechenised'.

At the same time, Putin expressed support for a Central Election Commission proposal to eliminate the single mandate constituencies that accounted for half of the seats in the Russian State *Duma*, thereafter requiring that all *Duma* representatives should be seated from lists compiled by the national parties. This move effectively eliminated independent deputies in the *Duma*, strengthened party control of the body, and effectively reduced the number of viable federal parties. At the time of the announcement, the pro-Kremlin, United Russia Party enjoyed a two-thirds majority in the *Duma*, sufficient to initiate amendments to the constitution. Proponents argued that these changes would reduce local corruption, streamline decision making, and strengthen government control in response to threats such as North Caucasian terrorism.

Appointment in Kabardino-Balkariya

In September 2005, Putin appointed Arsen Kanokov, a Moscow-based businessman, as president of Kabardino-Balkariya. Putin clearly hoped that his policy of giving free reign to an entrepreneur who had found success outside the republic would help to stem corruption and promote economic reform. One month later, Chechen and Ingush militants led local fighters in attacks against several sites in the capital city of Nalchik.

To his credit, Kanokov has marginally reduced federal subsidies, and some economic indicators have shown slight improvement. Yet the key agricultural and mining industries have gravely deteriorated, and lowland resorts, which traditionally provided jobs to thousands of local people, remain closed. Some highland ski resorts have opened, but these have been constructed on traditional Balkar grazing land. They have thereby benefited the Kabardin elite at the Balkar's expense, and have exacerbated smouldering ethnic tensions. The only flourishing industry is the production of alcoholic beverages. Clan elites have seized much of the remaining economy and respond to interference with tactics that range from the formal-legal to the unabashedly lawless. Unemployment is officially estimated at 23%—three times the national average—though the true figure is thought to be much greater.[7]

Appointment in Dagestan

On 16 February 2006, Putin passed over Magomedali Magomedov—the long-time chair of Dagestan's State Council—to appoint Mukhu Aliev as Dagestan's first president. Aliev is an ethnic Avar, who once served as leader of Dagestan's Communist Party (*Kommunisticheskaya Partiya Dagestana*), and went on to chair Dagestan's assembly while Magomedov led the State Council. Aliev's appointment suggested that the Kremlin had learned a lesson from its disastrous installation of Murat Zyazikov in Ingushetiya. Aliev was widely viewed as a principled leader without allegiance to any of Dagestan's clans or factions. Expectations rose following his early efforts to rationalise bureaucratic appointments and eliminate some corrupt local officials. These expectations culminated in a series of popular protests against local administrative abuses. Without warning, and with unprecedented brutality, some protests were suppressed by government forces. In defence of this suppression, Aliev stated that the government could not yield to popular protests because it would be a slippery slope to increasing demands and eventual chaos (Ware & Kisriev 2009).

This turn of events focused attention upon the fact that Aliev and other Dagestani administrators were no longer accountable to the local population, so much as to the central bureaucracy in Moscow. When this became evident, Aliev lost much of his popular support. Thereafter he proved to be no more effective at suppressing Islamist insurgency than at stimulating economic development. As leadership stalled, political power contracted into smaller circles. Protest was stifled, while economic disparities were ostentatiously flaunted. Corruption flourished in the increasingly malevolent social climate until it permeated all levels of public administration (Ware & Kisriev 2009). Then in a series of high-profile blunders, Aliev alienated key Moscow leaders, along with a Moscow-based billionaire named Suliman Kerimov. Kerimov is an ethnic Lezgin from southern Dagestan who has been working with Kremlin officials to organise investment in the republic, and who has proved to be instrumental in subsequent political appointments.

[7]'Kabardino-Balkaria Seeks to Break out of Economic Stagnation', *RFE/RL*, 1 February, available at: http://www.rferl.org/content/article/1079424.html, accessed 12 January 2011; see also Dzutsev (2009).

Second appointment in Ingushetiya

Under the brutal, weak and corrupt regime of Murat Zyazikov, Ingushetiya saw militant attacks upon law enforcement and government officials nearly every day from 2004 to 2008. Yet in contrast to Dagestan and Chechnya, the same years also saw the growth of a peaceful opposition movement that called for the removal of Zyazikov and his replacement by his popular predecessor, Ruslan Aushev. The opposition had grown to include well over 80% of the Ingush population by the summer of 2008. It was at that point when Russia's brief war with Georgia and its recognition of South Ossetiyan claims for independence from Tbilisi, threatened to revive a smouldering conflict between the Russian republics of Ingushetiya and North Ossetiya.

The Prigorodnyi territory was inhabited primarily by Ingushes until 1944, when Stalin deported the entire Ingush and Chechen populations to Central Asia and annexed Prigorodnyi to North Ossetiya. When the Ingushes returned to the region in the 1950s and 1960s, they found their homes inhabited by Ossetiyans. Since then many Ingush refugees have been consigned to squalid settlements. Conflict broke out in 1992, shortly after the dissolution of the Soviet Union. The Ossetiyans prevailed over the Ingush with the help of Russian troops, who defended established boundaries. Since then tensions have smouldered ominously.

As Stalin gave Prigorodnyi to North Ossetiya, so he awarded South Ossetiya to his Georgian homeland. Yet while Russia had defended Stalin's partition of Ingush land, it declined, in the aftermath of its war with Georgia in August 2008, to recognise Stalin's disposition of South Ossetiya. Perceptions of Moscow's inconsistency added to the bitterness that Ingushes felt toward Zyazikov. With a civil war already at hand in Ingushetiya, Moscow faced the prospect of a massive popular uprising.

Kremlin officials had four options: to retain Zyazikov, to replace Zyazikov with Aushev, to replace Zyazikov with someone else, or to reunite Ingushetiya with Chechnya. Retention was unlikely given the rapid escalation of instability; yet despite the support of Ingushetiya's peaceful opposition movement, Aushev's reprise was also improbable. While negotiating the Beslan hostage crisis, Aushev had prominently opposed Putin's tactics.

Ingushetiya separated from Chechnya in 1992, and its reunification has been periodically proposed by Chechen leaders; yet since most Ingushes have opposed reunification, this strategy would be unlikely to bring peace. Moreover, reunification would further strengthen Chechnya's autocratic ruler, Ramzan Kadyrov, whose triumph over Yamadaev, his neutralisation of the last GRU force in Chechnya, and his achievement of near autonomy, has disturbed top officials in Russia's Defence Ministry. This leaves the third option.

By some accounts Yunus-bek Yevkurov declined the presidency of Ingushetiya on two previous occasions, but finally agreed to an offer that also included some concessions by the Kremlin. Following this agreement, and without hesitation, Medvedev accepted Murat Zyazikov's resignation of 30 October 2008, and appointed Yevkurov as his replacement. On the following day, the Ingush Parliament endorsed the appointment and installed Yevkurov for a five-year term as Ingushetiya's third president. Yevkurov immediately embarked upon a series of populist overtures. By meeting with opposition leaders and preferring humble prayer to his own inaugural party he initially established his political credibility with the Ingush people, and especially with the opposition. While he got off to a good start in this way, his credibility eventually wore thin. Among his first policy measures, Yevkurov blocked officials from privatising public lands around the capital, moved to revive the Ingush oil industry, Ingushneftgazprom, and ordered the resumption of payments to workers.

Yevkurov and his Moscow supporters showed signs of having learned from preceding errors in neighbouring republics. Whereas Kadyrov rose up through rebel ranks (with help from his father), Yevkurov was a high-ranking official in the military intelligence bureaucracy. Yevkurov's appointment signalled that Ingushetiya would be controlled by the military/political bureaucracy, and would therefore never achieve the degree of autonomy that Ramzan Kadyrov attained in Chechnya. Yet, also as in Dagestan, militant attacks continued nearly every day and in July 2009, Yevkurov was critically injured in a suicide attack that killed one of his relatives. In January 2010, a suicide bomber killed five officers in a Dagestani police station. In these two republics, extremist violence was occurring with such frequency as to effectively terrorise significant portions of the populations.

North Caucasus Federal District

On 19 January 2010, Medvedev announced the creation of a new North Caucasus Federal District. The move signalled Moscow's recognition that conflict in the North Caucasus was spinning out of control, and that a new approach was required. Medvedev's announcement effectively divided the Southern Federal District into two parts. The regions remaining in the Southern District were Krasnodar, Astrakhan, Rostov, Volgograd, Adygeya and Kalmykiya. The new North Caucasus District included the republics of Dagestan, Chechnya, Ingushetiya, North Ossetiya, Kabardino-Balkariya, Karachayevo-Cherkessiya and Stavropol. The new district would be administered from the Stavropol resort town of Pyatigorsk.

Medvedev announced the appointment of Alexander Khloponin as deputy prime minister and the Kremlin's envoy to the North Caucasus District. Khloponin holds a degree from Moscow's Finance Academy, and made a fortune as chairman of Norilsk Nickel. In 2002, he was elected governor of Krasnoyarsk *Krai*. Aluminium has long made Krasnoyarsk one of Russia's richest regions, and in 2007 it attracted investments even greater than those in Moscow and St Petersburg. Since then Khloponin has been widely regarded as one of Russia's most effective regional governors. Significantly, he has also been associated with the Dagestani investor, Suiliman Kerimov.

Most of the Kremlin's federal envoys have lacked substantial power. An exception was Dmitry Kozak, a trouble-shooter whom Putin appointed to govern the Southern Federal District following the Beslan hostage crisis. Yet Medvedev announced that Khloponin was appointed both as envoy to the North Caucasus District and as deputy prime minister, making him the first of the envoys to combine presidential authority with ministerial financial influence. According to Medvedev, this 'unique situation' would allow Khloponin to combine socio-economic projects with the fight against extremism.[8]

From a Kremlin standpoint, Khloponin's dual status appeared to signify a power-sharing arrangement. As a presidential envoy, he would report to President Medvedev, while as a deputy prime minister he would answer to Prime Minister Putin. At the same time, Khloponin could be seen as a bureaucratic counterweight to Ramzan Kadyrov, who was becoming increasingly assertive beyond Chechnya's borders. Yet if Khloponin's appointment highlighted Kremlin politics, it also ignored the political realities of the North Caucasus. In this rugged region, economic credentials can count for little. Since Putin appointed billionaire Arsen Kanokov to govern Kabardino-Balkariya, the local economy has remained dormant while social unrest has increased.

Whilst Khloponin had the ability to succeed in Krasnoyarsk, his success there was partly due to the political legitimacy that he gained through popular election. As a Kremlin appointee however, he was denied that same legitimacy in the North Caucasus. Like most Kremlin appointees, Khloponin lacked a popular political base in the region. Moreover, those appointees who began with a popular base—like Kadyrov in Chechnya or Aliev in Dagestan—were delegitimised in the eyes of some members of the population by means of their appointment. This was because Kremlin selection denied genuine political expression and accountability to the local populous and precluded the formation of legitimate political opposition. As a result of the system of centralised appointment, the only possible opposition was illegitimate opposition, and the only functioning political opposition in the North Caucasus was that of Islamist extremism.

Thus, although Khloponin's appointment represents a long-overdue shift from the Kremlin's narrow focus on security, and a new commitment to regional economic development, it is unlikely that this structural alteration will prove sufficient to solve the region's problems. In order to improve the region's chronically dismal investment climate, and achieve genuine economic development, Khloponin would have to focus first on the political problems at the root of the insurgency: government incompetence and corruption. Moreover, unless corruption is effectively addressed, any economic development is likely to add to already destabilising economic disparities. Ironically, these objectives are at odds with Khloponin's own appointment.

Second appointment in Dagestan

When Putin appointed Mukhu Aliev as Dagestan's first president, Magomedali Magomedov successfully angled for the appointment of his son, businessman Magomedsalam Magomedov, to replace Aliev as assembly speaker. On 8 February 2010, a few weeks after Khloponin's appointment, Medvedev selected Magomedsalam as Dagestan's second president. Like Alexander Khloponin, Magomedsalam is connected to Suliman Kerimov, who was reportedly influential in his appointment. Thus Magomedov's appointment was consistent with the federal focus on regional economic development, signalling a central role for Kerimov and other oligarchs.

[8]Comments made by Medvedev on a segment of Russia's RT television, 19 January 2010, available at: http://www.encyclopedia.com/video/Ez4xJkJATXQ-russia-establishs-new-north-caucasian.aspx, accessed 12 January 2011.

Yet Magomedov's appointment was not initially assured. Following federal procedures on 19 November 2009, the chairman of the United Russia Party, Boris Gryzlov, presented Medvedev with a list of candidates for presidential appointment. While the candidate list in most republics offers three choices, the United Russia Party nominated five candidates for Dagestan. First was Mukhu Aliev, Dagestan's ruling president. Second was Magomed Abdullaev, an ethnic Avar attorney whom Aliev picked as deputy prime minister in late October. Though Abdullaev lacked administrative experience, there was media speculation that he would be appointed due to his early connections with Medvedev in the law faculty of St Petersburg University. Third was Magomed Magomedov, an Avar businessman active on Russia's Federation Council, and connected with prominent Kremlin officials. Fourth was Saygidguseyn Magomedov, the Avar head of the Dagestani subsidiary of the federal treasury, also with important Kremlin contacts. Fifth was Magomedsalam Magomedov, 45, who was the only Dargin candidate. He is an economist who succeeded in real estate and banking ventures while his father ran the republic. After serving as speaker of Dagestan's assembly, he was a legislative representative.

On 26 November, Dagestan's assembly voted overwhelmingly to appeal to Medvedev to hold further 'consultations' about suitable candidates. The Party list was widely viewed as tilting restrictively toward candidates with connections to the highest echelons of power in Moscow or Makhachkala rather than selecting those best qualified to address local problems. An obvious omission from the list was Said Amirov, the tough and often-effective, ethnic Dargin, Mayor of Makhachkala. In a later vote however, the legislators retracted their appeal.

Protocol was ignored when Medvedev failed to make the appointment, as expected, on 20 January, the day after Khloponin was appointed to head the new federal district. Amidst reports of disagreement between Medvedev and Putin, the choice of Magomedsalam Magomedov appears to reflect Kerimov's influence and Medvedev's interests in modernisation, ahead of a narrow focus on regional security. Yet his appointment pre-empts guarantees of government integrity and local accountability. Without these, it is likely that any economic development will favour the interests of established elites, thereby exacerbating Dagestan's cruel economic disparities, and further alienating the population.

Ironies of Chechenisation

In 2000, when the term 'Chechenisation' was coined, Chechnya was Russia's exceptional republic. At the time, the term signified the anticipation of a brutal civil war that deviated starkly from anything else in the Russian Federation. Yet, from the start, the term also suggested the opposite of its intent, and eight years later it culminated in levels of Chechen autonomy not altogether unlike those it was designed to prevent. In the meantime, it had influenced fundamental changes in the neighbouring republics, and had contributed to the evolution of Russian federalism. If Putin had been planning the centralised appointment of Russia's regional administrators more or less on the model of Akhmed Kadyrov, then Shamil Basaev gave him a cue in Beslan and provided him with a persuasive rationale.

Along the way, the policy of Chechenisation underwent an evolution of its own. Murat Zyazikov showed that it took more than brutality and corruption to make a Kadyrov from a bureaucratic appointee. Arsen Kanokov learned that the skills of a Moscow oligarch are insufficient to revive a North Caucasian economy. Mukhu Aliev proved that principled bureaucratic leadership could backfire in the absence of local accountability. Yunus-bek Yevkurov found that the well intentioned populism may not provide sufficient political legitimacy to a centrally appointed leader.

The intricacies of political appointment turned out to be more challenging in other parts of the region than in Chechnya. If Chechenisation had stabilised Chechnya beneath a centralised authority, then its export to Ingushetiya, Kabardino-Balkariya and Dagestan only seemed to provoke militant Islamist reactions. As Chechnya settled grimly into Moscow's backyard autonomy, other republics were 'Chechenised' in the sense of burgeoning instabilities that were contrary to Moscow's intent.

As its most volatile region, the North Caucasus has exerted a disproportionately strong influence upon the evolution of Russia's federal relations. The Kremlin's invasion of Chechnya in 1994 marked its rejection of a weaker, decentralised federal government. Since 2000, the Putin and Medvedev administrations have leveraged North Caucasian conflict in order to increase federal control and reduce local accountability, first in Chechnya, then in neighbouring North Caucasian republics, and finally throughout the remainder of the Russian Federation.

Yet if Russia's political evolution has involved a feedback loop between Moscow and the North Caucasus, the results have often been troubling. Conflicts in the North Caucasus seem to have contributed to authoritarian, bureaucratic, and centralising trends in the development of Russian federalism. By undermining local political access and accountability, these federal trends have inadvertently contributed to regional problems of corruption, alienation, and extremism. The Russian Federation appears to have fallen into a vicious cycle of horizontal resistance and vertical reaction that places it starkly at cross purposes with itself, a cycle that seems to be as self-perpetuating as it is self-defeating.

With the creation of the North Caucasus Federal District, the Kremlin is, once again, attempting to solve the stubborn problems of the region by establishing a new federal structure and appointing an official to administer it. Regardless of the qualifications of any Kremlin appointee, the imposition of an increasingly hierarchical and bureaucratic federal system is unlikely to produce the regional political stability that the Kremlin craves.

Many North Caucasian societies have ancient histories of democracy and egalitarianism. Contrary to the distinctive traditions and needs of this region, the federal system for the appointment of local governors has removed local accountability while doing nothing to ensure government integrity and efficacy. In societies as complex and pluralistic as those of the North Caucasus bureaucratic administration is useless without the active political involvement of the local population. Apart from the entrenched, self-serving bureaucracy and its closely affiliated United Russia party, the only viable political organisations available to the peoples of the North Caucasus are those of Salafi Islam.

Southern Illinois University Edwardsville

References

Dzutsev, V. (2009) 'Moscow Reduces Aid to North Caucasus: Jeopardising Precarious Security Situation', *Jamestown Foundation's Eurasian Daily Monitor*, 6, 169, available at: http://www.jamestown.org/single/?no_cache=1&tx_ttnews%5Btt_news%5D=35497, accessed 12 January 2011.

Evangelista, M. (2002) *The Chechen Wars: Will Russia Go the Way of the Soviet Union?* (Washington, DC, The Brookings Institution Press).

Goble, P. (2007) 'Kremlin Sending Ever More Money to North Caucasus as Ethnic Russians Flee, Writer Complains', *Window on Eurasia*, 14 November.

Goble, P. (2009) 'Moscow Cedes Control of Counter-terror Operation to Kadyrov, not to FSB', *Window on Eurasia*, 12 October.

Malashenko, A. (2010) 'Chechnya after Cancelation of the Counter-terrorist Operations', *Eurasia Review*, 29 March.

Reddaway, P., Lapidus, G. W., Ickes, B. W., Saivetz, C. & Breslauer, G. (2004) 'Russia in the Year 2003', *Post-Soviet Affairs*, 20, 1, pp. 1–45.

Smirnov, A. (2008) 'Who in Moscow Protects the Yamadaevs?', *Jamestown Foundation's Eurasian Daily Monitor*, 25 April.

Ware, R. (2005a) 'Revisiting Russia's Apartment Block Blasts', *Journal of Slavic Military Studies*, 18, 4, December.

Ware, R. (2005b) 'A Multitude of Evils', in Sakwa, R. (ed.) (2005) *Chechnya from Past to Future* (London, Anthem Press).

Ware, R. & Kisriev, E. (2001a) 'Ethnic Parity and Political Stability in Dagestan: A Consociational Approach', *Europe-Asia Studies*, 53, 1, January.

Ware, R. & Kisriev, E. (2001b) 'Russian Recentralisation Arrives in the Republic of Dagestan: Implications for Institutional Integrity and Political Stability', *Eastern European Constitutional Review*, 10, 1, Winter.

Ware, R. & Kisriev, E. (2009) *Dagestan: Russian Hegemony and Islamic Resistance in the North Caucasus* (Armonk, NY, M. E. Sharpe).

Kadyrov's Chechnya—Template, Test or Trouble for Russia's Regional Policy?

JOHN RUSSELL

On no account rear a lion in the city,
But if one is reared, then humour his ways.
(405 BC: Aristophanes, Frogs 1432–33, quoted in Gribble 1999, p. 1)

A little dragon has been raised by the Kremlin.
Now they need to feed it. Otherwise it will spit fire.
(2004 AD: Anna Politkovskaya, quoted in Knight 2010)

WHETHER OR NOT VLADIMIR PUTIN WAS AWARE OF Politkovskaya's observation, let alone that made by the Ancient Greek playwright nearly two and a half millennia earlier, the former Russian President appears to have been sufficiently politically astute to have worked out for himself the importance of keeping happy Ramzan Kadyrov, his young protégé in Chechnya, as the regional guarantor of territorial integrity and relative stability.

Although this essay is primarily addressed to the 'special' relationship between Putin's Russia and Kadyrov's Chechnya, its title reveals the difficult choices facing Dmitry Medvedev, Putin's hand-picked successor as Russian President, and raises the question of the extent to which he agrees with his predecessor and 'tandem' partner over how to handle 'arguably the most powerful—and dangerous—regional leader in the Russian Federation'.[1] Does Medvedev regard this legacy as a possible template for future Russian regional policy in the North Caucasus, does he fear that Kadyrov's idiosyncratic style of rule might test this strategy to its limits, or does he recognise that the spread of Islamic radicalism might be a result of Putin's misguided policies which could, in the end, prove troublesome for Russian control over the entire region?

In February 2008, Putin, in his valedictory address to the State Council, prior to handing over the presidency to Medvedev, asserted that:

> Through considerable effort we succeeded in ending the war in the North Caucasus. Separatism retreated and although terrorism remains an acute threat, we dealt it a decisive

[1] 'Holier than Thou: Ramzan Kadyrov and "Traditional Chechen Islam"', *RFE/RL*, available at: http://www.rferl.org/content/Holier_Than_Thou_Ramzan_Kadyrov_And_Traditional_Chechen_Islam_/2073626.html, accessed 16 June 2010.

> and crushing blow. Chechnya is now a full-fledged region within the Russian Federation. It has held democratic parliamentary and presidential elections and has adopted a regional constitution. Its economy and social sector are developing today.[2]

At this juncture the claim appeared to contain a lot more substance than those made on the many previous occasions that the region, according to Kremlin propaganda, had been 'pacified'; so much so, that even Britain's generally sceptical Russia watchers were obliged to reassess Putin's record in the North Caucasus, in general, and Chechnya, in particular. In August of that year Roland Dannreuther and Luke March broached the subject in an article entitled 'Chechnya: Has Moscow Won?' (Dannreuther & March 2008). A month later, in September 2008, journalist Jonathan Steele answered this question emphatically in *The Guardian* in a contribution headed 'It's Over, and Putin Won' (Steele 2008), identifying the accession of Ramzan Kadyrov to the Chechen presidency in March 2007 as the beginning of Chechnya's impressive renaissance.

Chechnya's *de facto*, if not *de jure*, 'special status' within Russia, to all appearances, was beginning to deliver undeniably positive results. In Georgia, moreover, not only had Russia conducted a short, victorious war against the Saakashvili regime, but Chechen *Vostok* troops, under Sulim Yamadaev, had fought heroically on the Russian side. This was proof positive, one might conclude, that Putin's policy of 'Chechenisation' (i.e. indigenisation, or the devolution of power to pro-Russian Chechens in order to counter the local insurgency) had paid off for both Russia and Chechnya. Indeed, the termination, in April 2009, of Russia's counterterrorism operation in Chechnya appeared to signal to the world that the conflict was over (Markedonov 2009).

Yet, within that same year, Sulim Yamadaev was dead, reputedly assassinated not by opponents of Moscow, but by one of Ramzan Kadyrov's own henchmen; suicide bombing had returned to the region; Chechen human-rights activist and long-time critic of Kadyrov, Nataliya Estemirova, had been kidnapped in Chechnya in broad daylight and subsequently murdered; and armed attacks on officials in neighbouring Dagestan and Ingushetiya had become near-daily occurrences. Russian observers opposed to the Putin–Medvedev 'tandem' once more were pointing to the gathering 'War clouds in the Caucasus' (Nemtsov 2009). Then, in November 2009, *jihadi*sts from the North Caucasus resistance exploded bombs on the Nevsky Express, running between the Russian capital and St Petersburg (Karpova 2009), and finally, in March 2010, targeted the centre of Moscow with suicide bombs on the metro, causing both Russian and Western commentators to question whether Putin's Chechenisation strategy had been derailed (Russell 2010).[3]

Putin's bold claims for his Chechen policy raise the very questions that this essay seeks to address. The answers to these questions revolve around four interconnected questions. Is Chechnya, as Putin claims, a full-fledged region, or effectively is it already

[2]See http://eng.kremlin.ru/speeches/2008/02/08/1137_type82912type82913_159643.shtml, accessed 31 May 2010.

[3]For a Russian commentary on Western reactions, see 'Mirovaya pressa o teraktakh v moskovskom metro', *newsland.ru*, 30 March 2010, available at: http://www.newsland.ru/News/Detail/id/481962/, accessed 31 May 2010.

beyond Kremlin control? Is the political situation in Chechnya the result of a unique set of circumstances that cannot be repeated elsewhere in the other North Caucasian republics (which, as will be argued, cannot have a 'Kadyrov' of their own)? Does the longevity of the rule of Kadyrov depend primarily upon the sustainability of his special relationship with Putin personally rather than with whoever is Russian President?[4] And, finally, is Ramzan Kadyrov politically astute enough to continue the delicate balancing act between being the supposed passionate supporter of Russia's territorial integrity and great power ambitions, on the one hand, and the 'energiser' of Chechnya's national and cultural renaissance, on the other?

In order to answer these questions a brief history of Chechenisation will be offered in the next section. This will be followed by a detailed investigation into the central role in Russo–Chechen relations of Ramzan Kadyrov in an attempt to determine whether he is, as he claims, 'Vladimir Putin's man' in Chechnya,[5] the inheritor of his father's legacy as nation-builder, or little more than a local warlord seeking to be rewarded handsomely for his loyalty to the Kremlin. The conclusion will assess which of the three perceptions of Kadyrov's Chechnya—template, test or trouble—Medvedev, should he seek re-election, is more likely to embrace in the run-up to the presidential elections of 2012. (This is an important consideration bearing in mind that the world's attention will be focused upon the region when Russia hosts the Winter Olympics at Sochi in 2014.)

Putin's Chechenisation strategy

Putin had opted for the policy of Chechenisation as early as June 2000 when the ex-mufti (and ex-rebel), Akhmet Kadyrov, was appointed head of administration in Chechnya. This appointment offered a means of avoiding either international mediation or negotiations with 'moderate' Chechen separatists, while seeking to 'normalise' the status of Chechnya within the Russian Federation. It also obliged the Russian President to draw a distinction between 'good' and 'bad' Chechens, which he belatedly did on 25 June 2002, when he declared that 'our task is to destroy this image (of Chechens) as terrorists'.[6]

To some extent, the Islamic radicals assisted Putin in drawing this distinction, since the launch of the Chechenisation strategy coincided almost exactly with the commencement of the Chechen suicide bombing campaign, characterised by the participation of 'black widows', Chechens who had purportedly lost their male relatives in the war against the federal forces (Speckhard & Akhmedova 2006). By October 2002 (after both the beginning of the second Palestinian *intifada* in September 2000 and the attacks of 9/11 in 2001), when some 30 'black widows' (dressed in *niqab* and carrying suicide belts) played a prominent part in the 'Nord-Ost' Moscow theatre siege, there really was no need to stress the *Chechen* origin of the terrorists. Those

[4]For a detailed analysis of the origins of Kadyrov's style of rule in Chechnya and its likely longevity, see Russell (2008).

[5]'Is Ramzan Kadyrov's Star on the Wane?', *RFE/RL*, 1 February 2010, available at: http://www.rferl.org/articleprintview/1945572.html, accessed 31 May 2010.

[6]'Putin Acknowledges that not all Chechens are Terrorists', *RFE/RL Newsline*, 25 June 2002, available at: www.rferl.org/content/Article/1142703.html, accessed 31 May 2010.

elements of the international community, which hitherto had been cautiously sympathetic to the Chechen separatist cause, drew obvious parallels between the Chechens, the Palestinian militants and *al-Qaeda*, and began to distance themselves from the insurgents.

In this propitious environment, Putin moved smartly to exploit the theatre siege in order to discredit further the idea of any negotiations with the Chechen 'separatists'. Prior to the siege, a major propaganda coup for Putin was the posting on a rebel website in June 2002 of a photograph of 'separatist' leader Aslan Maskhadov, posing before a Chechen flag adorned with Arabic script, alongside the mastermind of the theatre siege, Shamil Basaev, and the leader of the Arab *mujahideen* fighting in Chechnya, Abu Al-Walid (McGregor 2003). International sympathy and support for Putin's 'war on terror' took on a practical form in February 2003, when the US State Department responded to the theatre siege by placing three of Basaev's units on its list of terrorist organisations (US Department of State 2003). It was in the wake of the siege that Putin announced a three-step programme towards the implementation of his Chechenisation strategy (Russell 2007, pp. 82–88; Gilligan 2010, pp. 83–91).

The intensity of the suicide bombing campaign between the 'Nord-Ost' siege and that at Beslan in September 2004,[7] coupled with the Islamist terrorist attacks on Bali (October 2002) and Madrid (March 2004), sustained this distinction between 'bad Chechens linked to Al-Qaeda terrorists' which were equated with all Chechens fighting the federal forces, and 'good' Chechens, who were seen as those supporting Akhmet Kadyrov and, thus, supporting Russia. Against this background, Putin was able to push through the first two stages of his Chechenisation strategy: the referendum in March 2003 and a presidential election in October of that year, effectively dismissing complaints from international human rights organisations that neither poll was free or fair.[8]

When the victor in Chechnya's presidential election, Akhmet Kadyrov, was killed in an explosion at the main stadium in the Chechen capital Grozny on 'Victory Day' (9 May 2004), ostensibly by Basaev's group, it appeared at first that Putin's Chechenisation strategy had been derailed. There were even rumours circulating that those in Putin's entourage who had been against the policy of Chechenisation from the outset (Dunlop 2006, pp. 108–9), had used a protracted squabble over ownership of Chechen oil revenues to remove Kadyrov, while placing the blame on the militants (Doukaev 2008).

Due to the fact that, at 28, Ramzan Kadyrov was too young, according to the Chechen Constitution, to succeed his father, Putin proposed what was to prove to be the last election of a local leader in the Russian Federation. Alu Alkhanov, a local police chief with an unblemished record of loyalty to Moscow, was elected Chechen President at the end of August 2004 against the background of alleged electoral

[7]See 'Russia; A Timeline of Terrorism since 1995', *Radio Free Europe/Radio Liberty*, 30 August 2006, available at: http://www.rferl.org/content/article/1070937.html, accessed 31 May 2010.

[8]For example, the International Helsinki Federation for Human Rights' report on the referendum, in March 2003,was entitled 'The Constitutional Referendum in Chechnya was neither Free nor Fair', available at: www.osce-ngo.net/030328.pdf, accessed 25 September 2006.

irregularities and a concentrated series of suicide terror attacks.[9] These reached their apogee in September 2004, when a group of North Caucasians (mostly Chechens and Ingush) seized more than 1,000 hostages at School No. 1 in Beslan in the nearby North Caucasian republic of North Ossetiya. The bloody denouement left more than 338 dead, including at least 186 children, most apparently being killed during an assault by federal forces employing tanks and fire-throwers (Dunlop 2006, pp. 17–102).

Curiously, Putin avoided blaming the Chechens for this, the worst 'terrorist spectacular' of the entire Russo–Chechen conflict, blaming instead unnamed external forces, marking a definitive end to his post-9/11 'honeymoon' with Western leaders:

> Some want to tear off a big chunk of our country. Others help them to do it. They help because they think that Russia, as one of the greatest nuclear powers of the world, is still a threat, and this threat has to be eliminated. And terrorism is only an instrument to achieve these goals.[10]

In a domestic response to Beslan, Putin reorganised Russian regional policy by removing the right of regions (including Chechnya) to elect their own leaders (Lynch 2005), thus at a stroke both consolidating Russia's power 'vertical', which came to characterise his second term as Russian President, and also curbing the autonomy of regional elites, whose weakness and inefficiency he saw as a contributory factor to the tragedy in North Ossetiya. On the ground, however, the Russian forces were becoming increasingly successful in targeting a series of important insurgent commanders, culminating in March 2005 with the assassination of Maskhadov, an act which removed the last separatist politician with manifestly more legitimacy than that enjoyed by either Akhmet Kadyrov or Alu Alkhanov.

Meanwhile, Ramzan Kadyrov proved that he was the real power broker in Chechnya when he delivered in November 2005 a 'Soviet-style' victory for Putin's United Russia Party (*Edinaya Rossiya*) in the parliamentary elections, purportedly the final stage of the Russian President's Chechenisation programme. By February 2006, Putin was able to claim that other North Caucasus regions were 'more worrying' than Chechnya,[11] a trend that has continued to this day, albeit at low-level insurgency rather than the large-scale military operations which characterised the wars in Chechnya (Markedonov 2009). His critics, however, noted that his policies had created across the region the very *jihadi*sts that his war in Chechnya ostensibly had set out to eradicate (Torbakov 2005).

In 2006 Ramzan Kadyrov celebrated his 30th birthday and thus became qualified constitutionally to become Chechen President. In March of that year he had been promoted to the post of prime minister;[12] and by dint of a series of armed clashes and assassinations, gave notice that he wished to replace Alkhanov, a wish effectively

[9] 'Russia: A Timeline of Terrorism since 1995', *Radio Free Europe/Radio Liberty*, 30 August 2006, available at: http://www.rferl.org/content/article/1070937.html, accessed 31 May 2010.

[10] 'Putin Tells the Russians: "We Shall Be Stronger"', *The New York Times*, 5 September 2004.

[11] 'Putin: Other North Caucasus Regions "More Worrying" than Chechnya', *Jamestown Foundation's North Caucasus Weekly*, 2 February 2006.

[12] 'Chechen Parliament Approves Ramzan Kadyrov as President', *AP*, *ITAR-TASS* report published on 4 March 2006 on *Radio Free Europe/Radio Liberty*, available at: http://www.rferl.org/content/Article/1066351.html, accessed 31 May 2010.

granted in February 2007. In an early success for the young Kadyrov, Abdul-Khalim Sadulaev—Maskhadov's successor as leader of the Chechen resistance—was assassinated by Russian security forces in June 2006, just a few weeks before Shamil Basaev met the same fate. The importance of Basaev's elimination should not be underestimated, as it removed the one remaining leader of the armed resistance whose charisma extended beyond Chechnya across the North Caucasus. The separatist leadership was taken up by the long-serving Chechen field commander Doku Umarov. Lacking either Basaev's network of associates across the North Caucasus or Sadulaev's spiritual authority, Umarov presided over what was then little more than a disparate group of practically autonomous *jamaats*. In November 2007, in order to consolidate these structures, Umarov declared a Caucasian emirate, thus effectively abandoning the goal of national independence for Chechnya.[13]

If Basaev's death in July 2006 was greeted with a degree of relief and satisfaction in the West, another high-profile assassination in Russia later that year certainly was not. On 7 October journalist Anna Politkovskaya, an arch critic of both Putin and the Kadyrovs, was shot dead outside her Moscow apartment. The finger of suspicion pointed immediately to shady operators wishing to ingratiate themselves with Kadyrov or Putin.[14] The fact that an internationally well respected journalist should share the fate of Basaev, Russia's declared 'terrorist no. 1', provided the clearest example yet of how methods purportedly used to eliminate political adversaries in the Caucasus could be employed with apparent impunity against dissident, but law-abiding, members of Russian civil society (Chadaev 2007). Politkovskaya had been particularly damning in her criticism of Ramzan Kadyrov, calling him 'a Stalin of our times' in a last interview, '*Karatel'nyi sgovor*' (Punishment Pact), published in *Novaya gazeta* on 28 September 2006 just before she was murdered. The article ends:

> In other words, Chechenisation is not simply the transfer of authority to institutions consisting of local inhabitants, but an encouragement and legitimisation of those who are prepared to participate in punitive operations against their own population. In that way, Chechenisation is a policy for expanding the scope of the war, and the result of this policy has been a replacement of the genocide practised directly by Russian agencies in the early stages of the conflict by today's reign of terror by criminal and semi-criminal gangs, supported and directed from Moscow. (Politkovskaya 2010, p. 381)

The final, perhaps unintended, act of Putin's Chechenisation strategy occurred in March 2007, when Ramzan Kadyrov was confirmed as president.[15] Since then, the energetic young leader has intensified the re-Islamicisation of Chechnya along

[13]'The Official Version of Amir Dokka's Statement of Declaration of the Caucasian Emirate', 22 November 2007, available at: http://www.kavkazcenter.com/eng/content/2007/11/22/9107.shtml, accessed 18 June 2010.

[14]For the latest information on Politkovskaya's murder, see Committee to Protect Journalists (2010).

[15]In August 2010, ostensibly on Kadyrov's own initiative, it was proposed that all heads of state in the constituent republics of the Russian Federation would no longer use the title 'president', an honour henceforth to be reserved solely for the Russian head of state: '"Glava" zvuchit ne khuzhe, chem "president"', 29 August 2010, available at: http://www.chechnya.gov.ru/page.php?r=28&id=100, accessed 1 November 2010.

traditionally Chechen Sufi lines.[16] He has effectively suppressed all military forces within the republic that are not under his control, and he runs the country in what has been described as a personal fiefdom.[17] While his promotion of traditional Islam in Chechnya has made him eminently suitable as an ambassador to Arab and Muslim states with which Russia wishes to deal, his brutal and dictatorial style ensures that he would be unlikely to be welcomed in democratic countries, as was illustrated by the furore over his horse winning him prize money in Australia's Melbourne Cup in November 2009.[18]

It should not be forgotten that Putin's own political career was launched by exploiting the deep-seated fear of the Chechens—'Chechenophobia'—that became rampant in Russia from 1999,[19] and this, along with other forms of racism and xenophobia, has continued to grow in Russia (Bigg 2008). As a result he appears to have opened a Pandora's Box of future problems between ethnic Russians and Caucasians, especially Chechens. It has been suggested, for example, by some Russian commentators, that the bomb attack in Stavropol in May 2010 outside a theatre at which a Chechen dance troupe was due to perform, might have been carried out by anti-Caucasian Russian nationalists (Rechkalov & Fochkin 2010). The decision by Russia's NTV network to withdraw from its schedule a series of programmes that allegedly offended Chechen sensibilities, further fanned the flames of anti-Chechen sentiment.[20]

To the dismay of human rights groups within Russia and even governments abroad, the 'convenient' removal of opponents of the Kremlin administration or that of Kadyrov in Chechnya, continues with apparent impunity, as the spate of killings from January 2009 demonstrate: human rights lawyer Stanislav Markelov and *Novaya gazeta* journalist, Anastasia Baburova, were gunned down in that month in Moscow; Chechen exile, Umar Israilov, was killed in January in Vienna; Sulim Yamadaev was assassinated in Dubai in March 2009; and Natalya Estemirova was abducted in Chechnya and murdered in Ingushetiya in July 2009 (Bigg 2009).

Medvedev however, while having little to show in the way of convictions of those responsible for these murders, has been more outspoken than his predecessor on the need to respect human rights, meeting twice in 2009 with members of the presidential Council for Civil Society Institutions and Human Rights.[21] In May 2010, Medvedev

[16]'Is Kadyrov "Re-Islamicizing" Chechnya?', *The Jamestown Foundation's North Caucasus Weekly*, 31 October 2008.

[17]'Kadyrov's Horse Wins "President of Russia" Prize', *RFE/RL Transmission*, 1 June 2010, available at: http://www.rferl.org/content/Kadyrovs_Horse_Wins_President_Of_Russia_Prize/2059259.html, accessed 18 June 2010.

[18]'Kadyrov's Unlucky Day at the Races', *RFE/RL Transmission*, 20 November 2009, available at: http://www.rferl.org/content/Kadyrovs_Unlucky_Day_At_The_Races/1883657.html, accessed 18 June 2010.

[19]Vladimir Pribylovskii, of the Panorama political research group, coined this term after the Moscow apartment bombings (Feifer 1999).

[20]'NTV ubral iz veshchaniya oskorbitel'nyi dlya chechentsev serial', *APN*, 15 June 2010, available at: http://www.apn.ru/news/comments22883.htm#comments, accessed 18 June 2010.

[21]'ROAR: Medvedev Discusses "Painful Problems" with Human Rights Activists', *Russia Today Politics*, 24 November 2009, available at: http://rt.com/Politics/2009-11-24/roar-medvedev-human-rights.html, accessed 18 June 2010.

convened a further meeting devoted to the situation in the North Caucasus, at which such longstanding critics of Kadyrov as Tanya Lokshina of Human Rights Watch and Svetlana Gannushkina of *Memorial* brought to the Russian President's attention the string of human rights' abuses occurring daily under Kadyrov's rule.[22] Medvedev has made several attempts to limit Kadyrov's power, notably by the appointment of Aleksandr Khloponin as presidential plenipotentiary for the North Caucasus region in January 2010. However, the Russian President has not thus far shown any inclination to unseat Kadyrov, it being clear that his removal runs the risk of plunging Chechnya back into violent confrontation, thus derailing Chechenisation once more and potentially robbing Putin of his greatest domestic political triumph—the successful ending of the Chechen war.

The crunch for Russia and for its leaders will come, however, should they no longer be able or willing to satisfy Kadyrov's seemingly unlimited demands for more resources and power, something about which political analyst Dmitry Oreshkin has already warned: 'Kadyrov understands that the centre depends on him ... that if an alternative figure appears, then the configuration of power that Kadyrov built will collapse and chaos will rise again in Chechnya .... Correspondingly, he demands money as payment for his loyalty'.[23]

Despite claims that Chechnya is no longer a 'full-fledged territory of Russia' and persistent rumours that Kadyrov is planning for an Algerian-style separation from Russia (Feigin 2009), there is ample evidence that he is aware of how much he still has to gain by cooperating with Russia. For all of his shortcomings, Ramzan Kadyrov remains very much the key to the successful continuation of the Chechenisation strategy (Russell 2008).

Even Putin appears to have become less effusive in his support for the Chechen President than he has been in the past, as is demonstrated by his veiled criticism of Kadyrov among others in January 2010, at a meeting in Pyatigorsk with the heads of the seven regions of the North Caucasus Federal District, at which the local leaders were warned to 'do everything to ensure the normal work and functioning of human rights organizations whose activities do not contravene the constitution of the Russian Federation'.[24] However, if Putin's characterisation of Chechnya in his 2008 speech as a stable, intrinsic part of Russia is to have any credence, he will still have to rely heavily on the continued goodwill, support and cooperation of Ramzan Kadyrov. If, as Dmitry Medvedev has hinted, a new 'flexibility' and 'adaptability' are needed to replace his predecessor's 'stability' and 'predictability' in Russian society (Pismennaya 2010), then Kadyrov's ability to ensure a degree of the latter becomes significantly less important.

[22] 'Medvedev Meets with Local NGO Leaders in Bid to Stabilize North Caucasus', *The Jamestown Foundation's Eurasia Daily Monitor*, 7, 98, 20 May 2010.

[23] 'Oreshkin on Moscow and Kadyrov: Be Careful What You Wish For', *The Jamestown Foundation's North Caucasus Weekly*, 8, 14, 5 April 2007.

[24] 'Is Ramzan Kadyrov's Star on the Wane?', *RFE/RL*, 1 February 2010, available at: http://www.rferl.org/articleprintview/1945572.html, accessed 31 May 2010.

Ramzan Kadyrov—satrap *or son-king?*

Kadyrov has combined the trappings of a medieval warlord with those of modern jet-setter with a zeal befitting any Saudi playboy prince. From his menagerie of exotic pets and his fleet of high performance sports cars, to his string of world-class racehorses and his sumptuous palaces in Tsentrovoi and Gudermes, Kadyrov's style is distinctively glitzy. The menace of his authoritarian style of rule tends to go hand-in-hand with the glamour; his palaces are said to contain dungeons in which opponents are tortured, the wild animals and fighting dogs have clearly intimidated some visitors and Sulim Yamadaev allegedly was shot in Dubai by a stable hand who cared for Kadyrov's prize horse at the World Cup race meeting in the United Arab Emirates.[25]

The gulf between Ramzan's form of governance in practice and the norms laid down in the Russian Constitution appears to mirror the 'dual state' identified in the post-Soviet Russia (Sakwa 2010), in which real power is exercised by an opaque leadership network rather than by legitimate bodies in accordance with constitutional norms. However, despite the apparent proximity between Russian and Chechen politics in practice, Ramzan's extreme style prompted one commentator to ask: 'What does Chechen power in the guise of Ramzan Kadyrov have in common with the Russian juridical space and for what, in any case, did we conduct a years-long counter-terrorist operation that cost many thousands of lives?' (Sukhov 2005).

Whilst under Russia's semi-authoritarian system, the public is not consulted and seems quite content for its leaders to act in its name if this reduces the likelihood of further Chechen attacks, Kadyrov evokes indifference amongst a majority, and ambiguous feelings amongst a minority of ordinary Russians. In a Public Opinion Foundation poll conducted in February 2007, just after Putin had nominated him for the Chechen presidency, 39% of Russians questioned said they knew nothing at all about Kadyrov. Of the 61% who had heard of him, 73% were unable to list any of his positive or negative characteristics.[26] Given that Kadyrov wields significant political power in Russia,[27] this was hardly a ringing popular endorsement.

Within Chechnya, on the other hand, Kadyrov's cult status could hardly be higher, as demonstrated by the first verse of an entry in a poetry competition held in December 2006 for schoolchildren in Chechnya on the theme: 'Ramzan—hero of our time' (Markedonov 2007a).

> Praise to our radiant sun—Ramzan
> Mighty leader and fighting man
> To the faith and love and hope of Chechnya
> Grant a long life, O eternal Allah!

[25]For a good account of both the glitz and the menace, see Feifer (2009).

[26]FOM—Russia's Public Opinion Foundation poll on 'Ramzan Kadyrov—Acting President of Chechnya', published on 1 March 2007 (N=1,500, margin of error >3.6%), available at: http://bd.fom.ru/report/map/projects/dominant/dom0709/domt0709_5/d070923, accessed 20 March 2008.

[27]For example, Kadyrov was only the third leader in Russia, after Putin and Medvedev, to have been granted an international online conference (on 30 January 2008); see Krechetnikov (2008).

The question remains, however, what exactly is Kadyrov's role in Chechnya: *satrap*, warlord or nation-builder? I have chosen the term '*satrap*', aware that it originated in the ancient Median Empire which bordered the Caucasus. Moreover, the Old Persian word '*khšaçapâvâ*', which originally meant 'protector of the realm', was used to describe those indigenous vassal rulers who were chosen to represent the king's interests in the various provinces of the Achaemenid Empire. It is worth adding that Median and Persian kings regularly sent out their own inspectors (called the 'eye of the king') to exercise control and supervision over the *satraps*,[28] a course Medvedev might be seen to have taken, in order to check the flamboyant Kadyrov's apparently unlimited ambition, when he appointed Russian businessman and economist, Aleksandr Khloponin, as his plenipotentiary in the newly-established North Caucasus Federal District in January 2010 (Leahy 2010).

In the Russian context, this system of vassalage, dating from Muscovy's Grand Prince Vasily II in the fifteenth century, has been termed by Chantal Lemercier-Quelquejay as the 'Chingizid syndrome' (1992, pp. 18–44), a concept that has been applied to the relationship between the Kremlin and Kadyrov (Leahy 2006). Of the two means of recruitment of *satraps*, one would tend to assign the uneducated but powerful Ramzan Kadyrov to the category of feudal chieftain or warlord, rather than to the bureaucratic elite. Certainly, his many critics would recognise that his 'parasitic and exploitative power'[29] rests on retaining the old (Russian) imperial boundaries and strong (Russian) central government derived from imperial rule. However, it must be questioned as to whether, on the evidence available, it would be true to state that the last thing that Kadyrov wants is 'self-determination and national justice'[30] for the Chechen people. I would argue that Ramzan Kadyrov, at least in part, is fulfilling what he appears to perceive as his historic destiny as Chechnya's 'nation builder'.

It is worth noting, in this respect, that Kadyrov belongs to a very small group of current world leaders who are sons of previous presidents of their country. While the others (Bashir al-Assad of Syria, Ilham Aliev of Azerbaijan, Kim Jong-il of North Korea and Joseph Kabila of the Democratic Republic of Congo) might display the self-assurance one might expect from such a privileged background, Ramzan Kadyrov is the only one of the five to whom the label 'man with a mission' or 'nation builder' might readily be attached, marking him out amongst present leaders on the world stage.

Of course, although Chechnya, unlike the states listed, is not *de jure* an independent state, such is Kadyrov's scope for independent action that he acts, and to all intents and purposes is regarded both domestically and internationally, as a head of state. Compare his position with that of, for example, Magomedsalam Magomedov, whom Medvedev in February 2010 nominated as president of Chechnya's neighbour, Dagestan; Magomedov's father had held the post from its inception in 1992 until

[28]Jona Lendering, 'Satraps and Satrapies', *Livius Articles on Ancient History*, available at: http://www.livius.org/sao-sd/satrap/satrap.htm, accessed 18 June 2010.

[29]Taken from an analysis of the role of *satraps* in British and French colonies in Africa; see 'Biafra R.I.P.', *The Libertarian Forum*, 1 February 1970, available at: http://mises.org/journals/lf/1970/1970_02_01.pdf, accessed 14 July 2007.

[30]'Biafra R.I.P.', *The Libertarian Forum*, 1 February 1970, available at: http://mises.org/journals/lf/1970/1970_02_01.pdf, accessed 14 July 2007.

2006.[31] However, although Dagestan shares many of the problems of Chechnya, it does not enjoy its *de facto* 'special status' as a virtually autonomous republic, nor does Magomedov have anything like Ramzan Kadyrov's freedom of action on the international stage. On the other hand, Magomedov, like Ingushetiya's Yunus-bek Yevkurov and all the other leaders of republics in the North Caucasus, will resist strongly any attempt by Kadyrov to extend his realm beyond the borders of Chechnya.

Certainly, the five heads-of-state listed have all adopted an authoritarian style of rule and three (al-Assad, Aliev and Kadyrov) are Muslims. One writer has suggested that 'sultanism', albeit qualified as semi-authoritarian, might best describe post-Soviet Azerbaijan (Guliyev 2005), while others have described modern Belarus in these terms (Eke & Kuzio 2000, pp. 523–47). Moreover, speculation has been rife in the past that both Islam Karimov, President of Uzbekistan, and Nursultan Nazarbaev, President of Kazakhstan, in the absence of sons to continue their dynasties, considered promoting their daughters, Gulnara and Darigha, respectively, as their successors (Saidazimova 2006, 2008). This may be further evidence perhaps of a 'dynastic' trend emerging amongst former Soviet republics, especially (but not exclusively) those with a Muslim cultural background. Chechnya under Ramzan Kadyrov, I would argue, provides a further manifestation of this trend.

Unsurprisingly, the combination of authoritarianism, Islam and aspects of oriental despotism in Kadyrov's rule, particularly seen from a Western perspective, tempt some to conclude that 'sultanism' (Linz & Stepan 1996) might indeed best describe his style of leadership. One leading Russian expert on the region, Sergei Markedonov, has qualified this by stating that 'Kadyrov is a kind of Caucasus emir not unlike the Bukhara emir in the Russian empire',[32] the key difference between an emir (prince, commander) and a sultan (sovereign) being that the latter has no higher temporal authority above him. Ramzan Kadyrov would appear to defer only to the former Russian President, Vladimir Putin, who has given him his full personal and political protection since the assassination of Akhmet Kadyrov, and to Putin's half-Chechen advisor, Vladislav Surkov, two of the most powerful allies one could wish for in the Kremlin.[33]

However, it is becoming obvious that Ramzan Kadyrov's idiosyncratic behaviour, notably his attempts to remove each and every real or imagined political rival within Chechnya, is testing the patience even of his major backers in the Kremlin. It is significant, for example, that upon relinquishing the Russian presidency, Putin, in a wide-ranging interview with *Le Monde* on 1 June 2008, in the context of discussing Chechnya failed to mention Kadyrov at all.[34] Quite how the brash young Chechen leader's autocratic style fits into Medvedev's charm offensive on the world stage is less easy to determine; rumours were rife before his elevation to president that he wanted

[31]'Medvedev Nominates New Daghestan President', *RFE/RL News*, 8 February 2010, available at: http://www.rferl.org/content/Medvedev_Proposes_New_Chief_For_Russias_Daghestan/1952050.html, accessed 18 June 2010.

[32]'Zakaev Praises Kadyrov', *Chechnya Weekly*, 9, 20, 22 May 2008.

[33]Leahy (2010) claims that presidential aide Sergei Sobyanin took over as Kadyrov's 'minder' in the Kremlin. Sobyanin has since become Mayor of Moscow ('Putin Aide Sobyanin Confirmed as Moscow Mayor', *BBC News*, 21 October 2010, available at: http://www.bbc.co.uk/news/world-europe-11602794, accessed 22 October 2010).

[34]See http://www.russiatoday.ru/news/news/25525, accessed 31 May 2010.

to oust Kadyrov at the earliest opportunity (Smirnov 2008). Medvedev's aforementioned appointment of Aleksandr Khloponin[35], prompted some observers to speculate that Ramzan Kadyrov's star was, indeed, on the wane.[36]

The sustainability of the deal between the Kremlin and Kadyrov appears, therefore, to rest on the continuance of the personal relationship between Vladimir Putin and Ramzan Kadyrov himself, rather than on any firm legislative basis. Given the Byzantine nature of contemporary Russian politics this looks like an opportunistic policy for the short term rather than an arrangement that is destined to last. It is small wonder, therefore, that sceptical Russian commentators have already characterised the Kremlin's Chechen policy as a modern Russian version of the Roman Empire's ill-fated deal with its periphery: 'we will pay for the loyalty of local clans and officials—you can milk the Russian treasury, as long as you don't shoot us in the back' (Voronov 2006). If one accepts the findings of the opinion polls listed above, the same percentage of Russians consider Kadyrov a dictator as regard him to be honest, and twice as many think him a rebel fighter as recognise him as loyal to Russia.[37] This is not, I would suggest, the image of a politician in whom one would invest such a degree of trust as Putin appears to have done.

Ramzan Kadyrov—regional warlord?

In June 2006 *The Guardian* published an article about Chechnya (Walsh 2006), implying that Ramzan's domain could be ranked with Afghanistan, Iraq, Lebanon and Somalia, in which power was maintained through fear, intimidation and the barrel of a gun.

Lezhnev defines a 'warlord' thus:

> Warlords are powerful actors in weak states who base their control almost solely on rule by force for the overwhelming purpose of personal financial gain and glory rather than ideological struggle. They therefore prey on civilians through brutal armed intimidation instead of recruiting them for a greater cause. Conflicts between warlords bear more resemblance to criminal battles than societal struggles, with the population generally viewing the warlords as thieves and murderers rather than revolutionaries. (Lezhnev 2005, p. 2)

Aspects of Kadyrov's rule, such as his armed stand-offs with perceived opponents and the torture cells allegedly situated in his palaces, clearly fall into this definition. However, Lezhnev differentiates between 'partial' warlords (for example Fretelin in East Timor, the Tamil Tigers and Kurdish PKK) and 'absolute' warlords (such as Charles Taylor in Liberia), claiming that the former exhibit a lesser degree of warlordism, whereas the latter are motivated by unadulterated self-interest. Compared to some of his African and Asian contemporaries, whose sole primary aim appeared to

[35]'Medvedev Creates New North Caucasus Federal District', *RFE/RL*, 20 January 2010, available at: http://www.rferl.org/articleprintview/1934705.html, accessed 31 May 2010.

[36]'Is Ramzan Kadyrov's Star on the Wane?', *RFE/RL*, 1 February 2010, available at: http://www.rferl.org/articleprintview/1945572.html, accessed 31 May 2010.

[37]FOM—Russia's Public Opinion Foundation poll on 'Ramzan Kadyrov—Acting President of Chechnya', published on 1 March 2007 (N=1,500, margin of error >3.6%), available at: http://bd.fom.ru/report/map/projects/dominant/dom0709/domt0709_5/d070923, accessed 20 March 2008.

be personal enrichment to the detriment of their nations and, in particular, innocent civilians, rather than any commitment to nation building (Lezhnev 2005, p. 14), Ramzan Kadyrov seems to display at least a streak of altruism and patriotism, suggesting that he might be only a 'partial' warlord.

This preliminary conclusion may be tested further if one examines the five main elements that Lezhnev identifies as defining warlords as political actors (Lezhnev 2005, pp. 2–4). The first concerns the motivation of leaders which is driven overwhelmingly by personal power, glory and monetary gain, all elements that may be detected in Kadyrov's obvious lust for power. The second element concerns the social element of warlords who tend to come from a military background and have a very low level of education, often being school dropouts. Both of these characteristics clearly apply to Kadyrov, who left school at 15 to head his father's protection force—the *kadyrovtsy*. Such a background, argues Lezhnev, 'plays a role in their narrow view of the world, believing that only one person, rather than a complex series of political institutions, can wield power' (Lezhnev 2005, p. 3). Kadyrov's views on his own power and that of Putin clearly reflect this narrow interpretation.

The third element is the context of a political environment where law and order are extremely weak which facilitates the appearance of warlords. Such situations 'provide a vacuum of power and authority for warlords to fill with their rapacious method of ruling' (Lezhnev 2005, p. 3). Any student of Chechnya since the collapse of the Soviet Union would recognise that precisely such a context allowed warlords to flourish in the two periods of *de facto* Chechen independence (1991–1994 and 1996–1999) and facilitated the monopolisation of power in Kadyrov's hands since his father's death in 2004.

The fourth element is more problematic, relating to the distinctively brutal methods employed by warlords, who kill, rape, and rob civilians indiscriminately in order to establish zones of control, feed and house their forces and secure control of valuable resources. The leaders of the Sudanese *Janjaweed* and Ugandan Lord's Resistance Army are held up as classic examples of this element of warlordism. However, despite the overwhelming evidence concerning Ramzan's brutal methods against his political opponents, his manifest concern for the Chechen population means that he cannot easily be classed in this aspect alongside such absolute warlords.

The final element concerns organisation and control of people and resources. Control over such natural resources as oil, diamonds and coltan,[38] is an important feature of contemporary warlordism, allowing warlords to equip and pay their troops and undermine the loyalty of those that might oppose them. Kadyrov has been spectacularly successful in attracting 'fighters' from rebel groupings into his *kadyrovtsy* by promising them pay, weapons and security, while targeting ruthlessly the families of those that oppose him. For example, rebel leader Doku Umarov's septuagenarian father is said to have had his eyes gouged out by Kadyrov's cousin, Adam Delimkhanov.[39] His control of revenues emanating from the federal centre or

[38]Coltan is an industrial element used widely in mobile phones etc.

[39]As reported by *Kavkaz-Center*, see 'Dmitriya Medvedeva ub"yot snaiper', 7 March 2008, available at: http://www.kavkaz.org.uk/russ/content/2008/03/07/56823.shtml, accessed 18 June 2010.

the Akhmet Kadyrov memorial fund,[40] to which all who wish to operate in Chechnya are expected to contribute, provide him with more than adequate financial resources.

Thus, in four out of the five elements, Kadyrov might be said to be acting like a warlord, if not of the 'absolute' variety. However, as Lezhnev points out, the same could be said of professional criminal groupings (who lack only, in most cases, the direct control of natural resources) and the mafia (that tends to operate illegally in law-governed states), making explicit the link between warlordism and criminality, which both prize personal power, wealth or fame (Lezhnev 2005, pp. 4–5). One might conclude that as Kadyrov's state consolidates, his regime will resemble more the mafia state and less *ad hoc* criminal groupings.

Societies with a weak tradition of Western-style 'industrial' nationalism tend to facilitate the rise of feudal-type leaders who exploit this setting by surrounding themselves with members of their own clan or tribe and purporting to act and speak for the 'nation'. Such states tend to lack either a base for political parties or a merchant class, thus leading to a triumph of might over right and clientelism over market relations. The apparent inability to form an effective political wing within the Chechen insurgency would seem to prove this point, for, as James Kiras has noted, 'recent experience in Chechnya, Somalia, and the Democratic Republic of Congo, however, suggests that the warrior enabled by culture will face Western soldiers ... Warrior culture dictates goals—such as plunder, or killing to prove virility—instead of politics' (Kiras 2002, p. 227). This might well explain the predominance of Byzantine-style murders of political (and civilian) opponents under Kadyrov. However, although membership of the *Kunta-haji wird* (Arquilla & Karasik 1999), the Sufi brotherhood favoured by Ramzan, has grown exponentially under his rule, Kadyrov has been politically astute enough in Chechnya to spread his largesse beyond his own clan.

The apparent inability to form an effective political wing within the Chechen insurgency would seem to provide evidence of the pre-modern status of Chechen politics under Kadyrov. The absence of a political wing of the Chechen resistance under Maskhadov, strong enough to counter its violent warlords, would tend to suggest that such a warrior culture predominated in Chechnya right up to Kadyrov's assumption of power. The cult of personality that portrays 'King Ramzan' as a brave mountain warrior flourishes in such a culture.

It would appear that the key difference between absolute warlords and Kadyrov is that most of the former seized their power through insurgency, whereas Kadyrov inherited the mantle of head-of-state, giving him legitimacy and, perhaps due to inheriting his father's legacy, an altruistic motivation that his contemporaries lacked. All warlords use ethnicity ('creed') as a cover for their economic or political 'greed', but with Ramzan Kadyrov, as we have seen, there do appear to be genuine elements of 'nation building' in his rule. 'Nation builders' are held to be both those sent from the outside and those emerging from within failed states who are charged with the task of creating stability out of chaos and conflict, albeit often, especially in the case of

[40]See, for example, 'Statement of *Memorial*—On Our Work in Chechnya', 31 May 2007, available at: http://www.memo.ru/2007/06/08/0806071.html, accessed 31 May 2010.

insiders, through undemocratic, authoritarian measures. Ramzan Kadyrov would appear to belong to this category and, some would claim, thanks to the generous financial aid from Russia, is doing a better job of restoring his shattered country than any other 'nation builder' in Afghanistan, Iraq or Kosovo (Ignatieff 2003).

On the other hand, the peace that he has created is, in Galtung's terms, at best 'negative' (in the sense of an absence of widespread violence) rather than 'positive' (a harmonious society in which human rights are respected) (Galtung 1969). The non-democratic nature of Kadyrov's regime was reflected in the elections to the *Duma* in Chechnya in December 2007, during which 99.2% of voters allegedly participated in the poll, of which 99% voted for United Russia (Markedonov 2007b). These 'Soviet-style' figures give credence to the conclusion drawn by the Chechen analyst Mairbek Vatchagaev, when he stated:

> The situation in Chechnya and the entire North Caucasus is easy to understand if one harkens back to the days of the Soviet Union, when people's real lives bore no relation to what was shown and said in public. Such a situation cannot fail to cause disappointment and bewilderment among people forced to lead a double life, in which the government's propaganda is miles away from what the public actually believes. (Vatchagaev 2008)

Yet, for all of the negatives of Kadyrov's rule, there can be no doubt that the young president has raised the profile, morale and self-esteem of the Chechen people in a manner which no other leader could have delivered. As former Maskhadov aide, Magomed Khanbiev, has noted:

> Our President is a Chechen, the representatives of all branches of power are Chechens, and members of the law-enforcement organs are also Chechens .... We don't realize it, but it is possibly today that we have received the very independence that was fought for all those years. And when those who have not yet returned understand this, realize that it is the embodiment of their ideals, they will return home and become brothers-in-arms of the president.[41]

Even Akhmed Zakaev, arguably Kadyrov's leading separatist opponent still living in the West, apparently gave serious consideration in 2008–2009 to the Chechen President's offer of an amnesty and a return to Chechnya (Vatchagaev 2009). This followed a surprising, given his long record of opposition to Kadyrov, public statement in London in November 2008 that in his opinion, 'the decolonisation of Chechnya is now a fact', admitting that Ramzan Kadyrov had 'done very important work for the liberation of Chechnya'.[42]

Kadyrov's ability to attract Khanbiev and other former leading opponents to his side is indicative of the fact that loyalty to him, rather than to the Kremlin, is most important in Chechnya today. It also provides evidence that Chechen society and its structures of power retain many aspects of the warrior culture. For example, in

[41]As reported on the chechnyafree.ru website, 11 June 2008, available at: http://www.chechnya-free.ru/en/article.php?IBLOCK_ID=354&SECTION_ID=621&ELEMENT_ID=81353, accessed 18 June 2010.

[42]He made this remark at the Royal United Services Institute in London on 14 May 2008, as part of a panel of which I was a member (see de Waal 2008).

February 2009, Chechen's Grozny TV staged a remarkable live show in which Ramzan Kadyrov personally interrogated former leaders of the Chechen separatist movement who had been persuaded to throw in their lot with Kadyrov. The kowtowing of former opponents to Ramzan Kadyrov clearly emphasised to the watching Chechen public who was in charge in Chechnya (Are 2009).

Lezhnev's analysis would indicate that Kadyrov is a nation builder not so much along ideological lines, such as Nepal's Maoists for example, as on cultural and national grounds (Lezhnev 2005, p. 2). At the same time, clearly, he is emphatically not an absolute warlord in the mould of Charles Taylor. His position is secure only insofar as he is perceived by the Russian leaders as fulfilling the role of a *satrap*. In the final analysis, however, his legitimacy as a Chechen leader is built on such a fragile basis that holding on to the power he seized so improbably remains the greatest motivator of all. As Van Evera has noted, 'the less legitimate the governments or leaders of nationalist movements, the greater their propensity to purvey mystical nationalist beliefs, hence the greater the risk of war' (Van Evera 2001, p. 30).

The absence of strong market relations mentioned above also leads to a rent-seeking economy in which warlords are in cahoots with state and military officials, and in some cases, even with the insurgents, often helping them to circumvent the law in money laundering, tax evasion, smuggling, arms procurements, and protection. This has been a feature of the situation in Chechnya since the collapse of the USSR. Lezhnev states that: 'the final step on this scale of corruption is when warlords become state rulers, although they continue to treat the state as their own personal warlord domain' (Lezhnev 2005, p. 14). In place of budgetary probity and accountability, the warlord becomes the owner of his region's treasury and dispenses largesse as he thinks fit. Many would recognise this to be the current situation in Ramzan's Chechnya.

Chechnya's persistent claims for 'special' status, from the declaration of Grozny as an international airport[43] to the granting of huge subsidies from the Kremlin treasury (amounting to R120 billion for 2008–2011)[44] should consolidate further Chechen support for Kadyrov. By the same token, they are bound to irritate increasingly their neighbours in the North Caucasus, who receive nothing like as generous subsidies and, critically, never took up arms against Russia. The federal government, which seeks to curb the corruption and clannish nepotism rampant in the region, must strike a delicate balance between supporting the renaissance of Chechnya and alienating the rest of the North Caucasus. It is fortunate for Medvedev that the opinions of ordinary Russian citizens, who continue to pay the taxes that to a considerable extent fund Kadyrov's largesse, currently do not have to be taken seriously into account.

[43]'Aeroport Groznogo stal mezhdunarodnym', *RIA-Novosti*, 23 November 2009, available at: http://www.rian.ru/economy/20091113/193346634.html, accessed 21 June 2010.

[44]'Medvedev: "V Chechnyu vernulas' normal'nayu zhizn"', *LifeNews*, 14 June 2010, available at: http://lifenews.ru/news/27976, accessed 21 June 2010.

Conclusion

In June 2010, Ramzan Kadyrov appeared to have endorsed Putin's positive view of Chechenisation when he categorically denied that there existed within his realm any forces that sought to separate Chechnya from Russia:

> There are no Chechen separatist organisations. There are no forces wishing to separate Chechnya from Russia either. The republic had a referendum seven years ago, and local residents clearly pronounced their wish to remain within Russia. Russian laws are in effect in Chechnya, and all thc constitutional power bodies are operating there. It is impossible to disconnect Chechnya from Russia.[45]

Such a comprehensive endorsement of the Chechenisation strategy appears to reveal that Kadyrov still knows how important it is to keep on the good side of his major protector in the Kremlin, for it is hardly likely to displease Vladimir Putin. As long as Putin remains the most powerful political figure in Russia, it is difficult not to agree with Lyudmila Alekseyeva, head of the Moscow Helsinki Group, who states that: 'The impunity and omnipotence of Ramzan Kadyrov depends on the support ... of Putin. As long as Putin supports him nobody will touch a hair of Kadyrov's head, even if he kills us all' (Knight 2010).

Medvedev, clearly, is also prepared to defend Kadyrov, as illustrated by his comment in September 2009 that Ramzan Kadyrov 'was not the bad lad that some try to paint him'.[46] The Russian President remains less enamoured by Kadyrov's style, as shown by his comment reported by *Ekho Moskvy* radio station in May 2010 that those who cannot develop working relations with all the forces of the political spectrum must step down. However, as a sceptical commentator, Valery Dzutsev, from the *Jamestown Foundation's Eurasia Daily Monitor* points out:

> In reality, however, there is little or no opportunity in most of the republics of the North Caucasus to be a politician outside of the approved political spectrum. The lack of democratic process and severe restrictions on freedoms verging on oppression like that of the Stalin era are problems that pop up in every open-ended discussion on the North Caucasus. However, it invariably becomes clear that Moscow does not want and cannot afford political reforms in the North Caucasus.[47]

Given the lack of momentum from the centre for radical political change, a quintessentially Caucasian style of governance has restored a semblance of order in the region. As a Russian commentator noted, also on *Ekho Moskvy* radio in September 2009:

> Chechnya was a completely hopeless case. It seemed that it was irrevocably lost and the war there might last for decades. But the Kremlin has found a native among strangers, won him over and given him complete control over all this territory, and he has created a formal order

[45] *Itar-Tass*, 8 June 2010.

[46] 'Medvedev o Kadyrove: on ne takoi plokhoi mal'chik', *Korrespondent.ru*, 15 September 2009, available at: http://korrespondent.net/russia/968192, accessed 21 June 2010.

[47] 'Medvedev Meets with Local NGO Leaders in Bid to Stabilize North Caucasus', *The Jamestown Foundation's Eurasia Daily Monitor*, 7, 98, 20 May 2010.

> there. It is, of course, not the order liberals and human rights activists would like to see; it is not a democratic form of government. But the choice was simple: either the war or such a peace.[48]

The looming problem that Medvedev has belatedly recognised is that such authoritarian rule, with its poverty, corruption, nepotism and harsh treatment of all forms of opposition, is directly responsible for the growth of Islamic radicalism throughout the rest of the North Caucasus. Paradoxically, Ramzan Kadyrov's Chechnya, now home to Europe's largest mosque, has a relatively progressive attitude to manifestations of religious fervour, particularly of the local Sufi variety.

Elsewhere, particularly in Dagestan and Ingushetiya (despite the efforts of local leaders Magomedov and Yevkurov, respectively), the heavy-handed repression of such manifestations has proven to be a major cause for the rise in extremism. The extent to which Medvedev can contain this in the near future undoubtedly will be a factor in the 2012 presidential elections. There appears to be no appetite to use the Chechen experience as a template for policy in the North Caucasus. Indeed, the autonomy granted to Ramzan Kadyrov in Chechnya certainly does represent a serious test for Russian regional policy. Whether the continuation of Kadyrov's rule promises severe trouble for Russia's regional policy in the North Caucasus remains a moot point. The Russian government's recently-published 'Strategy for the Social and Economic Development of the North Caucasus Federal District until 2025'[49] appeared to gloss over the serious political and religious divisions within the region thus failing to engage publicly with this issue.

The dilemma for both Medvedev and the West is that Kadyrov's removal, by Chechens, by Russians or as a result of his own lifestyle, would almost certainly bring instability to a geopolitically sensitive part of the world, sitting between the Black and Caspian seas and astride some of the main oil, gas and communication lines in the region. The Chechen people are undoubtedly better off now than when they were occupied by Russian federal forces and Kadyrov is by no means the worst leader that has ever emerged from the Caucasus. On the other hand, how much better off the Chechens, and all North Caucasians, could be if their leaders were not so corrupt, is a question that could be addressed equally well to many nations, not least the Russians.

University of Bradford

References

Are, D. (2009) 'The Discrediting of Ichkeria', *Prague Watchdog*, 23 February.

Arquilla, J. & Karasik, T. (1999) 'Chechnya: A Glimpse of Future Conflict', *Studies in Conflict & Terrorism*, 22, 3, pp. 207–29.

Bigg, C. (2008) 'Russia: Hate-Crime Deaths Mounting, as Nationalists Close Ranks', *RFE/RL*, 11 June, available at: http://www.rferl.org/content/article/1144591.html, accessed 31 May 2010.

[48]'Kremlin's "Kadyrov Model" for Chechnya Now Failing', *Ekho Moskvy*, 16 September 2009, *BBC Monitoring*, reproduced in *Johnson's Russia List*, 18 September 2009.

[49]Government of the Russian Federation, Law approved 6 September 2010, No.1485-r on 'Strategy for the Social and Economic Development of the North Caucasus Federal District until 2025', available at: http://www.government.ru/media/2010/10/4/35578/file/1485.doc, accessed 2 November 2010.

Bigg, C. (2009) 'A String of Silenced Voices on Chechnya', *RFE/RL Features*, 16 July, available at: http://www.rferl.org/content/feature/1778554.html, accessed 31 May 2010.
Chadaev, U. (2007) 'First Anniversary of Shamil Basayev's Death', *Prague Watchdog*, 10 July.
Committee to Protect Journalists (2010) 'Russia Pledges to Pursue Journalist Murder Probes', 30 September, available at: http://cpj.org/2010/09/russia-pledges-to-pursue-journalist-murder-probes.php#more, accessed 15 October 2010.
Dannreuther, R. & March, L. (2008) 'Chechnya: Has Moscow Won?', *Survival*, 50, 4, pp. 97–112.
Deveraux, C. & Hayes, D. (2005) 'Chechnya: Elections versus Reality', *Open Democracy*, 25 November, available at: http://www.opendemocracy.net/democracy-caucasus/chechnya_3066.jsp, accessed 31 May 2010.
de Waal, T. (2008) 'Mysterious Shifts in Chechnya', *The Moscow Times*, 22 May.
Doukaev, A. (2008) 'Chechen Leader Takes On Three Powerful Adversaries, with Minimum Success', *RFE/RL Commentary*, 29 July.
Dunlop, J. B. (2006) *The 2002 Dubrovka and 2004 Beslan Hostage Crises: A Critique of Russian Counter-terrorism* (Stuttgart, Ibidem-verlag).
Eke, S. M. & Kuzio, T. (2000) 'Sultanism in Eastern Europe: The Socio-Political Roots of Authoritarian Populism in Belarus', *Europe-Asia Studies*, 52, 3, May.
Feifer, G. (1999) 'Russia Blames Chechens for Terrorism', *The Russia Journal*, 30, 20 September.
Feifer, G. (2009) 'The Price of Progress—Life in Kadyrov's Grozny Permeated by Fear', *RFE/RL*, 11 August, available at: http://www.rferl.org/articleprintview/1797452.html, accessed 18 June 2010.
Feigin, M. (2009) 'Malen'kii Alzhir', *Yezhednevnyi zhurnal*, 24 August.
Galtung, J. (1969) 'Violence, Peace and Peace Research', *Journal of Peace Research*, 6, 3, pp. 167–91.
Gilligan, E. (2010) *Terror in Chechnya* (Oxford, Princeton University Press).
Gribble, D. (1999) *Alcibiades and Athens: A Study in Literary Presentation* (Oxford, Clarendon Press).
Guliyev, F. (2005) 'Post-Soviet Azerbaijan: Transition to Sultanistic Semi-authoritarianism? An Attempt at Conceptualization', *Demokratizatsiya*, 13, 3, Summer.
Ignatieff, M. (2003) *Empire Lite: Nation Building in Bosnia, Kosovo, Afghanistan* (London, Vintage).
Karpova, L. (2009) 'Terror Attack on Nevsky Express Train', *Pravda Online*, 28 November, available at: http://english.pravda.ru/russia/politics/28-11-2009/110814-nevskyexpress-0, accessed 18 June 2010.
Kiras, J. D. (2002) 'Terrorism and Irregular Warfare', in Baylis, J., Wirtz, J., Cohen, E. & Gray, C. (eds) (2002) *Strategy in the Contemporary World: An Introduction to Strategic Studies* (Oxford, Oxford University Press).
Knight, A. (2010) 'The Kremlin's Chechen Demon', *The New York Review of Books*, 27 May, available at: http://www.nybooks.com/blogs/nyrblog/2010/may/27/kremlins-chechen-dragon/, accessed 31 May 2010.
Krechetnikov, A. (2008) 'Kadyrov ob''yavil o porazhenii separatistov', *BBC Russian*, 30 January, available at: http://news.bbc.co.uk/go/pr/fr/-/russian/russia/newsid_7218000/7218692.stm, accessed 2 February 2008.
Leahy, K. D. (2006) 'Russia's Relations with Ramzan Kadyrov: A "Chingizid Paradox"', *Central Asia-Caucasus Institute Analyst*, 22 February.
Leahy, K. D. (2010) 'Medvedev's New King-Makers in the Caucasus', *Central Asia-Caucasus Institute Analyst*, 13 May.
Lemercier-Quelquejay, C. (1992) 'Co-optation of the Elites of Kabarda and Daghestan in the Sixteenth Century', in Broxup, M. (ed.) (1992) *The North Caucasus Barrier: The Russian Advance towards the Muslim World* (New York, St. Martin's Press).
Lezhnev, S. (2005) *Crafting Peace: Strategies to Deal with Warlords in Collapsing States* (Lanham, MD, Rowman & Littlefield).
Linz, J. & Stepan, A. (1996) *Problems of Democratic Transition and Consolidation: Southern Europe, South America and Post-Communist Europe* (Baltimore, MD, Johns Hopkins University Press).
Lynch, D. (2005) 'The Enemy is at the Gate: Russia after Beslan', *International Affairs*, 81, 1, pp. 141–61.
Markedonov, S. (2007a) 'Ramzan solntselikii', *APN Publikatsii*, 9 April, available at: http://www.apn.ru/publications/article16854.htm, accessed 31 May 2010.
Markedonov, S. (2007b) 'Podavlayushchee bol'shinstvo', *PolitPortal*, 3 December, available at: http://.www.politportal.ru/analysis/detail.php?print=Y&ID=2325, accessed 11 December 2007.
Markedonov, S. (2009) 'Severnyi Kavkaz—2009: v zone povyshennoi turbulentnosti', 19 May, available at: http://www.politcom.ru/arc/2009/11.html, accessed 31 May 2010.
McGregor, A. (2003) 'Amir Abu Al-Walid and the Islamic Component of the Chechen War', *Central Asia-Caucasus Institute Analyst*, 26 February.
Nemtsov, B. (2009) 'War Clouds in the Caucasus', *The Wall Street Journal*, 26 August.

Pismennaya, Y. (2010) 'Chelovek Nedeli: Dmitry Medvedev', *Vedomosti*, 21 June 2010.
Politkovskaya, A. (2010) *Nothing But the Truth* (London, Harvill Secker).
Rechkalov, V. & Fochkin, O. (2010) 'Bomba neizvestnoi natsionalnosti', *Moskovskii komsomolets*, 27 May.
Russell, J. (2007) *Chechnya—Russia's 'War on Terror'* (Abingdon, Routledge).
Russell, J. (2008) 'Ramzan Kadyrov: The Indigenous Key to Success in Putin's "Chechenization" Strategy?', *Nationalities Papers*, 36, 4, September, pp. 659–87.
Russell, J. (2010) 'Monster in the Mountains', *The World Today*, 66, 5, May.
Saidazimova, G. (2006) 'Kazakhstan: Apparent Rift Opens within Nazarbaev Family', 19 May, available at: http://www.rferl.org/content/article/1068525.html, accessed 31 May 2010.
Saidazimova, G. (2008) 'Uzbekistan: President's Daughter Takes Another Step Toward "Throne"', *RFE/RL Features*, 5 February, available at: http://www.rferl.org/featuresarticle/2008/02/E129EECA-459F-4D23-B8C5-3D0AF2DB036F.html, accessed 31 May 2010.
Sakwa, R. (2010) 'The Revenge of the Caucasus: Chechenization and the Dual State in Russia', *Nationalities Papers*, 38, 5, pp. 601–22.
Smirnov, A. (2008) 'Who in Moscow Protects the Yamadaev Brothers?', *Chechnya Weekly*, 24 April.
Sourt, C. (2008) 'The Congo's Blood Metals', *The Guardian*, 25 December.
Speckhard, A. & Akhmedova, K. (2006) 'The Making of a Martyr: Chechen Suicide Terrorism', *The Journal of Studies in Conflict and Terrorism*, 29, 5, pp. 429–9
Steele, J. (2008) 'It's Over, and Putin Won', *The Guardian*, 30 September.
Sukhov, I. (2005) 'Chechenskii ochag', *APN Proyekt Instituta natsional'noi strategii*, 16 August, available at: http://www.apn.ru/publications/article1519.htm, accessed 18 June 2010.
Torbakov, I. (2005) 'War on Terrorism in the Caucasus: Russia Breeds Jihadists', *The Jamestown Foundation's North Caucasus Weekly*, 6, 42, 10 November.
US Department of State (2003) 'Three Chechen Groups Designated as Terrorists', 28 February, available at: http://www.america.gov/st/washfile-english/2003/February/20030228152333treceveur@pd.state.gov0.6110911.html, accessed 6 December 2010.
Van Evera, S. (2001) 'Hypotheses on Nationalism and War', in Brown, M. E., Coté, O. R., Lynne-Jones, S. & Miller, S. (eds) (2001) *Nationalism and Ethnic Conflict*, revised edition (Cambridge, MA, MIT Press).
Vatchagaev, M. (2008) 'Counting Chechnya's Rebel Fighters: Kadyrov's Fuzzy Math', *Chechnya Weekly*, 7 February.
Vatchagaev, M. (2009) 'Kadyrov Courts Akhmed Zakaev', *The Jamestown Foundation's North Caucasus Analysis*, 10, 5, 6 February.
Voronov, V. (2006) 'Chtoby tol'ko v spinu ne strelyali', *Sovershenno Sekretno*, January, reproduced at: http://www.compromat.ru/main/chechnya/kadyrovramnach.htm, accessed 7 February 2007.
Walsh, N. P. (2006) 'Land of the Warlords', *The Guardian*, 13 June.

Index